ONE SIGNAL
PUBLISHERS

ATRIA

The Lost and the Found

A TRUE STORY OF HOMELESSNESS, FOUND FAMILY, AND SECOND CHANCES

Kevin Fagan

ONE SIGNAL
PUBLISHERS

ATRIA

New York   Amsterdam/Antwerp   London   Toronto   Sydney   New Delhi

ONE SIGNAL
PUBLISHERS

ATRIA

An Imprint of Simon & Schuster, LLC
1230 Avenue of the Americas
New York, NY 10020

Copyright © 2025 by Kevin Fagan

First One Signal Publishers/Atria Books hardcover edition February 2025

ONE SIGNAL PUBLISHERS / ATRIA BOOKS and colophon
are trademarks of Simon & Schuster, LLC

For information about special discounts for bulk purchases,
please contact Simon & Schuster Special Sales at 1-866-506-1949
or business@simonandschuster.com.

The Simon & Schuster Speakers Bureau can bring authors to your
live event. For more information or to book an event, contact the
Simon & Schuster Speakers Bureau at 1-866-248-3049
or visit our website at www.simonspeakers.com.

Interior design by Davina Mock-Maniscalco

Manufactured in the United States of America

1   3   5   7   9   10   8   6   4   2

Library of Congress Cataloging-in-Publication Data has been applied for.

ISBN 978-1-6680-1711-1
ISBN 978-1-6680-1713-5 (ebook)

For Carolyn and Molly, the center of my universe,
and my parents, who filled our family with the wonder of words

Contents

CONTENTS

This Is Personal

started covering street life as a cub reporter in the 1980s, when the Reagan era's furious attack on federal support for poor people finally detonated the growing problem that began with the dismantling of mental institutions in the 1970s and crescendoed into what we now call homelessness. I've covered plenty of other topics since then, from mass shootings, executions, and serial killers to drought, disasters, and the American West—I'm a dyed-in-the-wool journalist. Which I believe means you try to become accomplished at most things in the newsroom as a reporter and editor, then specialize in something. Or in my case, a few somethings. Most of them grim.

But I got into journalism for a few core reasons, and taken together, they're not grim. First, I love writing. Second, I love studying people, drilling down on things other people can't or don't want to see—what I like to call shoving my face headfirst into life, up close. And third, I want to help make the world around me a better place, which has always inevitably led me back to writing about poverty and homelessness.

Beyond my reportorial impulses, there's also this: As the saying goes, "write what you know." I know what it's like to be poor. And to not have a home.

THE LOST AND THE FOUND

•   •   •

I GREW UP IN Northern California and Nevada in the 1960s and '70s, the child of parents who never really understood how to relate to kids, having both been raised as only children in somewhat odd circumstances. Dad grew up on farms in rural Oregon and Washington, left with relatives after his mother died when he was seven and his father became a traveling lumberjack and butcher. Mom was raised in hardscrabble mining-camp tents and shacks in Nevada and was tough as nails—knew how to kill rattlers a half dozen ways by age eight. She expected me to be the same way. So did Dad, who sat me down at twelve and said, "You're a man now, it's time to go to work." My first jobs were pulling weeds and cleaning carpets and sewer pipes. I have held some kind of job ever since.

My parents divorced when I was thirteen. My older sister was out of the house, so my ten-year-old brother and I were left with our mom, who promptly went to school full-time to "find herself" and finish her education so she could start what would later become a career teaching speed-reading, lobbying for mental health funding, and leading women's empowerment seminars. My dad on the other hand, anguished about the divorce, took a technical-editing job on a U.S. military missile base on the other side of the world, where no kids were allowed and he could retreat from the world. Meanwhile, my mom and I were having intense conflicts that were vexing for a single mom struggling through school on government aid, child support, and stray nonprofit jobs. I hung out with friends playing basketball or guitar and didn't come home on time, sneaked food beyond the tightly budgeted daily amount, rebuilt my beat-up motorcycle engine on the living room floor. I was a Boy Scout and didn't smoke dope or drink. But I didn't automatically obey, and that blew my navy-veteran mom's circuits. At sixteen, she told me to get out.

Years after we reconciled, my mom—whom I recognized as an awesome feminist once we got through our crisis period—told me she was only able to kick me out of our home because "I knew you could take care of yourself." Dad took the same view—"I always worked my way through school, you can do it, too," he said. And it turned out that, indeed, sixteen was an age to perfectly capably start life, for me at least.

This was probably because Dad, also a navy vet, had been chasing college degrees for most of my formative years, and with Mom mostly home taking care of three kids, much of the time we lived below the poverty line. They were both writers, and every wall in our house was covered with used books, but the whole money thing wasn't their forte. We moved every few years, food was short, clothes were ill-fitting hand-me-downs or once-a-year buys, student housing sucked. When whatever apartment we were living in needed paint or fixing, we did it ourselves. My parents taught us to work hard from the time we could hold a hammer. So struggling to get by was not new to me.

But I also had one other ace up my sleeve—I knew what direction I wanted to take in life. My father, who had taught high school and college English (among his many jobs), worshipped the written word and instilled that in all of us kids. My mom had been a navy journalist in the Korean War and always told me it was the best job in the world, and damned if she wasn't right. When I got on my Livermore High School newspaper in California at fourteen and wrote my first story—something about attitudes on recess at the Student Union—I was hooked. Talking to people, figuring out what was in their heads, helping my classmates understand things better, getting to write—now *this* was exhilarating, electrifying. From then on there was no doubt in my mind about what I was going to do with my life. I would be a journalist.

And even on my own at sixteen, I knew going to college was my ticket there. I had by then already couch surfed frequently at friends' houses to get away from the turmoil at home and had, at one point, run away for a week to sleep in a field (only to be found by the cops a week later at school—hey, I couldn't stand to skip classes). So I was descending through those phases where people become unanchored and potentially head toward the street. But I was determined not to wind up outside. When I got tossed out of the house, I sold my beat-up motorcycle for $100 and rented an unfinished garage in Hayward, building my furniture out of scrap wood, while I got started at Chabot Junior College and worked as a house cleaner. I was a slightly freaked-out teenager, but the family I rented the garage from was kind, and once I saw that making $80 a month, getting the occasional $100 check from Dad, and spending $50 on rent left me enough to eat—as long as I stuck to beans, veggies, and Velveeta—I was off to the races.

After a year I transferred to San José State University, where the dorms were cheap, but at the holiday, semester, and summer breaks, I had no home to go back to. So I crashed with friends if I was lucky, but by then I'd gotten some student poverty aid and jammed in some extra jobs to buy a battered old Volkswagen Bug—so most of the time for the first year or so, during breaks I slept in my car on the outskirts of campus. It was cold, wet, and scary for a kid, and the back seat was too small for me to stretch out past fetal position. I washed up in gas station bathrooms and cursed the world while I vowed that one day I would have a real paycheck and a place of my own.

Working, of course, was never a question for me. It's what you did, no matter what. So even when I was living out of my car, I had jobs. I pumped gas, painted houses, took office temp shifts, washed dishes, and did every other flexible job I could find until my senior year, when I finally got more sure of myself and scored a job editing the research office newsletter on campus. I figuratively pinched myself every day I went to work, thinking, "My God, they're paying me to write!" It made me ravenous for the day I would actually get a paycheck for being a newspaper reporter. I knew it would happen. I just had to endure the road to get there.

I was twenty when I graduated, and with journalism BA in hand I spent the next few years bouncing between Europe, the United States, New Zealand, and Australia as a street singer and journalist. In the times when I rooted in for a bit—a stint in London at BBC radio, a small-paper job in California, stringing for United Press International in New Zealand—I lived in apartments, and in England, a residential dive hotel before upgrading to a closet, in a shared apartment, with just enough room for a single mattress. But when I traveled as a street singer—Busker became my nickname among pals—I hopped between towns, taking buses or hitchhiking, and crashing with other musicians or just bedding down at the side of the road or in parks if I hadn't made it to a cheap hotel before nightfall. If it rained, I'd lay the guitar on one side of me, the backpack on the other, drape a tarp over the top, and sleep underneath. Great in the rain. None of it bothered me. The street was not a frightening place. I was technically homeless, but I knew in my heart I was going back to having a job and stability someday, kind of like a classic hobo. Many years later, I did ride the rails with hoboes through California just to give it a taste (and, of course, to write a newspaper story), and the feeling fit.

I smoked a bit of pot in those years, especially as a musician, and once while wandering via my thumb along the Australian coast I spent an entire week at a commune high on home-picked magic mushrooms. I was around plenty of addicts in the street, but somehow the hard stuff never tempted me. I didn't want to lose control of my mind, and I felt bad for those who were hooked—but I never felt afraid to talk, to offer some of my food, to connect with them. It became comfortable.

At every newspaper where I've worked, from the little *Lodi News-Sentinel* in Lodi, California—yes, the one from the Creedence song—to the *Oakland Tribune* and the *San Francisco Chronicle*, I've made reporting on trauma and distress a specialty. For me, that's mostly meant disaster, murder, poverty, and homelessness. I've been at the *San Francisco Chronicle* since 1992, and homelessness became my main focus after my dear friend Brant Ward—a *Chronicle* photographer who was as much a reporter as a photog—and I spent six months in the street in 2003 for a series examining why so many people were unhoused and desperate in San Francisco.

When asked about it, I say reporting on homelessness is "my happy place," and the tinge of dark humor there doesn't overshadow the fact that I actually do like street work more than anything else I do in journalism. It checks my boxes. I get to feel like I'm doing good in the world. By treating oppressed people with dignity, I get to hang with folks I love to talk to, and I get meaningful, emotionally rich things to write about. I get to feel like I'm making a difference.

I've always said that growing up the way I did made me strong, and I do believe that's true. But as therapists like to point out, leaving home the way I did, and being homeless even in the truncated way I was as a kid, left trauma. Anger. Pain. I have a severe flight impulse because running off to the next thing—the next town, the next gig, the next place to be in my life—was something I learned to do to survive, and it made me feel I was moving forward. That makes for some great adventures, but it's not altogether healthy. You carry your trauma and pain with you and it never disappears. To this day, in the far back of my mind, I still feel like some trapdoor about six feet in front of me might whisk me back to the street.

The thing to do is process all of that with perspective, learning which brass tacks matter and which don't. Try hard to make life what you need it to be so that the trauma that never really leaves your being becomes a minimal factor in your everyday life. Find stability.

I've found that stability—married, made a family, settled down, solid job. And, yes, I've still managed to avoid booze or drug addiction en route. The way I've reacted to my challenges has left me more empathetic than resentful, which is crucial for actually listening to the ragged people I write about, to care for them and want them to have better lives. And to exult whenever those lives actually do get better. Yeah, I've had a share of pain and trauma—but it's nothing like the stuff I've seen in the street.

Nothing like what the protagonists of this book, Rita Grant and Tyson Feilzer, have endured.

RITA'S AND TYSON'S JOURNEYS took them through unthinkable nightmares most people live very far from. To someone sipping a chardonnay in a white-tablecloth café, a disheveled down-and-outer lying passed out on the sidewalk outside can seem to be just part of the landscape. The decades-old tableau of our modern version of home-lessness is too often now something to look away from, or to glance sadly at, or maybe to visit for a moment while you hand over a dollar. But every one of those people was somebody's baby for at least a brief shining time, a child with potential, or an adult who wanted a life of security and love. You need to get past the grime and ruin to see it, to hear it, to feel it. But it's there.

Come with me while we find that in the lives of Rita and Tyson.

PART 1

Rita in high school
(Photo courtesy of her daughter Faith)

Rita, at right, homeless
(Photo taken by Brant Ward, provided courtesy of *San Francisco Chronicle*)

CHAPTER 1

Homeless Central

San Francisco prides itself on being the City That Knows How, the cooler older brother of Silicon Valley and Oakland, the Paris of the West, a progressive bastion with a caring populace. But it's not all shine. The city started out rough, booming into life with the 1840s Gold Rush to become a rollicking town of prospectors, shopkeepers, bankers, and everyone else trying to cash in on the gold being gouged and panned from the Sierra Nevada. Prostitutes and gangs proliferated, and the bustling seaport kept saloons, brothels, and dance halls filled with sailors, miners, and workers from the galaxy of businesses selling everything an adventurer needs, from shovels and chow to wagons and hydraulics.

Cocaine and morphine were easy to get, opium dens flourished. And there were plenty of unhoused people, too, notably when frigid winters in the mountains drove miners west with their families to sleep in the streets of San Francisco, waiting for better weather.

This wasn't the whole picture of the city, of course. There was a long history of Ohlone people thriving on the hilly oceanside peninsula that the occupying Spanish later dubbed San Francisco in honor of Saint Francis, patron saint of the poor. And along with all the hurly-burly that came with its occupation and transformation there was

3

artistry, a trade and wealth boom with the arrival of the Pacific Railroad, and colorful entrepreneurs from chocolatier Domingo Ghirardelli to pants-maker Levi Strauss. Nob Hill sprouted opulent mansions, one of the biggest Chinatowns in America expanded, and by the turn of the 1900s the city was known as a metropolis of style, hubbub, grace, debauchery, fancy hotels, and skid rows all happily rolled into one.

The 1906 Earthquake pretty much flattened the city through shaking and fire, but San Francisco was rebuilt even grander than before. In the century-plus since then, it's taken on layers of identity—military base, Haight-Ashbury birthplace of hippiedom, LGBTQ mecca, and tourist-magnet home of the gorgeous Golden Gate Bridge and Fisherman's Wharf and distinctly colorful neighborhoods of brightly painted Victorians from the Italian-centric North Beach to Latino-flavored Mission District. The city has world-class museums, a worthy rival to New York's Central Park in Golden Gate Park, village-like residential neighborhoods with local shops and a thriving financial center.

San Francisco has come a long way from those rollicking early days to become one of the most important cities in America, headquarters to global giants such as Uber and Salesforce. The city's annual budget of $14 billion is bigger than those of Maine and Rhode Island, and its seven-by-seven-mile space is the most densely populated metropolis outside of New York City.[1]

Then there's image, which is hugely important considering tourism is among the city's top industries. From the time of the city's 1850 incorporation to now, San Francisco solidified its reputation as the place where oddballs and the needy can always come to mix with the swells and notables—corporate titans from the Levi family to the Gettys, Clint Eastwood to Robin Williams, dockworkers to modern tech bros and moguls like Elon Musk. It's a fun city to visit, the place where that climb "halfway to the stars" takes cable cars past subsistence housing, high-end shopping, and multimillion-dollar mansions. And it always seems to adapt and innovate, keeping ahead of whatever societal waves are pushing forward, be it the Grateful Dead, Janis Joplin, et al., rock scene of the 1960s or the dot-com- and Twitter-era booms of the 2000s.

But since the early 2000s, the city has had another national reputation every bit as ingrained into the public consciousness: homeless central.

To be sure, there were always homeless people in San Francisco, as in the rest of the nation. And drugs. And booze. And addiction. In earlier times, homeless folks—the disabled, the unemployed, the mentally ill, those who didn't fit in, or people who just had phenomenal bad luck—were called bums, hoboes, winos, and worse. Every big city had its skid row. But that changed with the 1980s, when the decimation of public funding for the needy began in earnest as income got shoved toward the upper brackets. The word *homeless* made its way into wide use in the early part of that decade, and cities with good weather and compassionate aid systems such as San Francisco and Los Angeles started to see their streets filling with people who had nowhere else to go. San Francisco, like the saint it was named after, led its approach to the crisis with shelter and emergency-housing aid—but as in every other city, the problem quickly outstripped the efforts. Nobody in charge had ever had to handle a mushrooming problem like this before, and they scrambled.

Over the past decade or so, in fits and starts, there has been some progress in bringing street people indoors. The homeless veterans population was slashed by 55 percent between 2010 and 2022 through heavy spending by the federal Department of Veterans Affairs, and targeted spending by the U.S. Department of Housing and Urban Development (HUD) reduced some other segments of the street population a tad.[2]

Still, the statistical bright spots are rare. In 1990, a federal one-night count found 228,621 homeless people in America, and by 2023 that number had grown to 653,100.[3] Such one-night counts are inherently flawed undercounts, and many experts put the total throughout a year at more than 3.5 million—or by some estimates, more than 6 million.[4] It's become obvious that persistent poverty and economic backsliding for those who aren't rich has been a fountain of misery that continually pours new people into the streets every year, refreshing the ranks of the unhoused—by many estimates, more than a third of the United States is either impoverished or poor and struggling from paycheck to paycheck.[5]

In San Francisco alone, the city's Department of Homelessness and Supportive Housing estimates that for every homeless person who gets put under a roof, four more take the person's place.[6] That's a crisis in many ways, not the least of which is that there already isn't remotely enough housing to take them all in—let alone keep roofs over all of the poor who are hanging on by a thread, in danger of tumbling to the street. A 2023 report by the city's homelessness department revealed that San Francisco would have to build nearly 4,000 permanent supportive housing units and 2,250 new shelter beds to end unsheltered homelessness within three years, at a cost of $1 billion up front and nearly $400 million a year in operating costs.[7] That was immediately deemed unaffordable.

As for trying to plug the problem upstream? San Francisco's housing planners determined the city would have to build eighty-two thousand new housing units between 2023 and 2031 to meet new California requirements intended to force each municipality to fill the state's severe housing gap—and that more than half would have to be for affordable to low-to-moderate income earners. The number was seen as practically unreachable, requiring a tripling of the current construction rate in a city notorious for expensive, convoluted building approvals.[8]

The City by the Bay's homeless conundrum is unique for several reasons. Its homeless population of around eight thousand on any given night—and more than double that when counted overall throughout the year—is more centrally located, more prominently placed and therefore broadly visible, than anywhere else in the nation.[9] And San Francisco spends more money per capita on homelessness than nearly any other city—more than $600 million a year in all.[10] It's got more shelters per capita than anywhere else in the Bay Area, has nationally innovative aid programs like Project Homeless Connect, which convenes thousands of volunteers to hold assistance fairs for street folks, and has supportive housing and counseling services that have housed tens of thousands of formerly homeless people over the past two decades. And at times, particularly in the early 2000s, the street count dropped.

But all these efforts, all the money spent, all the analyses of who's where and who's been helped and which programs work best, haven't made enough of a dent, at least in the public eye. San Francisco still has what many experts across the country call the most obvious, most visible—in other words, to many, the worst—homeless problem in America, even though the street populations are bigger in the much-larger cities of Los Angeles and New York. And locally, homelessness is frequently named by its residents as the number one problem facing San Francisco.

It's been like this for decades.

IN 2003, I SPENT six months on the streets, working on what became a series of stories on homelessness called "Shame of the City" for the *Chronicle*.

The assignment came about because our managing editor, Robert "Rosey" Rosenthal, who had just arrived at the paper after leaving the *Philadelphia Inquirer*, decided we needed to take a deeper look into what he rightly considered the shocking scandal of homelessness in the city. One thing that tipped him over the edge came one day when he was driving through downtown San Francisco and saw a homeless guy snap the neck of a pigeon and then stuff it under his coat, seemingly to eat later.

Why are so many unhoused people screaming at telephone poles while folks just walk on by? he asked when he got back to the newsroom. Crapping on the sidewalk? Smoking and shooting up drugs right in the open? More than eighty-six hundred people were living in the city's streets at the time, with clearly not enough being done to help them. Rosey had never seen anything so widespread, so deeply dysfunctional.

Send out a reporter and a photographer who know the street, Rosey said. Try to figure it out.

That turned out to be me and photographer Brant Ward. The gig fit me easily. As it did for Brant, who had reported on war in Somalia and disaster in Haiti, disasters and poverty in Northern California, and the usual spread of hard-news stories everywhere. Brant and I had covered devastating floods and the Polly Klaas kidnapping in the 1990s together and spent about a week at Woodstock-famous hippie clown Wavy Gravy's summer camp for a magazine-length story, so we knew some shorthand with each other. But over the summer and fall of 2003 as we hit the streets, I came to regard him as a brother.

"Take as long as you need," Rosey told us. "Really get to know these people in the street—find out what's working and what's not."

I felt like I'd won the lottery. You don't often get told to "take as long as you need" in the newspaper trade, but Rosey knew his stuff. He knew what it took to get something in depth—and it turned out to be four immersive months on the streets, then two more intensive months combined with writing. I trusted him. And he trusted Brant and me.

So we headed out with camera, notepads, and blankets and utterly open minds. We didn't pretend to be homeless. We were just ourselves, which fortunately for the assignment didn't look too different from a lot of street folks—just a couple of guys in jeans and checked shirts and sneakers. Except for one stint in a shelter, we were upfront about being journalists. All we want to do is find out what the hell your lives are about so other people can understand, we'd say. (In the shelter we registered with our real names and stayed a couple of nights, but didn't offer that we were working for the paper until someone finally asked. If we'd told them from the jump that we were on the job, they would have given us a sanitized tour. This way we got to see the real deal.)

Brant and I trolled everywhere, separately and together, getting to know the homeless enclaves outside and in the shelters, often staying either all night or until wee hours. Our journeys began in the Mission District and the gritty Tenderloin, two swaths of San Francisco that were richly diverse, filled with artists and working-class folks with stretches of gentrification slicing through quite a bit of poverty. This is where you saw the biggest number of houseless wanderers and encampments. There weren't many tents back then—that came later, when tents sprang up everywhere with the 2011 Occupy social-justice movement and never left. What we saw was mostly makeshift tarp shelters and a lot of people sleeping on cardboard with blankets or sleeping bags—some gathered in small groups for protection, most just with a few pals or by themselves. The weather's mild here year-round, unlike pretty much anywhere north or far east of here, and it's just not that hard to sleep outside most of the time.

On one of the first days we were out, we were chatting up

Sunshine, a hefty houseless woman camped in a parking lot near the corner of busy Van Ness Avenue and Market Street, within eyesight of the stately, gold-domed City Hall, around lunchtime. I was asking her where she got her black eye—which I guessed was from her boyfriend, who was glaring at us from the other end of the parking lot—when I stupidly reached out to pet one of her two snarling German-shepherd–mix dogs. At that precise moment, the mutts decided to lunge and snap at each other, and my hand and arm got chewed in the middle with a couple of deep gashes. Sunshine barely noticed, her boyfriend smirked, and after I yelped in surprise I wrapped some Kleenex around my arm and tied it off with some string. It was just a street-life thing, like catching colds sleeping in the VW in college or cutting myself hitchhiking and wrapping a sock or whatever I had around it. You just put up with things. I didn't want to make a big deal out of it. Didn't want it to get in the way of the reporting. "You'd better get that looked at," Brant said. I shrugged it off. But by evening I had a fever and the blood wouldn't stop seeping.

So I checked into an emergency room to get patched up and filled with antibiotics, then went home and slept a day. Meanwhile, Brant wandered over to the corner where Van Ness becomes South Van Ness Avenue and crosses Mission Street. This is where he first spotted Little Bit, striding down the street, tiny legs pumping purposefully while she swung her arms back and forth like a kid skipping to the playground. She was only about four feet tall, so Brant thought she was a child. She wasn't.

She was thirty-two-year-old Susan Beach, known to street cleaners as the Midget, to her pals as Little Bit, and to anyone running a shop nearby watching her smoke crack, shoot heroin, and entice tricks as an exasperating paragon of tragedy. A dad, like me, Brant hurried over to talk to her, got the real skinny on who she was, and then met her crew. There were about a dozen of them, all hanging out on a wind-swept triangle of concrete with a couple of shading trees overlooking a cluster of tarps, cardboard, and shopping carts. This was just a few blocks from City Hall, and the traffic on busy South Van Ness and Mission roared by like metal rivers.

What do you call this spot on the traffic island? Brant asked.

"Homeless Island," they said.

When I got back into action after my emergency room visit and my one day of recuperating, we returned to that spot—and it hooked us. We still trolled all over the city, from forested Golden Gate Park to the industrial eastern-bayfront shoreline, but we always came back to Homeless Island every day or so.

These were desperate, fascinating people—the very definition of what the government calls the "chronically homeless," anyone who's lived outside for a year or more and has disabling conditions like mental illness or substance abuse.[12] That's a very different stratum of homeless from the majority. Most homeless people episodically slide into it because of emergencies like losing a job or fleeing domestic violence, then "self-resolve" (as caseworkers say) their way out of it by finding a job, moving permanently in with family, or the like.[13]

But the chronics? They are the most entrenched and most miserable of the unhoused, and they are the ones most people envision when they think of "the homeless." They're usually around 30 percent of the total homeless population. The other 70 percent, the ones you don't see all the time, are in shelters, couch surfing, or in institutions such as jail or rehab.[14]

The chronically homeless get the most attention because they are the most visible, outside all the time in tents or hanging out on the sidewalk, often shooting up or smoking dope. More than 75 percent of them are crushed by either mental difficulties or substance abuse, often both together.[15] They aren't going to just pull themselves off the street. No "up by the bootstraps" fantasy there. They are the ones most in need of help.

That chronic population was exactly whom I was looking for, and the Islanders were welcoming, in a street-rough way. Unusually street-smart. Messed up on drugs and desperation. But open to talking—and talking, and talking. They crept into our hearts. There was way more to them than met the eye, as there always is with homeless people.

And that's when we met Rita Grant.

I walked up to her as she sat on the concrete under the trees next to a shopping cart. In her lap was a big cardboard sign with HUNGER HURTS, ANYTHING HELPS scrawled on it with a Sharpie. She looked middle-aged and wore a sixties-style beige buckskin fringe jacket and jeans with piping around the pockets. Pretty stylish for a panhandler, I thought. She squinted at me for a long moment.

"Got a dollar?" she asked.

"Nah, I'm just here to talk," I said. "I'm a reporter. I'm writing about what life is like out here."

"Hmm, really?" Rita said, lips tightening. "Well, it's not good, I'll tell you that." She looked away, and I moved on to another shopping cart.

That one would take a little more time to open up, if she would at all, I thought. But something in her manner, her eyes, her moxie, told me it would be worth the effort.

CHAPTER 2

Rita—Subterranean World in Plain Sight

2003

The world of the most desperately homeless is a world all unto itself. Most people going about their daily business see the surface—like folks sitting on cardboard with bags, or panhandling signs—and mostly just keep walking by. Rita's Homeless Island stuck out like a human landslide.

If you rolled by the Island a few times in the spring of 2003, you couldn't help but notice Rita or her boyfriend, Tommy, standing in between the traffic lanes, holding cardboard signs reading Rita's favorite, HUNGER HURTS, ANYTHING HELPS, or Tommy's favorite, ANYTHING HELPS, EVEN-A-SMILE. Or Little Bit walking across the traffic island—here, at one of the busiest corners in San Francisco—looking for all the world like a lost little girl. Which is what her johns thought she was. That's why they'd drive up from places like Palo Alto in BMWs and the like to screw her at $50 a throw in the back seat. She was tough like a rat—snarling, telling you to fuck off or just plain giving you the cold shoulder until she got to know you. But then . . . then, she was heartbreaking, telling you about how she missed her four children, how she wanted a house with a yard and flowers. How she wanted love, how she had actually found it a few times in her life and had never given up hope of someday finding something that would last.

They were all like that, the Homeless Islanders—about a dozen regulars in all, with another dozen or so who drifted in and out. Tough or pathetic—but charming and gentle, and infinitely real under the surface.

And this place where they lived? Unlike anything else most people had seen before, even in a freewheeling lefty city of funky individualism. They lived on a *traffic island*. This forty-by-seventy-five-foot chunk of triangular concrete was ideal for them, with those two leafy trees giving shade, a nearby alley to do business in (mostly selling or buying dope and shoplifted stuff), and traffic streaming by on two major streets with stoplights in each direction so they could panhandle the stopped cars.

Rita and her friends were there all the time, their shopping carts parked around them as a barrier, as protection, as makeshift walls. In that circle they could hang out, eat, sleep, shoot up—do all the things they might do more privately inside what you'd call a home. Because this *was* their home. This was their reality, and they'd been in that reality for several years. So many, in fact, that dozens of others came and went at the little colony, some staying awhile, others just passing through, others still just showing up to buy dope or find out the best alley where they could pick up a john. The Island became so entrenched that it was known at least peripherally by nearly everyone who seriously dealt with entrenched street life in San Francisco.

The street counselors and panhandlers all knew Homeless Island was the hardest of the hard core in the city. They had talked with Rita and her pals, cajoling them, urging them to take services and move inside. Gave up. Then tried again. Failed again. This was anything but surprising, given the astonishing array of dysfunctions that had to be dealt with: Some were missing legs, some were deranged, some were hand-to-mouth pot, heroin, or crack dealers. Every one of them was addicted to something and usually shot up, snorted, or drank anything that became available. Aside from Little Bit, Tommy, and Rita, the main group included tough military vets, gay and straight alley hookers, and a society girl from Marin County who couldn't resist the needle. Most of the women had been dragged by bad-boy boyfriends onto life pathways that led to the gutter.

Memories of living in decent apartments or houses were long faded. They slept, injected and smoked drugs, dressed and undressed, and generally just hung out around their assembled bunch of shopping carts heaped with clothes, blankets, food, while the traffic from Van Ness and Mission roared alongside their little triangle of concrete. The traffic island actually lay at the end of a short stump of Twelfth Street that butted up to the corner of Van Ness and Mission, and the colony's mess spilled onto the sidewalks. Uneven heaps of food wrappers, empty beer cans and pint vodka bottles, clothes, stray shoes, blankets, cardboard—it all just lay where it was dropped, and the street cleaners, who came by with hoses and garbage trucks, swept the trash away every few days—along with whatever sleeping bags, piles of clothes, or other belongings the Islanders forgot to move before the trucks pulled up. They were a living-out-loud microcosm of all that can go the most wrong in the most dysfunctional homeless lives.

People who drove by or walked by on the way to shops or work saw the sprawl and the decay of Islanders doing drugs right out there in the open—a hallmark of modern San Francisco—and maybe wondered about how they got that way. But stopping to engage? Not many did. And even if they did, the conversations didn't last long. A lot of goodhearted people live and work in San Francisco, but getting into a deep talk with people who too often are jittery for the next hit is difficult. You have to pick your times and your spots. It takes effort.

And, yes, *crazy* is an offensive word to counselors and the mental health advocate community. But on the Island, when you had mental issues, the people around you called you "crazy." And like most chronically homeless people, everyone had at least some psychological trauma from living so hard outside. All those niceties about wordings could come later if you made it out of the streets alive and rejoined the more carefully worded society. *Midget?* Little Bit preferred to say she was "just small," but when her pals called her a "midget," she laughed. Everything was direct. Which meant the conversations with anyone who cared to stop and chat were direct. No pussyfooting around how hard it was to have to screw assholes for a pittance so you could pack your veins or pipe, or how desperately you wanted to get the hell off the street someday but had no real idea of how to do that.

No pretending that hunkering down outside wasn't miserable.

THE MOST IRONIC THING about Homeless Island was that this gritty little colony existed right in the middle of one of the prettiest, richest cities on earth—the Left Coast bastion of progressive compassion. That's the weird thing about San Francisco. It's got some of the prettiest buildings and homes in the country, but walking through the downbeat parts of San Francisco where I spend much of my time, you'd think you were in some gentrified version of Kolkata. The geography of homelessness in San Francisco is pretty specific, and it has its own demographics and dynamics—a subterranean world that goes way beyond tents and people with their hands out asking for cash.

The main populations are clustered in a few key regions.

There's the Mission, southwest of downtown, historically an economically spotty district with wonderful Latino flavor and Victorians that has in recent years gentrified with a tech boom but retains its bohemian essence. The Haight-Ashbury has been drawing would-be hippie transients and aging alcoholics to its spread of beautiful homes and shabby chic shops since the Summer of Love in 1967. For street folk who want to be near the water, there's the Embarcadero, the waterfront strip of cavernous piers and trendy restaurants and shops on the edge of the city's financial hub.

The Bayview–Hunters Point neighborhood, the historically Black sprawl of low-cost housing and shops on the southeast part of town, hosts hundreds of ramshackle vehicles and hard-to-find tent spots along the shoreline; and Golden Gate Park, an urban jewel of museums and nature, is studded with camping hideaways in thick underbrush or in groves of trees.

Among the first street folks I got to know were a half dozen panhandlers near City Hall on Market Street. The most colorful among them was Peg, a fortysomething guy with a titanium leg who panhandled by doing magic tricks with glow rings—snatching one from your ear, making them disappear from one hand to the other. He filled us in on life in his territory.

"The cops ping-pong us from block to block every few days or, if we're lucky, weeks," he said, sitting in a parking lot, where the little group was downing fried rice from a big carryout container some passerby had given them. "As long as you don't fight and just move on, it's all right. The cops don't really want to hassle you, but they have to move things around or the people who live here start complaining a lot. Who the hell wants to move, but what can you do? So we go up to the Castro [several blocks west] or up toward Fisherman's Wharf [several blocks north]. Doesn't really matter as long as you know where to get what you need—you know, the right food handouts, leftovers, good panhandling spots."

The ping-pong game is perennial. Shopkeepers and residents don't want indigents panhandling and crashing in front of their buildings, and indigents don't want to be hassled but can't really fight authority from a scrap of cardboard when they're ordered to move.

It's become more complicated over the years to move camps because of legal wrangling over sweeps—particularly over what the government's responsibility is to help the people being moved.[1] Just about every city, including San Francisco, finds ways to get around limits by forcing moves if the sidewalk is blocked or rampant drug dealing is going on, things like that—residents demand it, and business owners demand it. Homeless advocates fight back with new lawsuits, the city brass adjust the rules, and life goes on. Nobody's ever satisfied on any side.

It's been this way for decades.

This push-me, pull-you boiled over in a disturbingly emblematic way on a chilly January day in 2023 when art gallery owner Collier Gwin sprayed a homeless woman down with a garden hose in the posh Jackson Square neighborhood after fruitlessly telling her to move from in front of his shop. The woman, who went only by the name Q, had been a screaming disruption in the neighborhood for weeks despite residents asking emergency services to help her. The gallery owner snapped—and video someone shot of the confrontation went viral. Nobody with any authority publicly said what he did was okay, and even the shop owner, who was charged with misdemeanor battery, said he was sorry. But a lot of folks also sighed and said they could understand the frustration. They blamed the city for not housing or institutionalizing troublesome street people fast enough.

"I've called the Fire Department, 311 or the nonemergency line, many times over the years, and, yes, they come out," Dr. Kevin Miller, who lives on Van Ness Avenue near continuous encampments, told me. "I call to say there's a homeless person in need of assistance, there's garbage, there's a tent blocking the sidewalk, discarded needles—

you name it. It's the same complaints, but the same problems keep coming back again and again and again.

"People have the right to live on the street if they have no shelter. I wish them well, and I know they are in crisis and need help. But I also believe the public sidewalk should provide access to all, and how many times do we have to report the same problem?"

Even homeless advocates said they understood the frustration, but they also blamed the city—and called for compassion and patience from housed folks in situations like Gwin's.

"I think first and foremost, what's necessary is treating your un-housed neighbors with dignity and respect, getting to know them, and figuring out what they need," Jennifer Friedenbach told me when I talked with her about the hosing debacle. She is director of the Coalition on Homelessness in San Francisco, and one of the most thoughtful activists I've known—pushes her agenda, yes, as she should in that role, but tries to see both sides of debates.

"Getting to know what resources are available is important," Jennifer said. "You may have access to the internet in a way they don't, so you can look up resources like winter shelters, churches that offer support, drop-in centers. Just like you would with any neighbor, you want to communicate in a constructive way to resolve issues. Most of the times that works, and occasionally it doesn't. You just keep trying."

That's a pretty tall order. But if you live in San Francisco, it comes with the territory.

In this city, the biggest fights over what's right and wrong and whom to move and how have always swirled around the best-known center of homelessness—the Tenderloin. It's a tightly packed, poverty-pocked neighborhood of fifty square blocks spreading north of glittering City Hall, west of ritzy Union Square, and south of the mansions of Nob Hill. A compression of thirty-five thousand residents, most of whom are low income and struggling to get by in cheap housing that often dates back to the early 1900s, the TL (as locals call it) is a mix-and-match mess of worn-out old residential hotels, vibrant immigrant enclaves, creative businesses, and stop-n-robs, those little corner liquor and convenience stores where everything costs too much, there's usually a dope dealer within a few feet of the door, and a stickup empties the till with disturbing frequency.[2] Today? Twenty years ago? Blink, and much of it all looks the same.

Homeless Island was perched between the Tenderloin and the Mission. And just like everywhere else in the homeless world, not a single one of its campers *really* wanted to be there. Sure, sometimes you'd get bravado about freedom and living the outside life with nobody telling you what to do, but if you caught chronically homeless people in times when their heads were clear and they were being absolutely honest, they'd say it straight.

That is true to this day. Nobody wants to sleep facedown in the dirt or in a tent or on cardboard forever. You just learn to live with it in survival mode when you're hard-core. You have to, so you can put one foot in front of the other.

It takes a long time to fall that far, to slam through so many support struts in your life that there's nowhere left to go.

Rita rode that slide for years before she hit bottom.

CHAPTER 3

Surfer Girl

1965

Rita had been one of those so-called golden girls in high school, the athlete who knew how to dress up when she had to and just as easily shed finery for a bikini when she headed out to surf with the boys. By all reckoning, Rita—then known by her maiden name of Raimondo—had every chance to go out in the world and be what by 1960s standards would be considered a success. The only missing parts were these: she didn't like school, and she didn't have much ambition.

But in high school? Late 1960s? That didn't matter. Now was all that counted. The future wasn't even on the horizon.

"I guess in high school, I studied boys," she told me, always with an impish smile that I suspect looks like the same one she gave the boys on the beach. "Not much else, really." Back then—in the mid-1960s—she liked a mixture of cool boys who were good in class, and the fast boys who skipped class with their surfboards.

The term *golden girl* comes up a lot when talking to her family and her old classmates. *She* didn't think she was that "golden"—in fact, there was always a bit of doubt, that maybe she wasn't pretty enough. But others remember her as fun. Beautiful. Lean, not too tall or too short, honey hair falling to her shoulders, chatty with everyone. And being a surfer girl was pretty damn odd back then. Adventurous. The Beach Boys splashed "Surfer Girl" onto the charts in 1963, and by the time Rita was a freshman at Eau Gallie High School on the surf-happy Florida coast in 1965, the male-centric vibe hadn't changed.

"Rita was unusual—not many girls were surfers," Paul Le Fleur, a lean surfer boy a year ahead of Rita in school, told me. "She wasn't really a great surfer, but, man, was she in shape. And hot? Oh, man. That, and cute. But to be a really good surfer, you gotta put the hours in. And my buddies and me, we'd get up at six a.m. and put the work in—some great surfers came from around there. Kelly Slater [widely considered the greatest professional surfer of all time] came out of Cocoa Beach, right where we all surfed.

"Rita? She just really liked the surfing scene. She was certainly smart, but just like me, she didn't like school."

She was a creature of the times.

In 1965, *The Sound of Music* and *My Fair Lady* dominated movie screens. The Beatles still performed in suits as rock and roll started to hold its own against the likes of Tom Jones. Gas was thirty-one cents a gallon, the average house cost about $20,000, and the average annual income was about $7,000—a livable ratio we could only dream wistfully of today in California. Martin Luther King Jr. was leading marches against segregation, and the Voting Rights Act was signed in an attempt to squelch bigotry at the polls, but Black, brown, and Asian people were still generations behind white people in income and equality. The Watts riots erupted in Los Angeles that year and the Vietnam War was mushrooming into its full horror.

But for white folks in Eau Gallie, on the Space Coast of Florida, where Cape Canaveral was the hub of a cluster of space agency installations aiming for the moon shot, placidity and fitting into a traditional vision of sixties family life set the tone.

• • •

FLORIDA WAS A HUGE change from what Rita had grown up with a thousand miles north in Brewster, a village of about fifteen hundred people in New York State's Hudson Valley known as the hometown of the 1980s pop star Laura Branigan. That's where Rita's flame-haired, Irish-heritage mother, Joanne Raimondo, and Italian-heritage dad, Lee Raimondo, were raising their eight children.

Joanne was brilliant, but at a young age, her ability to pick a man who could stick to the straight and narrow and keep the bills paid was less so, at least at first. Unconventional.

Lee was quick-witted and worked hard, but he had one main flaw: he was irresponsible back then, an inveterate gambler. He bounced from job to job—driving an ice cream truck, delivering milk, doing sales—and always gambling on the side, which meant bills sometimes didn't get paid, debt collectors came to the door, and the family had to move several times.

Joanne was the opposite type. She was the steady parent, and the disciplinarian. Which came naturally to her.

She was a Depression baby, born in 1931 to an Irish immigrant woman and a bartender who got a job dishing drinks at the New York World's Fair in 1939. Life was tough, money short, and Joanne responded to the instability by buckling down and excelling at her studies. Before she graduated from high school the yearning to stand on her own two feet tugged too hard and she dropped out to work full-time. Decades later, she went back and earned her equivalency diploma—and even went to college and earned an AA degree, concentrating on writing—but for the time being, work was the priority.

Listening to the family describe her, she reminded me of my own mom, born one year earlier than Joanne and a take-no-crap, strong woman to the core. Mom helped start a NOW chapter in the early 1970s in the Bay Area—I have a picture on my mantel of her with Gloria Steinem, both wearing smoky sunglasses and looking equally fierce—and led women's empowerment seminars as the 1960s closed and the 1970s began. The moxie Joanne and my mom both needed to thrive in those times in the world was enormous. They each did it her own way—with my mom's way including tossing her son out of the house, of course, though that eventually worked out fine.

For Joanne, that meant pulling a full paycheck as a teenager. She was working at a store in New York at the age of sixteen when she met Lee. She married him soon after and started having children.

Rita and her sister Debbie, just one year younger, remember their dad as a good-time Charlie who wasn't around much.

"He was immature and irresponsible," Debbie said. "But he was a fun guy—when we lived in Brewster, there was a lake nearby and they had games like sack races and Hula-Hoops, tug-o'-war, stuff like that. And we'd always win because we were pretty athletic."

And that ice cream truck job? Heaven. "We got to eat ice cream all the time when he came home," Debbie said. "That was pretty great. But then, he wasn't around all that much. Out gambling, doing whatever."

As the kids spilled out one after the other, Joanne gave them the advice she gave herself growing up: try to do your best at whatever you're doing. She knew how to have fun, yes— "She was wonderful, would take us on picnics, to museums, once helped us make a carnival in the front yard for the neighborhood with booths and games," Rita's younger sister Pam Johnson remembers—but Joanne also drove them to be creative and strong. For Rita, that meant throwing herself into gymnastics.

It was the most ambitious thing Rita ever did, and she was great at it. In 1964, when she was fourteen, she represented New York State at the New York World's Fair national exhibition, and everyone who knew her figured she was next bound for the Olympics.

"Rita had everything," recalled Alice Wells, a gymnastics teammate in Brewster. "Blond, beautiful . . . everybody loved her, and, boy, was she good at gymnastics, especially uneven bars and floor exercises. She could do thirty backsprings in a row, and when we went to the Olympic trials, I thought she was going to be in for sure."

That dream ended when Rita tore a knee ligament that year. It healed, but not enough for competition.

Around that time, her mother decided she'd had enough of living with a gambling man who bounced between jobs and had a hard time keeping up with the bills. The family says that in later years, he became more responsible . . . but this was then. Rita had just finished middle school.

One day in 1965 Joanne suddenly gathered seven of her children together and said, "We're going to visit your grandparents in Michigan, kids." But when the car headed south instead of west, the older kids caught on. Rita cried; most of the others were confused and worried.

"Pam said, 'Oh, boy, a trip!'—but the rest of us did not want to move at all," Rita recalled. "But it was probably the best thing for us. Yeah, it actually was the best thing. Changed our lives, that's for sure."

Danny, the oldest of the kids—one year older than Rita—stayed behind with his father. A freshman in high school, he was already getting into trouble—staying out late, a juvenile-law scrape with theft and the like—and his sister Debbie says their mom just didn't have the bandwidth at the time to deal with it. He later moved to Florida and reconnected with the rest of the family, but for quite a while it was just mom and the other children.

Joanne had hidden more than $2,000 under her mattress to pay for the journey, and she had a friend on the Space Coast of Florida, so that's where they headed.

They wound up in Eau Gallie, the coastal town of about ten thousand just twenty minutes from the surfing mecca of Cocoa Beach. The name in French means "rocky water." It was prophetic.

RITA FIT IN QUICKLY at school and easily made it onto the cheerleading team, scoring a coveted spot as one of the team's two "mascots," meaning she wore a uniform evoking the school mascot, a sailor, and wowed the game crowds with cartwheels and splits. And the surfing? That skill set in quickly, and it helped seal that "golden girl" image.

"She was sweet and always had a big ol' smile on her face," recalled classmate Debbee Hicks Combs, who now lives in Tennessee. "I never heard her say a harsh or unkind word about anyone. She did front flips and backflips all the way down the court. And at that time in the late sixties there weren't so many girls who could do that. She was just phenomenal at doing that."

Yes, she was a knockout for the boys and the fans. But classes? They just floated by. She doesn't remember a single thing she studied except for—always said with a smile—"boys." Somewhat prophetically, or maybe just appropriately, the face page on Rita's junior-year yearbook quotes *The Prophet*: "Let there be no scales to weigh your unknown treasure; And seek not the depths of your knowledge with staff or sounding line. For self is a sea boundless and measureless." Rita took the "seek not the depths" bit to heart. And the bit about "self."

Meanwhile, Joanne was working as many as three waitress jobs at once, and though she had less time with the kids than some moms, she still drove them toward achievement. She was kind and loving, but tough.

"My mom was a very strong woman—she had to be," said Rita's younger sister by three years, Valerie Boecker. "She had us involved in everything—sports, dance classes, everything—but she could rarely show up, like when I was a cheerleader. She was always working.

"The good part about growing up with that many brothers and sisters is having all of us together. I loved that we were all a baseball team—literally, in the neighborhood when we'd play with the other kids, we were a baseball team all by ourselves. We had a great child-hood. We were very happy children.

"Some of what she gave us in the way of a strong upbringing I only appreciated later," Valerie said with a laugh. "Like, my mom used to make us clean up the house every Saturday—I hated it then, but after having two kids of my own, now I can appreciate it."

Rita, the oldest of the brood with Danny still back in New York with their dad, kept on the straight and narrow—with that surfing twist. "Mom just wanted me to do well in life, and I really just loved the beach and boys," Rita said.

Her senior-year yearbook picture in the Wheelindas public-service club for girls shows her in the front row, standing in a prim white dress to the knees with a white sweater and blond hair falling lightly below her shoulders. Her hands are politely half-clasped in front of her.

That same year, she also ran for homecoming queen. Most of the family remembered her as winning the crown, but in reality she was the first runner-up—memories can be like that. Runner-up was still a big honor. Classmate Le Fleur laughed hard when I reminded him of the yearbook photo of her standing alongside the winner, Janet Lee "Jan" Dover, and Rita with white gloves above her elbows and her hair pulled up into a tower on her head in the beehive style of the day.

"Oh, man, I cannot imagine her like that," he said. "In the surfing crowd, we all hated the cheerleaders and all that shit. But Rita—she pretty much got along with everyone."

Le Fleur took her to his senior dance in 1967, and even though the Summer of Love and the advent of movies like *The Graduate* were reflecting a loosening of culture, being a surfer or a band nerd still meant the same thing: you kept things fairly proper.

"We didn't have sex, that's for sure," Le Fleur said. "I only asked her out because I was one of the so-called bad boys in surfing, and she was a surfer girl, and she was hot, and she understood what surfing was about. And she was very sweet, I tell you. Kind. Very nice. What you'd call 'a good girl' back then, even though she had that bit of wild about her."

The actual winner of the homecoming queen title that year, Janet Dover, recalled Rita as being gracious in second place.

"It was a real honor, her being runner-up—it spoke very highly of her," said Dover, a schoolteacher and aerobics-business owner who retired to a house near Eau Gallie. "Rita was a surfer, and I thought that was so cool because I never learned how to do that. But she sure did. To be athletic and a surfer and so attractive—Rita had it all. She was a keeper for sure."

Rita chuckles when the homecoming queen thing comes up. "It's what we did back then," she told me when I first learned of it. "Nice thing to do. But it was just the thing you did. Different times."

Rita's sister Debbie remembered her "as being super-popular, super-pretty, and got any boy she wanted. She liked girlie stuff, fashion magazines. And she was fearless. I mean, she'd cut class to go surfing. She was the golden girl. I was the dependable daughter."

"It wasn't just all about me. Debbie always had whatever boyfriends she wanted," Rita said. "She was really pretty, too."

The good-looks thing comes up again and again when spending

time with this family because, well, the women in it all pretty much look like they stepped out of a fashion magazine. Sister Pam's daughter Amanda Grace Johnson even took the leap as a teenager into modeling and wound up gracing magazine pages and runways all over the world, leading to a role as a beautiful maiden in distress in Robert Downey Jr.'s 2009 hit, *Sherlock Holmes*.

"I guess we got good genes," Rita deadpanned. But she only partially meant that. "To tell you the truth, I never thought I was pretty," she confided to me. I told her everyone I've talked to who grew up with her uses words like *pretty*, *hot*, and *beautiful* to describe her, and she laughed it off.

"I was jealous of the other girls because I didn't have a great body," she said. She thought about that awhile, then added, "But I was really full of life back then."

The captain of Rita's cheerleader squad, Marsha Holbrook Wicks, was in Rita's class all through high school and still lives in that part of Florida, near Orlando. It was her turn to laugh when I told her Rita didn't remember herself as anything special in school.

"What I remember of Rita was her smile. So pretty, and she just lit up," Marsha said. "You could tell she just loved what she was doing—being in gymnastics, being with the crowd, being on the cheerleading squad. It made her light up, being so involved.

"It was great that she added that spirit to what we did. We all appreciated it.

"Running for homecoming queen, the cheer squad, being in the Wheelindas service club—yeah, those weren't academic notches aimed at college, but they did show initiative," Marsha went on. "She always had a goal, and she worked hard at it." That grit probably helped keep her alive later on, Marsha said.

The trouble for the golden girl came, as with so many people who hit a popular peak in high school, after the classes ended and the cap and gown finished their moments in the sun and were put away. The surfboard got stashed, the beach crowd all went off to marriage, college, or the draft and Vietnam, and the structured carefree nature of teenage life ended.

That's when real life began.

CHAPTER 4

Beaches, Boats, and Freedom

1969

I t was one of those humid Florida summer days, and Rita had headed to the beach to hang in the sun, ogle the surfer boys, and maybe buy some weed, something she'd just started to dig now that she'd been out of high school a year or so. That's when she saw him—tanned and lean, lithe and handsome, with long blond hair. A surfer dude, and he seemed to be selling pot, but he was darting back and forth in the crowd, yakking with everyone—like a busy social bee, she mused.

"What are you doing?" Rita asked.

Doug Grant looked the equally lithe, bikini-clad Rita up and down and smiled.

"Do you want to spend the night with me?" he said.

Thoughts of pot dashed from her mind. Things were suddenly moving fast in a direction she hadn't anticipated—but she liked it. And she wanted her head to be clear for whatever happened.

They hung out that day, and by the time they actually did spend that night together, Rita was in love. Another night followed, then another, and soon they were pretty much full-time together. It was 1969, songs like "Hot Fun in the Summertime" and "Get Together" ruling the airwaves, and Rita hadn't decided what to do with her life after dropping out of the local community college and living at home. But as always, she liked boys, and now she actually loved this one.

"He was quite the handsome guy, and kind of the leader of the pack on the beach," Rita recalled. "He could surf, he always had a little weed, and he could dive for fish better than anyone anywhere. He was even living at the beach and fished with a cane pole. He was so cool.

"I wasn't going anywhere else in my life, so I went along with him. But really, I was totally slayed by the energy coming out of his body. It was like—no other person affected me the way he did."

Doug remembered her being fun to hang with, but mostly what drew him was that she was a knockout.

"It was my eyeballs that made me fall in love with her," he said with a laugh. "She was an Olympic-class gymnast and looked great. I mean, really—she was beautiful."

They became beach people. Doug fished and dove for crab and lobsters, selling them onshore, Rita did waitressing jobs, and by 1976 they were married (she took Doug's last name) and had their first child, who they named Faith. A year later came daughter Joy, and they wound up in Sebastian, a little town on Florida's Treasure Coast, so called because a fleet of Spanish treasure ships heading home from the New World sank there in a 1715 hurricane, spewing gold and silver all over the coastline waters. With treasure hunters and tourists swarming the shoreline towns, the place is a good one for selling seafood and scoring waitressing jobs, so the couple did well. There was no talk of college, of any mainstream careers. It was a form of 1970s hippiedom, not caring about money, smoking a bit of pot, living for the moment.

Then in 1979 a hurricane tore off the roof of the rental house they were in, so they loaded their car and headed south. They'd heard life was even easier for beach people in Key West, so three hundred miles later they parked there and took a look around.

The island town of Key West could hardly have fit better. It had always been a sun-and-fun getaway spot with great fishing and laid-back charm, while also being a military base dating from the early 1800s. President Harry Truman had kept a winter White House there, a slew of literary giants including Ernest Hemingway and Tennessee Williams had lived there, and tobacco from nearby Cuba—just ninety miles away—made the town a cigar capital at one point. But by the time Rita and Doug arrived with kids in tow, the vibe had morphed into something even looser.

A history chapter on the Vacation Homes of Key West website captures the feel: "With more bars and more churches per capita than anywhere else in North America, the 1970s and '80s attracted a whole new wave of creative free-thinkers with the arrival of literary groups, actors, musicians, treasure hunters, artists, designers, photographers and film makers, entrepreneurs, trades people, sailors, philanthropists, self-proclaimed 'pirates' and members of the hippie 'counter-culture,' openly gay and lesbian people from every walk of life, and expatriates."[1] For freewheeling wanderers like Rita and Doug, it was like coming home to a place they'd never been before, like the John Denver song says.

This dot of an island is only four miles long and about a mile wide, and the 1980 census put the population at just about 24,400.[2] After asking around a bit, Rita and Doug wound up at Simonton Street Beach, a tiny stretch of sand at the end of a road. A few hundred yards off the beach lay a swarm of liveaboard boats anchored just off what was known to locals as Christmas Tree Island, a twenty-two-acre oval of fill created by military dredging and covered by pine trees. Simonton Beach was called Bum Beach, and the island—officially called Wisteria Island—and its boats were inhabited by people who lived hand to mouth thanks to odd jobs. It was an enclave of free spirits.

"We felt at home right away," Rita said. "You weren't allowed to park and sleep in your car for too long, so we rented a boat for one hundred dollars."

That boat sank before too long, so they rented another for $150. It sprang a leak, so they got another. And another. In between, there were times sleeping in a tent on Christmas Tree Island, where the kids could play and people shared food and there was a sense of community. Sometimes they'd take a motel room in town, sometimes they'd have a camper van onshore, but nothing ever lasted for long.

The term *homeless* hadn't really caught on when they first got there, but nobody in the island liveaboard bunch thought of themselves like that anyway. By now, Rita and Doug were in their early thirties, in the prime of life, elastic enough to roll loose and love it.

"We all lived pretty free back then—being a boat bum was easy," recalled Jeff Erwin, one of the crowd and a close friend of Rita's and Doug's. "There were plenty of railroad riders, travelers, and people who knew where to get a free meal. And we all loved the water.

"And Christmas Tree Island? It was pretty nice. We'd have meals together and respected each other."

Jeff was a Vietnam War navy veteran, and he'd come to Key West the long and hard way—though he just considered it part of his journey, no big deal. He had dropped out of college in Wisconsin in the 1970s, hand-built a thirty-five-foot outrigger canoe fitted with an outboard motor, and sailed it on various waterways, including the Mississippi River, until he wound up in Florida—then Key West, because it was as far south as you could go in the United States. It was an adventure. Freedom. The same kinds of things that drew Rita and the other island liveaboards.

"Rita and Doug were the nicest people," Jeff said. "Nice family. Doug was tough as nails and good at diving. But Rita? She never seemed like she had any ambition." Jeff laughed. "But neither did I. She just took care of the kids."

Rita and Doug went through at least four boats (*Sailboat, Captain Sleepy, Dauntless,* and *Entropy*), ranging from thirty-six to sixty feet long, over the next several years. They were beat-up crafts costing a few hundred bucks at best to buy or rent, and Faith remembers one springing a leak so bad that cockroaches floated up around them on deck. Rita kept a skiff to ferry the kids to shore for school, as the oldest reached school age in the early eighties—and the count of tots swelled to four with the arrival of Penelope in 1980 and Doug "Dougie" Jr. in 1982.

But everyone involved remembers the time as pretty magical—both on the boats and in town. At least for a while.

The kids learned to swim like fishes, stayed tanned as berries in the year-round balmy sun, and loved the open air. When they got old enough, they roamed the town, played on the beaches, ran free.

Rita was perpetually fit from being in the water all the time and helping Doug with the fishing. And Doug? He could hold his breath for four minutes underwater and became one of the island's premier divers for lobster, crab, conch—anything that squatted in the water, he could grab and sell onshore. He dragged up anchors and other metal and sold that, too. Before long, he was dubbed Diver Doug and was making enough money to use dive tanks to go deeper. He also worked on lobster boats. A lot of the family meals were just snatched from the ocean.

"We'd say, 'Dad, what's for dinner?' And he'd say, 'Give me a few minutes,' and jump overboard," said Faith. "Then he'd come back ten minutes later with crab or lobster or whatever, and we'd have dinner. It was pretty cool."

Doug and Rita felt like they'd found a floating life they didn't even know they'd been hoping for. It was a mix of Robinson Crusoe and Swiss Family Robinson through a hippie lens.

"Shit happens our whole lives, and you just adjust," Doug told me. "That's what we did. Everything kept progressing, and living around that Christmas Tree Island, well, it was just fun. There wasn't any paperwork. We never had a phone, address, none of that stuff.

"The fun thing about it was—we did our thing, we didn't bother anybody, didn't have to steal. We always ate good—stone crabs, oysters, pompano in parchment, lobsters. And conches—you eat 'em raw. They're the Florida abalone. Money didn't make any difference to me. I'd seen that people who had a lot of it had nothing but headaches. As far as I was concerned, the real collateral was food. And we always had plenty of that."

FOR THE KIDS IN particular, Key West life was a blend of conventional and unconventional.

Rita always had a bit of a spiritual side—"I do believe in God, you know," she'd tell me with eyes wide, as if that might be a surprise for someone who doesn't fit a lot of norms. So she took the kids to a Seventh-day Adventist church in town on Saturdays. But when it came to pitching in with the parent volunteering at school—no way. "Mom was never the PTA kind of mom," Faith said. "Not my thing," Rita said.

And food? The main rule was no junk food. With fresh seafood available all the time, and mangoes, bananas, and avocados growing all over Key West, ready for picking, there was a baseline of decent eating. The diet Rita enforced was vegetables, fish, clams, and the like. It went with the outdoor, beach-swim lifestyle—which persists there to this day, with Rita's kids all still looking like they belong on the cover of a beach-resort magazine. They're stunning, in the way their mother was at their ages.

"My mom was a really healthy person—was totally into health food, super-healthy and fit," Joy told me in 2022. "Like, the only kind of dessert we could have would be carob graham crackers. And that's funny because my only addiction to this day is sugar, which I keep pretty good control of now.

"I remember one time when I was a kid, I was eating a mint chocolate-chip ice cream cone, and I was eating it on the beach. Mom came out, looked at me, and smacked it out of my hand and said, 'I told you a million times I don't want you eating that green shit!'" Joy chuckled at the memory. "Yes, sugar. Not healthy."

Junk TV was also not allowed in the home, which was a lot easier to achieve since the family didn't watch TV. But they did have a videotape player to watch movies.

"We kids wanted to watch *Dark Crystal*, kid stuff like that, not *Gandhi*. But our parents wanted only the serious stuff. So that's what we'd watch."

And then there were the drugs.

Doug and Rita had liked pot since the 1960s, and Doug had experimented with heroin back then, but not until they immersed in the island-boat culture of Key West did they start dabbling more regularly in opioids or cocaine. They both told me they weren't full-on addicts, and the kids say their parents never used in front of them—which would have been tough to pull off if they were strung out.

"We didn't want the kids to see any of that stuff," Rita recalled. "It wasn't until later that things got out of control." She and her family say she didn't use dope when she was pregnant with any of the kids, and none of them displayed complications that could have come from that kind of use.

Meanwhile, as the kids grew, the family became woven into the bohemian world of onshore Key West.

I got a look at that world in hindsight a few years ago when Rita, Faith, Joy, Pam, and I all strolled and drove through Key West to look at the family's touchstones—a motel they stayed in, the spots they parked a van at to sleep in, the houses they stayed at in between boats and Christmas Tree Island, the places where they liked to hang out. For me, it was like finally opening a book that's grown dust on a shelf.

I had never been to this part of their geographical history that so formed who they were—and I found myself so moved I choked up every few hours. Everywhere we went, I could picture the young Rita and her kids from photos she'd sent me over the decades in Christmas cards and letters, and contrasting that with the pain I knew had pocked their lifetimes was vividly illuminating. It was a real-time reminder of that peculiar archaeology of place and era that shapes people into success, failure, happiness, sorrow, tragedy, and contentment, and how our early lives propel us more than any other period toward where we wind up.

This was where this family's early lives happened. It was a beautiful place. I loved seeing it.

On a skinny island that's only four miles long, most people get to know one another. The beach and the family's wide circle of friends were "great babysitters," Rita cracked.

Down one alley was the cottage where "Popeye," a corncob-pipe-smoking old man, lived. On Saturdays he'd hold competitions for the island kids in making puzzles and casting nets; they'd come for gumdrops and to play marbles. "He had frozen pineapple juice for us . . . he was wonderful and kind," remembered Joy. When he died, he left thousands of dollars for several kids' education—it helped Joy pay for massage school.

Another lane held a house they'd stayed in briefly with Doug, while Rita stayed on the boat. Another was where family friend Jeff had the kids over for extended stays when they needed a break from the water or when the parents were in between boats and wanted a break themselves. We visited health food stores they'd buy vegetables at. And everywhere were spots where they'd hung out with characters like Tightrope Man, Cookie Lady, and Banana Bread Man, who peddled homemade banana bread from a cooler on a bicycle. The kids used to spend endless hours at the library and strolled up and down touristy Duval Street, window-shopping the jewelry, clothing, and souvenir shops.

But perhaps the most fun was street performing—busking—at Mallory Square, a wide plaza at the water's edge stuffed with arts and crafts booths and restaurants. In early adolescence, the kids had taken a "Circus of the Kids" performance class at school for fun, and they put it to use for loose change on the dock. Joy did fire eating, Faith played clarinet, Penelope performed as a fake statue—but Doug Jr. was too young to even do that, so he just played on the beach. (Later on, when their littlest sibling, Scooter, came onto the scene, he also played on the beach.) While the kids worked the crowd, Diver Doug would paddle up to the pier's edge in the family skiff, blowing a conch shell to sell seashells, and Rita sold conch shells she'd picked up diving. It was a family affair, and the pickings were easy. Every night tourists packed the place to watch the sun sink over the Gulf of Mexico.

One night we stood and watched that same sunset in a glorious profusion of orange and pink, and it was like an electric energy went through Rita as she and the kids remembered what they were doing on this very dock four decades ago. Mallory Square is every bit as hopping today as it was then, super-touristy and fun, reminding me of San Francisco's Fisherman's Wharf. Only with more reliable sunshine and warmth.

"I loved my kids performing like that," Rita said. "It got them off the boat, they had a chance to be with their friends doing something fun, and Doug—everyone loved to hear his conch horn."

Joy laughed. "Our parents' main involvement in our performing? 'Be back before night gets too dark because the running lights aren't working on the skiff,' they'd say."

Everywhere we drove, up and down the island from Simonton Beach to Hemingway's house and the classic tropical bars from Sloppy Joe's to the Green Parrot, the memories sparked. When they became adults, the kids came back and worked here, and though not all of them stayed, Key West stayed in them. In the early to mid-1980s, the island-boat life was—a word that usually comes up when they recall it—"magical." Pictures at the time show Rita, Doug, and the kids arm in arm, smiling, looking happy and healthy.

"We had a fucked-up life, but my mom was a loving mom, and she really does love us," said Joy, who still lives in the Keys but up a few islands from Key West. "That's never in doubt. Our family is all free mentally—we're kinda like free birds. And I do love my mom, but she's like a giant fifteen-year-old. She likes to have fun. And I say this with real love, but she can be a bit of an airhead.

"One-half of her is a super-clean hippie person, and the other half is someone who doesn't want any rules or regulations, to do whatever she wanted to do. I've learned as a parent, though, that if you're not really committed to really putting in the time and effort, it doesn't really work. Just loving your kids isn't enough."

Faith kept a house in Key West until she moved to a spacious home in Orlando with her growing family a couple of years ago, and though her life has evolved light-years from those childhood days, she appreciates the strength she got from them.

"This is an island of misfits," Faith said. "I don't think Mom felt like she belonged in her family—they were too normal for her—so she came out here where no one was normal. The castaways and misfits are the ones she always feels the most comfortable with. And we kids wanted to be normal.

"The community took care of us. It's what Key West was like. It was a tribe, everybody knew everybody. There were our little guardian angels all over the island."

When the kids got frustrated at having to ferry in and out of town for school, or at cold nights on the rickety liveaboard boats, or later when they were older at the erratic behavior by their parents as they were splitting apart, the kids had shoulders to lean on in Key West. It was a true community.

Faith sighed and gazed at the sunset. "You didn't have to have a lot of money here to be happy."

CHAPTER 5

Homeless Island

1986

In the mid- to late 1980s, as the kids were heading toward early teen-agerhood, that carefree Robinson Crusoe vibe started to unravel.

By now known as an ace deckhand who could dive for any-thing, Diver Doug was taking spot gigs on lobster boats as well as boats run by treasure hunter Mel Fisher, operating equipment and poking around for shipwrecks. Fisher's outfit is world-renowned for finding the wreck of the Spanish treasure ship *Nuestra Señora de Atocha* in 1985—a mother lode of silver, gold, coins, and more that, worth around $400 million, is considered the greatest sunken trea-sure ever recovered. Doug was doing jobs for Fisher during the time period of the big find, and it didn't make him rich, but that didn't really matter.

"I just loved diving . . . it was unbelievable, so cool. You'd see history down there," he said. I told him friends said he spent more time underwater than most fish, and he chuckled. "That sounds about right."

The boat gigs took him away for as much as a week at a time, though. And in his absence, Rita liked to party. Too much, she admits. "I started thinking the grass would be greener somewhere else. We just weren't getting along."

The two split up around 1986, and Rita soon had a new boyfriend, a shrimp boat captain named Mark Cotter. Their son, Mark "Scooter" Jr., was born the next year, and island life continued on a liveaboard boat, with the kids splitting time between Mom and Dad and pals like Jeff. Faith, who at eleven was the oldest, felt protective of all the others and didn't like Mark, saw him as trouble. But Rita was mostly glad just to have another man to lean on.

"I had a lack of respect for myself and was just going along with what was in front of me," Rita says.

Rita kept the kids in the Seventh-day Adventist church and attending school and tried to maintain a family unit through the 1980s. But then, in 1991, nine-year-old Dougie peed off the side of the boat they were living on, spattering one of his sisters swimming in the water. An angry Rita picked up a board and paddled him with it, leaving a bruise—which a teacher saw at school and called the authorities.

In short order, Rita was arrested on a child-abuse charge, according to the Monroe County Sheriff's Office, which maintains jail records for Key West—and the kids were ferried off to foster care. Rita soon got them back, but the die was cast. Life was deteriorating. In 1992, she got arrested for public drunkenness, and again the kids were temporarily taken away. Then came the hammer blow.

The following year, in 1993, Mark hooked up with a pot-smuggling operation in between his shrimp boat gigs and was running a full load from Jamaica to Key West when he drowned in suspicious circumstances. Court documents indicate Mark's boat had eight hundred pounds of dope on it, and though the sheriff's office investigated extensively, nobody got nailed for murder. The 847-page case file says he was found floating in a life jacket, that he had been struck in the head and had suffered a broken neck bone, but it could only conclude that "during a smuggling operation the victim somehow went into the water and drowned. . . . Cause of death: Saltwater drowning and the manner of death was Undetermined." Case closed.

But for Rita, there was nothing closed about it. "I didn't really understand everything that went on there," she said. "I just know that Mark dying like that was awful for me. I kind of lost it."

She started spiraling from boyfriend to boyfriend. Alcoholism had dug its talons into her. She was depressed. Her three youngest kids wound up with relatives or in foster care, but Faith and Joy were already in high school, and the Seventh-day Adventist church became a bit of a lifeline for them. They got paid spots at a church boarding school near Orlando, hundreds of miles north, and though Joy opted to come back to the Keys to finish school while staying at a foster home, Faith stayed—with Rita's sister Lynda taking on guardianship while Faith finished out her schooling and went on to Smith College.

"I did what I could, and I didn't know the extent of all the trouble going on in the Keys at the time until later," Lynda said. "And becoming guardian for Faith was easy—she kind of raised herself. Super-responsible and serious about school."

Back in Key West, Rita tried to get the kids back by taking a job as a maid, but it didn't pay enough to cover rent. She applied for but couldn't get past a waiting list for public housing. Then she started hanging out with a new boyfriend named Steve, who was even more of an alcoholic than she was. Plus he shot heroin. Rita believes he's the one who gave her HIV—something she found out about years later in a medical checkup; "I can't remember when, it was all a kind of haze," she told me. "Just more bad news, is what it was."

That period is such a haze that she doesn't even remember Steve's last name. Neither does any of the rest of her family.

"I felt defeated," Rita told me. "I couldn't really get my kids back because I had nowhere to take them."

But she still hadn't bottomed out.

In 1997, Steve decided to ramble out to the Bay Area, where he had relatives. Rita's kids were all off with foster parents, relatives, or grown by then, so she said fine, I'll go, too. "I left my children because I was so upset with so many things. My boyfriend had been murdered—that's what I believed—I started drinking hard, my heart was broken. I was used to leaving my kids with hippie friends, and Steve was a shoulder I was crying on."

Soon after they hit San Francisco, though, Steve ditched her. She never saw or heard from him again, but he left one legacy: she was now a heroin addict. Rita got on General Assistance—welfare—of about $400 a month, which required her to clean buses and do landscaping.

"I was lost," she said.

In 1999, Faith took time off her studies at Smith College and flew to San Francisco to visit her mother in her room at the Bristol Hotel, then a bottom-end flophouse in the gritty Tenderloin. Faith was horrified by her mom's living conditions, but couldn't convince Rita to leave. "I played Scrabble with a pimp across the hall, and he said he'd learned it in prison," Faith recalls. "I thought, 'How can my mother be living like this?'"

Rita tried going to massage school, couldn't stick with it. Couldn't shake heroin. The sorrow of losing her kids, losing Mark, relocating West, and being abandoned by Steve—it was crushing. Within a year, she gave up on the whole housing thing and hit the streets. She was fifty, entering a homeless scene that, as the twenty-first century dawned, had settled in as an intractable bleak aspect of the landscape.

AT THE TURN OF the millennium, homelessness in San Francisco, as in most places, had rumbled from the shock of the 1980s through earnest efforts at shelter and aid in the 1990s—as Rita's life dissolved—and on to compassion fatigue. Nothing seemed able to stem the tide of destitute people flowing into the streets, and the periodic one-night counts taken by the government had settled in to around eight thousand.[1] This was before tent cities—remember, the 2011 Occupy movement helped create that trend by injecting untold thousands of tents into the streets—so homeless people mostly hunkered down under tarps, doorways, cardboard.

When Rita first hit the panhandling corners of the Tenderloin, drugs had become so easy to score you could find a cheap dealer on nearly every block. Between panhandling and welfare, she netted enough to feed herself and her habit, about $10 to $20 a day for not just heroin and booze now, but crack as well. The crowd was rough, scary. Her inclination, as always, was to find another man—and soon that desire had a name, a big red beard, and a shy smile. He was thirty-eight-year-old Tommy Rettig.

Tommy was kind. By now the symptoms of the HIV Rita had picked up from Steve were starting to scare her—she tired more easily—and Tommy was the protector type. Plus he was another heroin addict. Peas in a pod.

A broke drifter from Iowa, scarred by a childhood with a drunken father who abandoned the family and a ne'er-do-well mom who died in an apartment fire, Tommy was a master panhandler, using the same cardboard-sign slogan he'd used all over the country since he was a kid: ANYTHING HELPS, EVEN-A-SMILE. Mild brown eyes, that smile, those shy ways—he had the unthreatening-begging hustle down cold.

"I was on Mason Street in the TL and so tired of all the lowlives there, and that's where I met Tommy," Rita said. "We went to cop drugs at Mission and [South] Van Ness, and that's where Tommy showed me this traffic island. It was perfect."

Just like a homeowner, Tommy had picked that corner for "location, location, location." Four-lane Mission Street and six-lane South Van Ness Avenue meeting just a few blocks southwest of City Hall, teeming with traffic—perfect. A big Honda dealership was on one side of the island, and the sprawling A&M Carpets showroom was on the other side, meaning you had no homeowners to complain. Tourists and workers walked by, drivers stopped at the four-way traffic lights—they were all rich targets for panhandling.

And the traffic island itself, this little triangle of concrete? The Island's two big leafy trees offered shade from the summer sun and helped fend off the rain, and a tall streetlamp gave light. The place was central enough so that pretty much everyone wandering from the crack center of the Tenderloin to the heroin center of the Mission District pulled through with gossip and dope to sell. It was the perfect spot for camping or just hanging out. Tommy had panhandled there before, and a few unhoused people were parking shopping carts there, but when Rita and Tommy started camping there full-time, it soon blossomed into its full colony of more than a dozen people, parking their carts near the trees in a circle like a Conestoga wagon train.

Street cleaners called it Pigeon Island because of the flocks of pigeons that roosted there. But for the people homesteading the concrete it was always just Homeless Island.

The name fit. Streams of traffic on the asphalt, streams of passersby on the sidewalk, and this little chunk of concrete in the middle. Before long, Tommy and Rita and the settlement became part of the landscape, like the trees, the hundreds of pigeons who roosted and crapped on the traffic median, the workers, the cars.

They were all well dug in when, in summer 2003, I drifted onto the Island.

• • •

I FOUND THIS BATCH of tough, street-smart, and achingly sad people more extreme than anything else I'd seen. And Rita? You could tell a special person was deep inside, but the only vestige of that once-sparkling, derring-do past was a hint here and there, way behind the eyes, that spoke of something better, something just a little in the way she moved. Sometimes she could startle me with a graceful swing of the arm or smooth straightening as she stood up, a tiny thing that registered in the back of the brain telling you this was a body that once had steel and flow.

But her childhood? She didn't bring that up until much, much later.

"Go talk to Tommy, he'll tell you everything you need to know," she said snidely one day early on, when I was just getting to know her. "You don't want to talk to me."

She was right on one count: Tommy was the fulcrum of life on the Island. The founder.

"Probably the best thing I ever did was start this thing up here at the Island," Tommy told me. "It's good to have people around you, y'know? There's that safety-in-numbers thing, we watch each other's backs. Plus, I've picked up a few tricks from everywhere.

"I guess I have some things to show people."

His main skill was in panhandling, or "signing," as they called the art of using those hand-lettered cardboard signs. Coming up with a catchy phrase on the sign was key, and Tommy's—ANYTHING HELPS, EVEN-A-SMILE—was the best. He'd hold it out with his almost-shy smile and mild eyes, and drivers and passersby would either chat him up briefly or get sad looks on their faces—then hand over cash.

Signing on the Island fetched anywhere from $10 to even $100 a day, plenty to buy $10 hits of smack, $5 crack rocks, or $2.50 bottles of Royal Gate vodka to tide a junkie over when the dope got scarce. It was like a job, occupying several hours off and on throughout most days.

And if Key West, the other island Rita had called home, was full of misfits—this one was misfits on a whole other, most dissolute level.

There was Vina, the one-legged former artist with broken teeth whose boyfriend had shot her leg off years before. She weaved her wheelchair in and out of traffic with a cardboard sign that riffed off Tommy's, reading ANYTHING HELPS, and with her pitiful appearance she could rake in $100 on a good day. Slender Michelle had been sexually abused as a child, and after her dad was shotgunned to death and her drug-addicted mother died of cancer, she fled to San Francisco, where being Black and trans was more accepted than in most places. She had worked as a home health aide in pressed, clean dresses before heroin dragged her into the streets.

Bobby Ray Wright was an army Ranger vet who showed people how to stitch up knife wounds with Krazy glue, One-Leg Mike McFarlane was a great late-night conversationalist, and Wild Woman Angel— whose family didn't want her name used—was his girlfriend, and known for wild freak-outs in the street, screeching and rolling in the dirt.

Little Bit was the most eye-catching of the bunch. She came from Kentucky, and after her father drank himself to death and her mother was found unfit, Little Bit wound up in a group home. She had four kids somewhere. When she was dope sick, she was the most fearsome of the Islanders, snarling and charging around the camp, snatching a needle out of someone's hand if she could get to it—but when she'd shot up and was clearheaded, she was sweet and as introspective as Rita.

Other characters came and went, like bone-skinny street sex worker Jill May, who mostly stayed in the TL with her pimp/boyfriend,

Ricky, but rolled through the Island for a change of pace. It was a safe place.

Rita gradually came around to chatting more with Brant and me after a lot of our hanging out.

"I don't know what to make of you," she said one afternoon while she was leaning against one of the Island's trees, having a peanut butter sandwich, no jelly, with Little Bit. "You really just want to see how we live?"

"Absolutely," I said. "If we can show how hard it is out here for you all to live like this, maybe people can learn and do something more about it."

Rita thought about that for a moment. "Here"—she handed the rest of the sandwich to Little Bit—"not my kinda sandwich anyway."

"Oh, that's right, you're the health nut," Little Bit said, taking the sandwich. They both chortled. Little Bit took the last bites, then stood up. "Watch out for the cleaners," she said. "Someone said they might be coming tonight for some stupid reason. I'm gonna move my cart and you should move your stuff. Don't want everything hosed down."

Rita nodded. She looked back at me. "You gotta understand, we look out for each other, and that means a lot out here. Nobody else gives a damn."

By the time I met her in 2003, Rita was fifty-three years old, had hepatitis C, and between that and the HIV she qualified for an $800 monthly federal disability check, so she had a little more flexibility on dope money. Every now and then, she and Tommy would rent some fleabag room for $50 to wash up and feel an actual mattress, but most of the time they were on the concrete with blankets and sleeping bags like everyone else. Life had a predictable cycle: panhandle, buy heroin or crack, get high, panhandle, then get heroin or crack again, depending on whether you needed to come down or ricochet up. Sleep, maybe get laid if you had enough energy. Get up and do it again.

This is survival mode. When you've been on the streets longer than a bounce through, staying alive becomes the driving force in your life—and if you're messed up on dope, that becomes the main pain driver. The minute the heroin, methamphetamine, crack, or whatever your poison is wears off, the hunger begins to build until it's a pounding pile driver in your brain and your body that can only be dulled by another hit. I've seen it over and over in most of the chronically homeless I've come to know: that manic look in the eyes and hair-trigger temper of someone who's too high on meth. The fidgety desperation of the opioid addict who's overdue for a hit. The drooped head and body of a heroin or fentanyl addict who's just shot up or smoked and has "the nods."

This was the reality that Rita came to know intimately: Being homeless in a big city, even with a lot of pals around, actually takes a lot of work. Not having a home to go to means every night is a coin toss, hoping someone won't cave in your teeth with a boot just to steal whatever you have in your pockets. You can find your regular haunts, and if you're lucky, you wind up at some place like Homeless Island—but even then it means putting up the tent or tarp or cardboard, arranging the shopping carts like a wall, or finding blankets to replace the ones ripped off while you were off copping dope.

Those people who say, "Hey, I just love the outdoor life so I'm homeless"? Bullshit. Some social workers call them "service resistant," and what they're really saying when they profess to love the outdoor life is that they have their routine for staying alive, and damned if they want to change it because that is terrifying. Move into a shelter, and the fear is someone will steal your stuff either in the shelter or on the street where you had to leave it because you can't haul it all inside. Trust someone official to help you? After having most of the key officials you have to confront most days tell you to move off the sidewalk (cops) or kick dope cold turkey (jailers when you get busted), your trust is about zilch.

It's no surprise that street counselors in San Francisco, Philadelphia, and New York consistently tell me it takes about two years of regular visits with a hard-core homeless person to convince him or her to take the help offered.

"You can't force anyone to take help," said Dr. Josh Bamberger, a city health specialist, professor at the University of California at San Francisco, and a key architect of the city's outreach strategies for the chronically homeless. "Throw them in jail, sure, but they just come out trusting you even less. You have to convince them they will get more out of being off the street than being on it. As counterintuitive as that sounds, it's reality."

As for the Homeless Islanders? "They were about the toughest ones to ever try to help," said Rann Parker, a longtime street-outreach counselor who was just one of many offering rehab, shelter, and housing to the Islanders over the years. "They were just really dug in."

For Rita, thoughts of being inside with sheets that were regularly cleaned and a door that locks were more than unfeasible by the time she'd been on the Island for a couple of years. They were forgotten niceties. The one thing that worked in her life became Tommy—he was security, kindness, predictability.

One day, Rita and I sat under the trees at the Island while she tied off her left arm with a rubber strap for a hit. She sprinkled a pinch of brown heroin onto a spoon, sparked a Bic lighter, and melted the stash into liquid.

"You don't meet a lot of great guys out here," she mused, pulling a fresh syringe from a wad of clothes and bags at her side; clean needles then, as now, were handed out freely at city health sites to help prevent the spread of disease that can come with sharing hypodermics. She pulled off the orange protector sleeve on the needle, stuck the needle into the spoonload, and pulled back on the hypo's plunger to suck up the hit. By now a fat vein had throbbed up near the rubber strap on her arm. She slid the needle carefully in and pushed down the plunger.

Her head drooped toward her chest for a slight case of the nods, then she perked up. "That's more like it," Rita said, and smiled.

"So—Tommy?" she went on. "He's my guy, that's all, and he treats me better than anyone has in a long time. I haven't had a lot of those lately."

She peered up through the leaves of the huge sheltering tree, where she was again sitting in the heap of blankets and shopping carts while Tommy and a few others panhandled the traffic.

Normalcy was impossible on the Island, she told me. Whatever she tried to store there got hosed away or carted off to trash by periodic street-cleaning crews while she and Tommy and the rest of the colony were out copping dope, wandering, or, in Little Bit's case, turning tricks. Rita would get antibiotics at the hospital clinics—they're all free for homeless folks—for the abscesses (open, oozing sores) from dirty needles, and if she forgot to take them with her when she was away, they'd get hosed away. She'd stash a few changes of clothes in the Island's shopping carts or bags, and same thing if she forgot to grab them—they'd get tossed into a garbage truck.

"It's just the way it is." Rita shrugged. "When they take your stuff, you go get new stuff."

By 2003, her silky hair was like straw, the ravages of sleeping out-doors had carved deep lines in her face, and that lithe, toned body of youth had wasted to a stick. All but a few stumps of her teeth were rotted out from "meth mouth," the affliction that hits every junkie through a combination of methamphetamine or other dope (the term has become a catchall) drying up protective saliva, and a craving for sugar doing the rest of the damage.

Real food, the nonsugar kind, wasn't really an issue. So many passersby handed over leftovers from restaurants that food largely, literally, just came to the Island. Dumpster diving behind the local groceries filled in a few gaps.

Here's another reality that might not be obvious to people who day in, day out, walk by substance users like Tommy and Rita and others all over downtown San Francisco: That's not some frivolous lifestyle choice. If you're as acutely down-and-out as the Islanders were, you're on dope or booze and probably both. You've shattered through every support system you have—family, friends, counseling and housing programs that you ditched or that tossed you out, and now you have nothing. It's the definition of the bottom.

Climbing out from there is not a matter of getting a little hand up, or pulling yourself up by your bootstraps. It takes creating a whole new life. And that takes massive assistance, which means providing welfare housing with counseling right there in the building to keep people from crashing back into the street. It's called supportive housing, and it's the only thing I ever saw that worked for most desperate folks other than a family rescue of some kind.

Rita and Tommy and Bobby Ray couldn't even begin to wrap their minds around that concept.

"Who the hell wants to give me a place to live?" Tommy said. "I'd just fuck it up like everything else."

CHAPTER 6

"She Had to Hit Bottom"

2003

The day everything finally hit rock bottom for Rita was hot and hopeless.

It was September 16, 2003, the summer sun was beating down, the morning traffic on South Van Ness and Mission was already in full commute roar. Rivers of workers strode by on the sidewalk, heading to jobs or shopping. Some glanced furtively at the grubby dozen homeless junkies and their heaped-up shopping carts on Homeless Island—but most just kept their eyes straight ahead. The Islanders snored on obliviously.

Tommy hadn't been around for a couple of days, but it wasn't unusual for people to disappear from their little colony now and then in the middle of their relentless cycle of doping, sleeping, scoring drugs, eating, and wandering.

"He's probably just out on a bender somewhere," Bobby Ray told Rita.

"I'm getting a little worried," she said. They'd just crawled out of their sleeping bags, and Rita was already a little dope sick. She hadn't shot smack since dinnertime, and as the drugs wore off, her deeply lined forehead was starting to pound and get clammy. "Not seeing him for so long just doesn't feel right. He's been sick, and you know how he doesn't take care of himself."

"Yeah," said Bobby Ray, idly scratching a track mark on his forearm. "But that's the way it is, isn't it? Stop worrying."

Rita smiled tiredly, shook her head. "Yeah, he always comes out okay." She slowly struggled to her feet, stretched her bony body for a moment, then headed into traffic with her HUNGER HURTS cardboard sign to panhandle enough cash for her own hit of smack. At that moment, she really did expect he would just roll up again with his panhandling sign and sleepy smile.

BRANT AND I HAD also noticed Tommy wasn't around, and it didn't sound good to us, either, so I started looking. Calling hospitals, checking nearby gullies, asking around.

"See what you can find," Rita told me. "You guys know how to look for stuff, right?"

She and Brant and I were sitting on the Island cement having lunch—cinnamon twists and dishwater-thin coffee from the nearby All Star Café on Van Ness Avenue. My legs itched from another bout of pigeon mites I'd picked up from pitching my blanket on the Island the night before. Damn, I thought. I'd have to throw another pair of pants away next time I made it home to clean up a bit. My wife would tolerate a lot, but not mites or lice in the house—she often met me at the door with a Lysol sprayer when I'd come home, and I sometimes had to throw my infested clothes away or burn them.

But mites weren't the assignment. And I pretty much didn't care. It was the people whom I was there for.

"Sure," I said.

Brant glanced sideways at me, then back to Rita. "Sometimes you don't want to know what you don't know," he said.

Rita shrugged. "It'll be okay."

I finally called up the medical examiner's office to see if it knew anything. It did. An investigator there told me Tommy had walked into S.F. General Hospital the previous night, September 15, around 11:00, feverish with deadly necrotizing fasciitis—commonly called flesh-eating disease—which he'd gotten from shooting up with dirty needles and not keeping the wounds clean. The infection had already gone too far by the time he came in.

The medical staff tried to save him, but he died a bit after 4:00 a.m. He was forty-four years old.

We went back to Homeless Island to find Rita, but she was nowhere in sight. So we walked over to Bobby Ray a little after noon while he panhandled the stoplight at Mission. None of the Islanders liked hedging around things, and neither did we.

"We found Tommy," I told him. Brant nodded, looked hard into Bobby Ray's eyes.

Bobby Ray, a rangy army vet who was damn hard to rattle, stared back through narrowed lids. "Well, where the hell is he?"

"Sorry, bud, he's dead," Brant said. Another long stare.

"Fuck," Bobby Ray whispered. "Fuck."

Bobby Ray dropped his sign to the asphalt at his feet and stood looking down at it, not really seeing it. Then he shuffled over to the edge of the Island where the rest of the colony was.

Rita was still gone, out trying to cop a hit. Cowboy, a longtime Islander, was cleaning a crack pipe. Michelle, the slender trans woman, had just shot her first bag of smack for the day and was nodding off on Vina's shoulder as they sat in the snarl of heaped shopping carts. In her right hand, Michelle clutched a box of .38-caliber bullets she'd found in an alley that morning.

"Hey, listen . . . Tommy's dead," Bobby Ray called out, shifting from one foot to the other in front of the crowd.

"What?" someone gasped.

Michelle and Vina broke out sobbing, and then the whole Island freaked out as only cracked-out homeless heroin junkies can: screaming. Scratching wildly. Crying. Slamming their fists against trees and walls.

"When that flesh-eating disease gets you, there's nothing you can do," Bobby Ray let out after a few minutes. "Lying on a slab at the General right now. That's that."

"Damn, I loved that man like a brother—what was his last name?" said Cowboy with a groan. Michelle stood up and started swaying in place, two used-up syringes crunching under her feet as she wailed and cried and nodded off, then wailed again. She had the box of bullets in her hand.

"At least he's not suffering anymore," Vina said softy.

"What the fuck, what the fuck . . . ," Michelle muttered, then let out one last, wet screech. She closed her eyes. A calm came over her. "Do you know where I can sell these bullets?" she asked, eyes still closed.

That's when Rita shambled back onto Homeless Island.

She headed for her sleeping bag where she'd left it, next to one of the Island trees so everyone could keep an eye on it. Bobby Ray met her on the sidewalk and gave her the news. It wasn't sinking in. "You're just shitting me," she said. Then she looked over and saw everyone crying.

"Oh, my God," she moaned. In her hands she held a pair of jeans she'd found, and she started whipping them against a picture of Tommy one of the Islanders had just tacked to one of the trees. Whap, whap, whap. Scream, whap, scream, getting louder and louder.

"Damn you!" she howled. "Why'd you die? Why didn't you take care of yourself?"

Bobby Ray had just started methadone a few weeks before, going daily to the clinic, waiting in line with the rest who were trying to kick heroin, but this was too much. He signed a bit, then asked Vina for a fix. Said he'd pay her later, then sat down alongside one of the carts and jammed the needle into the underside of his left arm.

"Goddammit," he whispered. The screeching went on around him and he nodded off while the sweet flow of dope seeped throughout his body.

Then, after about an hour, it was over. Everyone just ran out of grief gas. The pain wasn't gone, but there was the business of survival to get back to.

They simply stopped gnashing and screeching and crying and went back to normal: wandering off a few blocks to score crack and smack. Coming back to smoke or inject. Staggering around in traffic with panhandling signs. Leading tricks into the nearby alleys for $10 blow jobs, or maybe a quick $20 screw in a car. Buying Ding Dongs or Twinkies at the local convenience shop for lunch, sharing a cheap burrito or handout food from passersby for dinner.

Except for Rita. It wasn't time to score her next hit of heroin yet. So she lay by the tree, crying until she passed out.

In late afternoon she woke up. Without a word, she got to her feet, looked around, and shuffled onto Mission Street. The dope sickness was setting in again. She had to go score.

Two days later, Brant and I went with Bobby Ray and Michelle — we couldn't find Rita — to see Tommy's corpse on a slab at the hospital morgue. He was a mess. Necrotizing fasciitis advances and dissolves tissue rapidly when it takes hold, and the hospital staff had clearly worked hard, with tubes still jutting from Tommy's nose and mouth, eyes taped shut, dried blood coming out of every opening, the skin around his abscessed leg a wet, raw flesh goo. I have seen plenty of dead people, even friends, in my time of covering homelessness, disaster, and crime—victims with gaping bullet wounds, mauled by dogs, charred by flames, drowned, executed, you name it. They're always awful in one way or another. This was, too. Michelle fainted with a groan.

Tommy's uncle, Ron Rettig, had him cremated and flew his ashes back to his hometown of Burlington, Iowa, where Ron owned a construction company. He told me Tommy had been doomed from the start.

"His father was a drunk, never had much going, left Tommy's mother when he was little and never sent child support," Ron said. "And Tommy's mother—well, she laid with this one and that one and was not too picky, if you know what I mean. She died in an apartment fire. Cigarette lit the place, burned her right up."

That's when I learned Tommy had lived with his grandparents, dropped out of high school, married twice and had five kids, then wandered until winding up in San Francisco. None of the family had seen him since the late 1980s. "He was always a charmer, very sweet. He was no dummy, but school was not his thing," Ron told me. "I just wish he could have had more of a life. Such suffering, such a waste."

LIFE ON THE ISLAND didn't really change. With Tommy dead, Little Bit became the quasi-leader of the bunch, meaning she was the one everyone went to if they wanted to know where anyone was. She just kept tabs on people. And Rita—she felt even more unmoored. She screwed up her resolve and went to a health clinic to try to get onto methadone, but the several-months-long waiting list for every rehab clinic seemed hopeless, and she sank deeper into despair. The HIV she had contracted had flared into AIDS, but all that had done so far was make her more tired. So she just carried on.

Panhandling, sleeping, copping dope, eating. Trying to find a few moments to read a book, share a laugh, maybe hit up the thrift store across the street that had $1 bins in the back to buy some clothes. All of this living out loud was just normal life for the Islanders, but for nearby shopkeepers it was intolerable.

"It's horrible for the city, and it's horrible for us," Barry De Vincenzi, service director at San Francisco Honda, told me. "They leave their needles on our sidewalk, bury their dope in the dirt of our plants, shoot up in front of our business. Yesterday, they stuck mirrors in our fence wire so they could shoot up under their tongues."

The Honda dealership spent thousands of dollars fencing off a lunch area on the side of the building, strengthening doors, and putting up security lights. But that didn't do anything to keep trash from being left on the sidewalks in front of the business, or to keep the obviously sketchy drug dealers from rambling through—one trio was so obvious locals called them the Penguins because they kept their pants so low they waddled like the birds.

One of the worst moments, Barry said, came in June 2003 while Brant and I were away somewhere else and Randy, an old alcoholic, was sitting as usual in his wheelchair by the front Honda entrance. A hooker and he were deep in conversation over a bottle of vodka when he suddenly slumped over and died. His organs had simply given out from years of hitting the bottle, and when emergency crews cut open his shirt, his stomach was an open, crawling mass of maggots.

"I call the city, but all they do is come out every week and hose off that traffic island," Barry said. "Nobody in the city seems to know how bad all this is."

One morning an hour or so before dawn when we were still on

the "Shame of the City" project, I was sleeping on the sidewalk across the street from the Island—too many people were around the tree, snoring too loudly—when One-Leg Mike woke me up with angry noise. "Damn! Damn!" he was yelling. It was October, chilly, and Rita was obliviously sacked out in her blankets on the Island with Little Bit and a few others. Mike—who got his name because like so many other addicts living outside, he lost his leg when an abscess got too infected from dirty needles—was sitting with his girlfriend, Wild Woman Angel, a syringe in one hand and a spoon with a dirty cotton ball in the other. He jammed the needle into the cotton ball, trying to suck out a few drops from the heroin that he'd screened through the ball earlier in the day—a shot Rita shared with him because he was out of cash—and it was only dragging up the tiniest dribble. Mike stabbed the needle into the stump of his hacked-off leg and shoved the plunger down. He stabbed it again, grunting as the needle bit in. Angel gibbered senselessly while she watched, then on the second stab couldn't resist anymore.

"Gimme gimme gimme," she breathed, and bent her head next to Mike's stump, licking the needle hole and then the needle. "Gimme gimme."

Mike batted her head away. "You'll get your turn, Angel," he snapped. Back to the cotton ball, and another stab in the stump. Nothing was getting through, and both of them were now wearing out. Mike tipped his head back and closed his eyes, finger caressing the end of the needle, as if he could coax out some smack that might make a difference. Angel passed out next to his stump; Mike fell asleep, moaning.

Rita slept through it all. As did the others.

A few days later, Rita showed me a gaping, oozing abscess on her hip that alarmed me—it looked like the one Tommy had had on his leg, the one that killed him. I pleaded with her to go to a hospital, but she was too discouraged by everything in her life to make the move. She was fifty-three years old.

This was not the Rita of twenty years before. Or ten. Or even six—which was about when everything went down the dumper for her. After years of being lost, being so crushed by life on the street, she was trapped in a survival cycle. All the Islanders were. But the heart was still there. She knew, deep down, what it was like to have a home, be dope-free, have a future.

"I have kids, I used to work, I used to have a life in Florida," she said. "I remember that." We were leaning against one of the Island's trees having a couple of doughnuts I'd brought. She stared at the ground. "I do know what it's like to be normal," she said softly. "I did used to have a home."

AFTER THOSE SIX MONTHS on the streets in 2003 for the "Shame of the City" project with Brant, watching the most broken people of the Island, Golden Gate Park, the Mission, the Tenderloin, and everywhere else hopelessly mired in street life with no real way to pull themselves up, I became convinced that either supportive housing with counseling or reconnecting with family and friends was the only way to save them.

Our "Shame of the City" series began running on November 30, 2003, and by the time it finished five days later, we'd made a national splash. The goal was to show the depth of the problem, how we got here, and then how to fix it, and we were pretty cynical but hoped we could make a difference.

We concluded that moving people inside rooms or apartments with rehab on-site, rather than waiting for them to clean up, was the best government fix for the crisis—since everyone we saw who tried to shake dope and booze in the street failed, even if they briefly hit sobriety after a stint in jail. And the message hit a nerve. Politically, conservatives liked that housing the chronically homeless saves money, and liberals liked it because it was humane. President George W. Bush's national homelessness czar, Philip Mangano, already a fan of supportive housing, passed the series around all over the country, and as 2004 set in, he began requiring that governmental agencies getting federal homeless funding make permanent supportive housing a priority.[1]

ON THE OTHER END of the nation from San Francisco, Rita's high school pal Alice Wells read my story on Homeless Island online. She lived in New York State still.

"I had this image of Rita, knowing how wonderful she was in high school, of her being married and living in a nice home somewhere," Alice said. "Instead it was an absolute heartbreak.

"She once had such a great life, such promise. I just sat there and cried. I thought, 'How did she come to this?'"

She forwarded the article to Rita's family, who sent the article to Rita's sister Pam, a furniture maker and painter living just north of Orlando, Florida. The Homeless Island story floored her. Pam and her five nieces and nephews—Rita's kids—had lost track of Rita and practically given up hope of reconnecting. But after reading about how hellacious life was on the Island, Pam, forty-seven, and Rita's daughter Joy, twenty-six, resolved to fly out to find her—on their own.

They didn't tell me the precise time or details. But Pam did leave me a voicemail in late March 2004 on my newsroom desk phone. She left no callback number and our phone system didn't register one.

"My name is Pam and I am the sister of the girl Rita that you wrote the story about in the *Chronicle*," she began. "I called because I wanted to thank you for writing that story, and the harsh reality, and how nobody really wanted to look at it. I knew my sister was homeless and I knew she had problems, but I didn't really know how bad, and the story sort of put light on the situation for me.

"I made arrangements to come out there and hopefully will be getting her into a clinic, and bringing her back home to Florida where I live. If you happen to see Rita again and are doing any kind of follow-up story, tell her that I called and to please contact me because we all care about her. She has a family here. You probably wouldn't believe it, but she was homecoming queen of her high school and she used to be an Olympic hopeful for gymnastics. We gotta get her back here. Hopefully she'll have a chance if she gets out of that environment.

"I'm not leaving my number because I really don't want you to call me, but I just wanted to let you know that these kinds of stories are helpful. And I hope that there's some kind of solution out there, because otherwise now people are going to keep dying."

THIS WASN'T THE FIRST time Rita's family had tried to find her. In late 2001, Faith and Joy had flown out to San Francisco and found Rita at the Island. "I was shocked and horrified at what I saw, how she was living," Faith told me many years later. Faith was working in financial services at the time, living in New Orleans, and somehow managed to convince Rita to come back to stay with her—and even got her briefly on methadone, "which wasn't easy because Louisiana wasn't very supportive on that." It lasted about a month. Faith had to fly to London and Paris for a long-planned vacation with a friend, left Rita some cash to get by while Faith was gone, and the money went straight into a bus ticket back to Homeless Island.

"I couldn't stay away from Tommy," Rita admitted to me years later with a shrug. "I loved him."

Faith and Joy had known where to look because several months before they flew out, Penelope had been hitchhiking through Northern California with a boyfriend and stopped in San Francisco to look for her mom. "I went walking through the streets praying that I could find her—praying, 'God, I know you know where she is, please help me find her,'" Penelope told me years later. "At the end of the day we went to a shelter so my boyfriend could take a shower, and I was sitting on the sidewalk and started talking to a blind man about looking for my mom.

"He said, 'Rita with five kids from Florida?' And I said, 'Yes!' He took me to see her at this camp under the highway."

This camp was several blocks south of Homeless Island, underneath Highway 101 as it cuts through the south-middle end of town—it's a camp I know well, since it comes and goes all the time. Now, as then, authorities roust it, the campers move, and then a few days or a week later, a new bunch comes in along with some repeaters, and the cycle starts over. Rita was hanging out and shocked to see her daughter walk up. Penelope said she wanted to take her home with her.

"She said, 'You can't save me, honey, I have AIDS,'" Penelope said. "She said, 'Don't worry about me, I love it here.' I tried. I couldn't convince her." That night Penelope, her boyfriend, and Rita all slept in the sand dunes on Ocean Beach. The couple went back downtown and dropped Rita at the Island, then headed off to Nevada City, where they'd been staying.

"I woke up that morning and I just felt heartbroken because I knew I wasn't going to be able to take her with us and give her what she needed, to take care of her," Penelope said. "I've never felt so torn in my life between knowing what I wanted to do and what I had to do."

Rita never told me about this visit, or the 2001 stint in New Orleans, until many years later.

Pam remembers of that time when she first read the Homeless Island story that "nobody, really, back here had heard from her in ages. A lot of my family just kind of gave up on her." But after seeing my story, the family started talking.

Pam says, "I cried when I read it, did some thinking and talking about it, and then Joy and I came out. It was one of those times when you do something and it feels like it's not you doing it, know what I mean? It's like, instead, it was meant to be."

It was time for them to take action.

ON MARCH 30, 2004, Pam and Joy landed in San Francisco and immediately made their way to Homeless Island. They were horrified by what they saw in broad daylight—the shopping carts, the heaps of soggy clothing, the panhandlers in traffic, used needles and crack pipes scattered on the cement. They gave Danny, one of the Islanders, $5 to tell them where Rita was. He smiled and pointed to the wasted wraith sitting on a bench nearby.

It was Rita, so emaciated that they could barely recognize her. She was hunched over, bundled in several layers of clothes. Pam sat next to her and lifted up her face. "Rita, Joy's here. I'm here. We're here to help you," Pam said, looking her sister straight in the eyes.

Rita didn't say a word. She rested her head on Pam's shoulder. Joy sat down on the other side of her mother and put her arm around her. They all sat that way for a few long moments.

"Okay," Rita said. That simple.

She told me later she was more than just ready—she'd had a bizarre epiphany a few days before they showed up, and it primed her.

"I was at a little camp with Vina under the freeway [Highway 101], just to get away from the Island a bit, and I had a vision," Rita said. "I felt the miracle of God, and I saw Jesus—but I thought he was the Zig-Zag Man [the bearded emblem of Zig-Zag cigarette and joint rolling papers]. He told me, 'One side of the fence or the other, Rita, you can't do both.'

"Tommy was dead. I was so sick I probably wasn't far from death. That vision did it for me. That's when I chose life. And that's right around when Pam and Joy showed up."

Pam knew the score even before she walked up to the Island.

"We didn't want to make her do anything—we'd already learned that wouldn't work if we forced anything, because she wasn't ready before," Pam told me much later. "But this time she was. She had to hit bottom." The first thing Pam and Joy did was take her to the city's "wound clinic," where doctors gave the seven-inch-long abscesses on her backside and close to her spine their first good look. They'd been brought on by shooting heroin with dirty needles, and the doctors were alarmed. They cleaned, stitched, and medicated her and got it all under control.

"The doctor told us, 'You got her just in time,'" Pam said. "He said with those abscesses, two more weeks and she'd be dead."

Next was a trip to a methadone clinic. And getting her on AZT, the AIDS medication. Then it was just hanging out in a hotel room, taking the methadone, resting up with healthy food, visiting Golden Gate Park to get a taste of clean outdoors and getting ready for the flight back to the land of sun and family that she had left in the 1990s.

All of these things had been available to Rita before—but the key thing with help for the unhoused is that they have to be ready to accept it. They can't be legally forced to accept help unless they are a danger to themselves or to others, which is a high bar for street counselors to declare, and Rita hadn't met that bar. It took the love of her sister and daughter to get it done.

"I was lost," Rita said later. "Just couldn't work it all out. I guess I needed them."

I ROLLED OVER TO the Island in late April 2004 to see if this sister of Rita's had shown up, but I was too late. Rita, Pam, and Joy had already left. By then, the cops had mostly broken up the little colony—partly finally in response to complaints by local businesses, but also driven by my story, which had laid out for them in greater detail just how addicted and dug in the Islanders were. They didn't camp there full-time anymore, but the spot was too good for panhandling to abandon, and it remained a crossroads for dealers, users, and homeless folks who just wanted to connect.

One of the panhandlers there said Little Bit was in S.F. General Hospital again with infected abscesses, so I visited her to see if she'd heard anything. I found her in one of the rooms, on methadone again, and reading *All He Ever Wanted*, by Anita Shreve.

"Her family took her back to Florida all right, and I think that was the best thing that could have happened to her," Little Bit said. "After Tommy died, it was like she was losing her mind. I guess that's the story of our lives. All of us females on the street seem to do this—hook up with the wrong guys.

"I sure as hell hope she makes it."

I had my doubts. So many rehab efforts flame out after a few months. In my six months on the street working on the series, I watched several people like Little Bit give programs like Walden House—or earlier detoxifying stints in the hospital—a stab, only to wind up right back at Homeless Island.

But I was pulling for Rita; I thought she had it in her to succeed. She hadn't told me much about her family during our time together on the Island, but she had an inner quality, a strength that made her seem not lost beyond repair. I hoped her family was the kind that could help her make a new life. Not just a refit back to what she had before—but a truly new one. Healthy, levelheaded, dope-free, and unencumbered by disease.

I waited nearly a year, figuring that would be long enough to determine if this rescue attempt was going to stick. Alice had filled me in a bit by then, and I had Pam's phone number, but I hadn't used it because I was respecting Rita's family's privacy—I didn't want my reporter's intrusion to mess anything up. I hadn't seen Rita at the Island that whole time, though, which I took as a good sign.

So about two weeks before Christmas in 2004, I picked up the phone and dialed Pam's number.

PART 2

Tyson as a kid in Danville, California
(Photo courtesy of his brother, Baron)

Tyson, homeless
(Photo taken by Jessica Christian, provided courtesy of *San Francisco Chronicle*)

CHAPTER 7

Tyson—Cardboard Despair

2019

The sun was warm and bright with none of those all-too-often chilly San Francisco breezes, just another beautiful day to be trolling the waterfront working a story. Thrashing about for new places to open up "navigation center" homeless shelters (enhanced with extra counselors and privileges like 24-7 open hours that engage chronically homeless people as never before), San Francisco mayor London Breed had decided a great location for one would be on a parking lot outside a stretch of million-dollar condos along the pricey, touristy Embarcadero waterfront.[1] A sizable homeless population had been entrenched nearby for years, and the thinking was that this could bring them inside. But the mere suggestion was like tossing a political grenade into the economic war zone of San Francisco housing, where for years the price of housing and rent had been outstripping typical incomes, and people were digging in their heels to avoid changes in their neighborhoods that might bring down the quality or price of what they were hanging on to.

The neighborhood revolted in rage against Mayor Breed's plan. Residents complained that a more inclusive shelter like this—nav centers, as they're commonly called—would be a magnet for transients to hang around on doorsteps and sidewalks. The residents sued and packed meetings to protest, saying their real estate prices would plummet as the shelter roiled their neighborhood with panhandlers, fights, and open-air drug use. For the unhoused, the shelter could be a lifeline. But for the housed, a lot of cash was at stake.

San Francisco is the third-most expensive city in America to live in, with the median price of a home at $1.2 million, and the average rent for a one-bedroom apartment at $3,000. The overall cost of living is 79 percent higher than the national average—and the city has been obscenely expensive like this for decades. After spending that much money on a place to live, any percentage drop in home price hurts in proportionately big chunks. As for renters—after forking over exorbitant monthly checks, they want the best neighborhood bang for their bucks.

Nav centers were conceived in 2015 by the city's then homelessness-policy adviser Bevan Dufty as a way of enticing unhoused people who would normally chafe at typical shelter restrictions. The centers have no curfews, you can bring your pets and partners in, and they have more personal space than the usual cot-by-cot shelter configuration. Many even have individual rooms you can stay in, like tiny apartments. The whole idea is to give as few restrictions as possible to outside-living people, so they'll stay and engage long enough to make use of the housing, rehab, health, and other counselors who station themselves there to help. The rules from the start said you can't get a spot inside unless an outreach counselor picks you. So hanging around outside the center does no good—you need that tap on the shoulder by a counselor, which happens when the outreach teams rove the neighborhoods looking for the most needy cases, or the biggest homeless encampments of tents clustered in alleys, on sidewalks, and in stray parking lots. The camps were—and are—usually easy to find except for the small ones packed into bushes or groves on the edge of town or in Golden Gate Park by loners who don't want to be found.

Some people did congregate outside the nav centers anyway—to meet with friends staying there, or just to be around something that seemed to be a hub of hope or at least presence for the homeless. The first nav center, opened in 2015 near the corner of Mission and Sixteenth Streets, came to have a steady string of couches and chairs with tarps set up on the sidewalk outside, and neighbors complained.[2] But that part of the neighborhood had always been a hub of homelessness anyway, so it was hard to judge just what change there really was. To me, it just seemed like some of the usual folks had shifted a bit from one block to the other. And the routine for nav centers has been that they get moved every few years, so they don't become a permanent fixture in the neighborhood. But even though neighbors are polled and educated with community meetings before a center goes in, there are always at least some complaints.[3] Few people want a shelter next door. And when it came to the Embarcadero nav center proposal, the opposition was off the charts.

On April 9, 2019, a hot sunny day, I trolled the waterfront, not to find out how the residents felt about this proposed Embarcadero nav center—that was already abundantly clear—but what the homeless people themselves thought. One of the myths about street people is that they hate shelters, but the opposite is often true—everyone wants a roof and warm bed. They just don't want to be told what to do, when they can sleep and eat, who can visit, and especially about when, where, and how they can score and smoke, snort, or shoot dope to feed their aching habits if they have them. Sure enough, I found most of the Embarcadero gutter regulars liked the idea of a nav center and said they'd move in.

"Yeah, if they made it just right," said Shorty, one of my off-and-on longtime street guys. "But I don't really trust the system that much. Too many disappointments."

THE LOST AND THE FOUND

Shorty knew from disappointments. His nonstreet name was Alex Pierson, and throughout his tumultuous thirty-six years as a "little person" Black man with nonfunctional legs, he'd been shunted from one home situation to another until he wound up years before in the street with a methamphetamine addiction, propelling himself around in a manual wheelchair. That's how I'd met him.

He hung with a band of fellow homeless addicts that rotated between the nightlife-and-café-heavy North Beach neighborhood and a palm-tree-studded strip of park a mile away on the Embarcadero, across from the historic Ferry Building, where foodie restaurants offered bowls of soup in the $20 range and bottles of wine in the $60 range. This would have been maddening to the street folks if they focused on it too much, but the high prices just meant they got better handouts from good-hearted diners—leftover quiche lorraine slices, sushi, Thai curry, and the like. Some of it sat around in the sun a few hours before being chowed down, but it beat the hell out of scraping the leavings off McDonald's wrappers in a dumpster.

The palm-tree guys took good care of Shorty, pushing him in his wheelchair to drop-in homeless facilities for bathroom or shower breaks, fetching him food when he needed it, copping dope when he was dry. They were pretty set and embedded in their ways, and, sure, they said they'd move into a nav center, too—but only on their own terms.

"Go talk to people down the road a bit, over where they want to put that nav center," Shorty said. "Maybe you'll get something a little different."

I walked about a mile south of the Ferry Building, connecting along the way with *Chronicle* photographer Jessica Christian, and at the end of that walk I found Tyson Feilzer.

He sat on a scrap of cardboard across the street from the parking lot that was proposed for the nav center, soaking in the sun. He looked thoughtful and calm. Hair closely cropped to his head, clean black jeans ending in equally neat running shoes. He wore a sweatshirt with a huge rendering of a tiger on the front, and his hands were neatly clasped in his lap. He had a small black backpack, but not mounds of gear like other homeless folks. I could tell he was an addict—call it forty years of instinct—but one with some measure of control.

"How you doin', man?" I said, holding out my hand.

He gazed up thoughtfully and shook it. "Fine, I suppose." Tyson let the beginnings of a smile dawn on his face. "Pretty nice day at least."

I sat down next to him on the cardboard. "You look like a guy who's been out here awhile."

"You could say that. Been quite a few years."

The backpack and a coat lay at his side, and one of the pack pockets had a meth pipe sticking out. I pointed to it. "Long time using meth?"

"Yeah, and heroin." He chuckled. "Not a fun habit."

I chuckled back. "Yep. But this seems like a nice quiet place to do what you've got to do if you're into it."

Tyson nodded. "You want to see crack dealers, you go to the TL [the Tenderloin, the poverty-stricken downtown neighborhood]. You want some peace and quiet and a nice view, you come here."

I paused a beat and then asked if he'd heard of the plan to put a nav center near where he sat. I'm a reporter for the *San Francisco Chronicle*, and I'm doing a story about this plan, I said.

Tyson brightened. "I hadn't heard of it, but great idea. Those navigation programs work well, and the city needs more shelters. There's not enough path from homelessness to not homelessness here, or pretty much anywhere. I've been out here for a lot of years . . . around seven outside. If I could get a place for a few months, I could get back to a real life."

He waved a hand absently at the waterfront. "You know, I worked thirteen years before I wound up out here. Sales, flooring, but quit in a bad economy." He'd lived with his grandmother, he said, and then she died at ninety-four, and as the money and opportunities dissolved, he hit the streets.

"I've learned a lot out here, the hard way. Look, San Francisco's always had homeless people. When you think of this city, you think liberals, free love, hippies. But also you think of some of the most expensive real estate in the country. I don't think a nav center would screw up their house prices. I think it would benefit them because you'd have fewer people like me out here all the time."

What about some people's idea of forcing all the unhoused people onto giant ships turned into shelters in the bay, or onto Treasure Island? I asked. Or just continuing to convert the city's century-old residential hotels into supportive housing in the Tenderloin, concentrating the population there?

"That's not fair," he said calmly. "And let's face it, it's not practical."

The idea of being fair or practical would be debatable for people who just want the homeless population to go away by all means necessary, I said—not a politically popular concept in liberal San Francisco, but one that does get talked about. He just smiled. That vein of conversation could go a long way, I thought. This guy was a thinker. Forcing homeless people into a shelter anywhere, if they're not breaking the law, doesn't legally fly in California, and Tyson obviously knew both that, and that homeless people wouldn't stay marooned. And he clearly knew that it had been hard for homeless addicts who got housed in the dope-riddled Tenderloin to shake off drugs when, as soon as you walked out your door there, you could find a dealer in three minutes.

What about the idea that a new nav center would just be a magnet for trouble?

"People think a navigation center would draw more homeless people? Like I said, it would actually benefit business and housing prices here because then we'd be off the streets and inside. Face it. We're already here. You either own and handle it right where it's happening, or you let it get worse."

A giant container ship heaved into view on the bay and we all looked over. The Bay Bridge, with its looping cables, arched over to Yerba Buena Island just to our left on its way to Oakland, and beyond that the deep blue water spread all the way to hilly Richmond and over to Sausalito, with its tourist-ready waterfront of expensive restaurants and shops and *House Beautiful*–worthy homes climbing up woodsy slopes. It was magnificent, a view free to anyone from the swells in the million-dollar condos above us to the fellow sitting alongside me on the cardboard. "Helluva view," I said.

"Yeah," Tyson said quietly.

Jessica had snapped enough shots, and I knew they would be good because she is a terrific photographer. I stood up.

"Well, I hope you find some place quiet and safe to sleep tonight," I said.

Tyson nodded. "I sleep wherever I can, but it would sure be nice to sleep right there"—and he pointed to the parking lot where the nav center was planned. We both smiled.

"I hope you do," I said.

A few days later, my story ran with Tyson's photo in the lead position.

That nav center did get built, with two hundred beds, within a year, over the neighbors' objections, and it's still there. The neighborhood did not go to hell, and dozens of miserable lives have been made better because of it.

CHAPTER 8

All the Chances in the World

1979

Across the Bay Bridge and thirty-four miles east of San Francisco lies the tony little community of Danville, where people like Rita are a rarity, if seen at all. It's there, in 1979, while Rita was eating fish on liveaboard boats and before homelessness was even a widespread term, that James Tyson Feilzer was born into privilege.

Rita's never been to Danville. By the time she rambled to the San Francisco Bay Area, it was the furthest thing from any place that had anything she needed. Danville is one of the most affluent suburbs in America, and if you're homeless there, you're pretty much invisible and have to hoof it for miles to a more downscale suburb — or twenty miles back across the East Bay hills to Oakland and Berkeley — to find dope, shelter, clothes, panhandling spots, and other homeless people to hang with.

For Tyson — who used his middle name to differentiate himself from his father and uncle, both also named James — it was an idyllic place to grow up.

With a population of about forty thousand, Danville officially refers to itself as a "town," not a city — a heavily wooded suburb of million-dollar-plus homes spread around an upscale-folksy downtown of boutiques, cozy plazas, and high-end restaurants. The big-reveal restaurant dining scene from *Mrs. Doubtfire* was filmed in one of them. Tyson's dad, Jim Feilzer, was an accountant, mom, Patricia, was a real estate agent, and at Monte Vista High School Tyson played football, breezed through classes, and was a popular campus jokester. He was a handsome kid, thoughtful. One of the smart ones—a good student with a good future, his friends said.

The high school is one of the nation's best—consistently ranked in the top one hundred among California's three-thousand-plus high schools.¹ The campus is a pretty, graceful spread of modern, vaguely Spanish-style buildings with red roofs overlooked by what folk singer Kate Wolf called "the golden rolling hills of California," gentle slopes layered with tan grass in summer, green in winter.² Famous alumni include Congressman Adam Schiff and model Christy Turlington, and from the 1960s to the late 1990s, Tyson's time, the school drew Bay Area rock-star acts including Journey, the Doobie Brothers, and Huey Lewis and the News to put on concerts so the students could practice sound recording and editing. It was the kind of place where a kid with ambitions could find ways to soar.

Tyson was more into gliding along.

"Tyson could have done anything if he applied himself," Jim told me. "Plenty smart. In fact, he was a brainiac—he just couldn't use it in the right way. Back in high school, he didn't really study, just relied on memory of what he saw in the class. He once brought home a letter in high school that said he had gotten into an advanced course, and he said, 'Look, Dad, I'm smart!' I said, 'Yes, you are, but you have to work at your schooling if you want to get ahead.' But working hard—that wasn't really him."

But when he was very young? Ah, well, as with most kids, that was a more innocent time. More unwritten pages of what could have been, unseen promise. He was a sweet kid.

"Tyson was in my Cub Scout troop for two or three years, so probably when he was seven to ten years old," recalled his den mother, Barbara Van Dyne, now seventy-two years old. "He was very sweet, friendly and kind to everyone. He was always helpful, cooperative, and was never a discipline problem. He was a gentle soul."

Danville and the even tinier upscale towns around it have trails, parks, and part of the east Bay Area's only real mountain, craggy and arid Mt. Diablo, rising at its eastern edge. For two boys with a lot of energy, it was one big playland. Tyson and his younger brother, Baron, had their run of the outdoors with their bicycles, and in the summers they went to the Sierra Nevada with their cousins to camp and fish and swim the lakes. Their favorite spot there was Pinecrest Lake, an idyllic splash of blue surrounded by thickly forested slopes and flats, just off the winding Highway 108. It's fifty-six hundred feet up in the Stanislaus National Forest, and the Feilzer boys and their cousins went with their fathers, a camper, and fishing poles.

With nothing around but towering pine and cedar trees and a smattering of nearby campers, Pinecrest was the perfect getaway for suburban San Francisco Bay Area kids to clear their heads. They did typical stuff—roasting marshmallows, hiking the trails, swimming the lake.

"We spent a lot of time camping at Pinecrest growing up, and, oh, we did a lot of fishing up there—a *lot* of fishing," said Stephanie Feilzer, Tyson's cousin. She's an attorney, working with the nonprofit Central California Appellate Program, which helps represent low-income defendants. Stephanie is a live wire, quick to laugh and quick on the memories. She lives in Stockton with her husband and young son, and she's such a sunny presence that the minute I met her I thought how life could have been different for Tyson if he'd tapped his brainy attorney cousin for more help.

On a warm summer day in 2022, I was sitting in Stephanie's kitchen listening to her rhapsodize about the fun they all had in the mountains as kids. Her dad, Fred, and Tyson's dad, Jim, led the expeditions up to Pinecrest, she said, and as she scrolled through a string of photos on her cell phone, her whole being lit up.

"Oh, man, did we have fun," she said, paging through until she found one particular shot. "Okay, here's a famous picture in the family." She pulled up a faded photo from 1986 showing Baron, Tyson, Stephanie, and her little brother, Jason, standing in a forest clearing. Tyson's eight years old. Stephanie's nine, the oldest, and she's beaming as she holds a string of three trout.

"The three of us—Tyson, Baron, and I—had caught our first fishes that day," she said. The dads had to help toss the fishing lines and pull in the hooked trout—but for these little kids it was like hauling in whales with their bare hands. A big deal.

"It was pretty exciting," Stephanie said. "And we got a lot better. A lot better."

I've only ever caught one trout myself, but I remember the thrill. And I can see that thrill on Stephanie's and Baron's faces. But Tyson? Here's what struck me about that picture: He looks already grown-up. Or self-possessed. Not like a little kid of eight.

In the shot, he's standing at the far right in a Mickey Mouse T-shirt with his name lettered below the collar, and the look on his face is that of a contemplative adult. Not like that of six-year-old Baron, who's next to him in red overalls, face scrunched up with delight. Tyson's eyes drill directly into the camera, mouth in a straight line. He's holding out his right fist to do an eighties precursor of a fist bump with Baron and Stephanie, but it's like his mind is already ahead of this accomplishment they're reveling in.

Even as a tot, he was a kid in a hurry. To get where? He was never fully sure. But he was always headed there.

"I looked up to Tyson all my life," said cousin Jason, who is three years younger. "He was the guy—*that* guy we followed everywhere. Off the cuff, fun. Like one night we were at the beach and he just takes his flashlight and chucks it out into the lake. He says, 'I just wanted to see how long it would take for it to die.' I mean, who does that?"

Unpredictable is a word that comes up again and again about this man.

"Tyson was very smart, all right, and very creative," Stephanie said. "I mean, I could have seen him being a writer if he wanted to. He could tell a story."

But schoolwork? As with Rita—not his thing.

"There were situations where he tried to hide a bad grade in the garbage can and the cat pulled it out," Stephanie said—not kidding. "And his dad saw the bad grade because the cat was playing with the paper.

"Yeah, Tyson got in trouble." She stopped, gazed into the distance a moment. "I guess you could see what was coming a long time before it did, the downward spiral, I mean. But did we? Not like that."

Tyson's dad, who took the parental lead as disciplinarian, tried hard to bear down on the boy, make him study, make him try. But it never took.

BEING TWO YEARS TYSON'S junior, Baron had the right vantage point to watch his big brother screw up as they grew up. Tyson was cool, sure. But that didn't cut it, Baron could see. He was the kind of kid who paid attention. He was quieter—and steady, always steady, albeit with the usual occasional teenage wobbles.

It didn't help that the boys were still learning how to tie their shoes when their parents divorced—Baron was in preschool, Tyson in first grade. "I was so young I don't remember them being married," Baron said. So that meant the boys grew up living the usual shuffle life, about half the time at Dad's and then half the time at Mom's. But again, given the upscale community location, life could have been a lot worse.

Patricia kept the house in the divorce, and it was a suburban jewel—a sprawling ranch home backing up against a hill coated with wild grasses and oaks, baby grand piano in the living room, wooden clubhouse in the backyard and a pen with a couple of sheep and actual boars in it just for fun. "My brother and I would go in the backyard and we'd play, catch ladybugs, and the sheep would head butt us," Baron said. "It was pretty great."

Their mom got remarried, but that didn't last long, and then she married another man, named Ray Williamson, who moved them across town to a roomy, dark green ranch home. Patricia's new house had a pool with a waterfall that was so tall the boys could dive from the top of it, and another of those "golden rolling hills" rising behind the backyard. It was home until after the kids graduated from high school, when Patricia divorced again shortly after the boys left.

Meanwhile, the digs were also fine when they were with their dad, Jim, in the house he bought soon after the divorce in next-door San Ramon—an upscale little enclave of big tract houses and no downtown that bleeds into Danville against the hills. It was slightly more modest, but this was still in the Danville-dominated land of good living, so it had plenty of room for the boys—a big park just behind the earth-toned ranch house that they could play in, a big rock garden with koi ponds. It was in a cul-de-sac with a couple of other kids, but Tyson and Baron spent most of their kid time back in Danville, where all their school pals were.

"It wasn't fun at all having to live in two different homes," Baron said. "So when we were at Dad's, especially in summer when we were old enough to be left alone, Tyson and I would just stick to ourselves."

While Tyson meandered through high school with mediocre grades and a ready wisecrack, he did have a stint on the football team. Baron became a star on the wrestling team and stuck to his studies. Both boys partied and drank too much in that suburban way of privileged kids, but the difference was that Baron knew when to stop. Tyson liked it a little too much—which in high school made him kind of cool. He hung out with a group of pals who called themselves the Owls because they liked to hang out together and laugh it up, calling out hoots like owls for yuks.

"It's crazy how many people really liked Tyson," Baron recalled. "Always."

Their mom remembers that, too. She also recalls both her boys being into sports, but that from the get-go Tyson was different.

"Baron was very athletic, but Tyson was a little bit on the back shoulder when he played football," Patricia said. "He would help you up if he knocked you over—he didn't have that killer instinct for sports, and the coach was merciless to him. He really just liked to be with the other boys, with his friends."

There was one sport Tyson was good at, though—Ultimate Frisbee. Both Feilzer brothers played it, and it was one of the few things they bonded tightly on. "He really knew how to throw the Frisbee, better than me back then," Baron said.

The Frisbee thing actually started with the Owls, which started with Tyson's friend Alton Glimme. Alton was out sailing with his father one day, he said, and "my dad said he used to have a gang of friends called the Owls, but it broke up. So we revived it.

"We would meet at my house once every few months, about thirty of us eventually, and we'd have breakfast," Alton said. "Then we'd put on sweater vests and walk to school—I lived right nearby—yelling 'Hoo! Hoo!' like owls, or whatever came to mind. It had no clear purpose, it was just a peaceful gang, of sorts."

The main thing they did was play Frisbee. Not exactly a rebel thing to do, or something whacked-out leading to dissolution and drugs. Though a *little* bit of drugs was involved.

"Okay, we'd often cut school to play Frisbee," Alton admitted, sounding a little sheepish about it even decades later. "We'd smoke a little weed, play Frisbee, hang out. It was good times. Innocent."

After bouncing over the East Bay hills to live in Oakland for a few years after high school, Alton wound up back in Danville with a wife and two kids and a career as an electrician. He's proud of his friendship with Tyson, and the times they had together as schoolmates. Looking back now, he can almost understand how his friend wound up dissolving later in life. But only almost.

"We were just messing around with a little pot and some drinking back then, really starting around junior year," Alton said. "But you could tell Tyson was going to get kind of heavy into that stuff. He just seemed to like it a little too much."

Alton and Tyson were on the football team together as freshmen and sophomores—Tyson a linebacker and Alton a cornerback—and Alton thinks that it gave Tyson "structure, and he needed it."

But Baron saw it differently, believing the organized-sports shtick was too conventional for his brother. "He couldn't stick long with something so normal," Baron said. Too bad. Tyson was a bit stockier than his brother, but all muscle like him, and football was a good fit. Instead, Tyson chose to make his mark as the school funny guy.

"He was goofy, clowny. I cannot imagine Tyson being quiet. That's not him," recalled Kristin Schnauz, a screenwriter and actor who was in the same class as Tyson. In the few years after high school, "Tyson did improv [comedy] in Oakland around the time I did improv with the Groundlings in Los Angeles. There was definitely an ego to him—it was a double-edged sword."

Tyson felt he needed the wit to get through his parents' divorce when he was still a kid. It served him well, said Chris Van Dyne, who was a good friend from the time he and Tyson were Cub Scouts together in his mother's den.

"Was he always funny, even after the drugs? Yes. He was an incredibly smart guy," said Chris, who now is an entrepreneur in Santa Fe, New Mexico. "And I mean that in terms of being incredibly witty and quick to the point of being infuriating almost. He knew how to get under my skin. He knew exactly the right thing to say to piss you off."

They didn't keep in as close contact after high school, as Tyson started edging into using cocaine and other party drugs. But Tyson left his mark in many ways on Chris—both as a cautionary tale, and for "certain habits I still have because of him.

"Like for instance, whenever I brush my teeth, and this may sound a little weird, I do my tongue with my toothbrush and I think of Tyson. I remember once I told him I don't brush my tongue—and he said, 'What, you don't fucking brush your tongue?!' He was just pushy like that. But I'll tell you this—I've done it ever since. Because he was right."

Stephanie remembers the same spirit from the time the cousins—she, her brother, and the Feilzer boys—all grew old enough to remember what was being said.

"When we were kids, Tyson was always the leader," she said. "He always came up with what we were going to do. I was the oldest, but Tyson was the most headstrong of the four of us. And I think Baron was always the most go-along. I had a joke that when we were kids, every terrible great idea that we came up with as a group originated from Tyson."

It was silly kid things, like tossing water balloons, secretly taping visiting kids and making fun of them with the recordings, blasting out fart noises at exactly the right-wrong time.

"They were never anything bad," Stephanie said. "But we were— we were a lot. I'm sure we were a handful."

After Tyson got his high school diploma in 1997, he started general studies at Chico State University, 155 miles north of Danville. Onward and upward was the plan.

CHAPTER 9

Cool and Smart and Spiraling

1997

I t was late Halloween night and the party in Chico had been great, but freshman Tyson was so hammered he couldn't find his car. He had to get back to his room on campus, and he kept stumbling around with a couple of pals until he gave up. "Screw it," he thought, "I'll just steal a car"—God knows how he knew how to do that; he was a smart guy.

So he did. Drove home. And the next day, what did he do? He drove the car back and left it where he'd swiped it.

"If I remember correctly, Tyson and Mark [one of his pals] were detained by the police that night, after I had gone home," said a friend who was there that night, Tyson's old high school classmate Dave Stapely. He couldn't scrape up more memories than that, and there's no record that Tyson got arrested. The recollections I heard were that he talked his way out of whatever happened with the cops.

"The next day I guess he returned the car," said Kristin, "but it was an odd choice and foreshadowed how he would wind up in jail later on."

Very Tyson. Bad boy. Good boy. Weird mix. And not great for chasing a BA at a four-year college.

Inevitably, Chico State lasted only about a year, followed by a much shorter stab at nearby Butte College, and then Tyson was done. He discovered that cocaine was a fun fit with booze for him, and he grew impatient. Chico lived up to its reputation as a party college, and with his attention scantily spread on his business-oriented classes, Tyson partied. That part stuck—even after he finally left for good in 1999 and returned to splitting time living in his parents' houses. Tales of him getting too snockered on booze and blow began about then and raised alarms among friends who were still around.

"We'd drive back to Chico together and he'd just disappear for a while, then come back," said longtime pal Jeff Sutherland. "We were all doing a bunch of cocaine back then. But it wasn't terrible—just a bunch of young guys messing around."

With four-year university out of the running, Tyson turned to the local two-year Diablo Valley College (DVC), the main community college for the area where his parents lived. General studies again, with business orientation, and he'd commute with Jeff, who was also taking classes there—and who today owns a local construction company and a cannabinoid (CBD) medicine shop in Danville.

"He lasted about a year there, too, but was working and very social," Jeff said. "He really loved his friends, and we all had a great time together. The whole classroom thing really wasn't what he was into."

The 1999 DVC try was mostly to mollify his dad, and after that failed, Tyson decided it was time to take the nonacademic work world by storm. He wanted to make good money like his parents and told himself a degree would just slow him down. But nothing stuck.

Being a young man in a hurry with no stomach for paying dues was a classic pathway to ruin, and he trotted right onto it.

He tried out the mortgage business. Didn't take. Tried being a phone salesman. Didn't take. Home Depot. Didn't take.

His best jobs, but also only in spurts of several months at a time, were waiter gigs. He could turn on that wry appeal of his, and he had fun—especially at Applebee's in San Ramon, where he made new pals he could hit the bars with after work. One of them was waitress Kate Hauser, and like a lot of other women, she was impressed by Tyson's "really good-looking, kind-of-chubby preppy charm."

"He was sassy, kind of sexual, funny, and he liked a little bit of a power trip over people because he knew he was smart," said Kate, who is one year younger than Tyson. She now lives in Germany, working with horses, but back then she was a nineteen-year-old community college student. Tyson and their other work pals were great drinking buddies.

"I don't know what he dabbled in, in Chico, but when he came back to stay with his mom in Danville he had a couple DUIs," she said. "He had a little Mazda and was always asking me to blow into the tube in it that he'd gotten from the DUI convictions. He was a cool smart guy, but living under his potential. And, hey, he was charming, good at what he did, and fun."

After work they'd take their fake IDs and head to TGI Fridays or any of the plethora of other suburban bars and live it up doing karaoke, dancing, whatever.

"Once we got totally smashed and my future husband was puking out of the car and a cop was following us," Kate said. "Tyson was saying, 'Just keep your speed, they don't have a reason to pull you over. Turn into my mom's driveway.' And then when the cop pulled up, Tyson said, 'You have nothing to see here,' and you know what? It worked. The cop left.

"That's one thing about Tyson. He kept his cool. He had a serious poker face."

It was clear that by the age of twenty, the path was being set for Tyson. Drugs, booze, aimlessness with intermittent attempts to move forward. It all reads like one step short of street life to me. All he needed was a stiff setback or two to kick him all the way there.

But that wasn't in the cards yet. He still had parents to fall back on, and he had more potholes to stumble into first.

"He didn't like the nine-to-five thing. Doing something that would get him rich quick—it was always his thing," said his father, Jim.

Jim moved away to Lebanon, Missouri, with his wife, Becky, in the early 2000s. A burg of about fourteen thousand known mostly as a motel stop on historic Route 66, it was far from the bad influences more easily found in cities or sprawling suburbs—and it soon occurred to the struggling Tyson that this could be a lifeline. Why not start out someplace completely new? he thought. So in 2008, when his brief stab at getting into the mortgage industry had failed, Tyson gave the lifeline a tug. He called his dad.

The idea was to get clean and reorient himself toward some better way forward, far away from the homegrown influences that were dragging him down—to essentially give in once more to his father's guiding hand. As always, there was a core in Tyson that knew when he was screwing up, knew there was a better way to be, and knew he had resources.

Jim was game for helping his older boy. "I remember the call when he went through another hard patch," Jim said. "He'd lost his license, had IRS troubles, a DUI. He'd gotten into trouble with cocaine and called me and said, 'Dad, can I come there?' So he lived downstairs with us."

Lebanon is the kind of small town where the city council's pressing agenda is usually dominated by things like buying a new street sweeper, planning parades, or authorizing major purchases of deicing salt for the winter roads. Lots of hunting and fishing in the woods surrounding the quaint brick-walled downtown. It defined placid; the motto on its website is Friendly People, Friendly Place.

The move worked. Within a few months, Tyson found a 12-step rehab program, breezed through it, and was sober. "He really blossomed again," Jim said. "Got a great job at Lowe's. Was doing great."

Tyson got so stable that high school classmate Kristin says he encouraged *her* to get sober when he was living back East.

"We reconnected by Facebook," she said. "I couldn't imagine anything beyond my alcoholism, and he caught me at a moment when he was in Missouri, living sober, and he talked about this whole big life. Coming from Tyson, this promise of life being big, bigger—that was very enticing. I'd tried AA, talked to another alcoholic, but then with Tyson something sunk in.

"I got sober in 2010, and I credit him very much with my coming to accept my own addiction."

But beneath Tyson's optimism, his desire for a big life still nagged at him. He wanted to be a big shot of some kind, to make good money like his dad, to drive a fancy car and have a great job, like selling big-ticket real estate. But—again—deep down, he just didn't want to take the time to work his way up in a career. He was smart and he knew it. Surely he could skip the drudgery steps, he reckoned. And beyond that—he just plain liked to have fun, to party with pals, to be around a bigger city's sense of action. So once stability took hold, the healing and quiet of Lebanon started to grate. Wanting some place with a little more action going on, Tyson found it about forty miles southwest in the Queen City of the Ozarks—Springfield, Missouri, population 160,000. It was no San Francisco, but it wasn't Danville either, having plenty of metro to keep humming, with universities, theaters, opera, and bars in a thriving city center. Tyson scored a part-time job running the karaoke show at a bar there and found a tiny apartment on the north side of town.

He stayed off the bottle and the coke lines for about a year. Got a job at a phone company answering calls for assistance. Met friends like Staci Sue, a technician at an optometrist's office. She was cute and dark haired, single and chatty, and at twenty-four she was five years younger than Tyson. She also had two young sons, aged two and six—which the newly sober Tyson took to right away.

"It was funny. I'd met him through mutual friends on Myspace, and then we ran into each other at a Halloween pub crawl with friends," Staci said. "He was a lot of person—very outgoing, fun, wasn't drinking. We became good friends—that's all, just friends. We'd hang out, go get something to eat. I'd text him and tell him I was hungry, and he'd show up with a huge bag of tacos from Taco Bell."

Staci was very protective of her boys. "But Tyson? He was just a trustworthy, honest person. He was always smiling, real good with kids, and we just all got real comfortable with each other. He'd play with my two-year-old, he liked joking around. There was one time I had a bunch of cupcakes in my car for my son's birthday, and he just helped himself to them. It was hilarious, and it was just fine."

The trouble was, Tyson just found it too familiar and fun to be in bars. He followed the same template as he had back home—go out for a few pops after work with friends. At first, he stayed sober.

"We'd go for karaoke, and he didn't do the karaoke but he did sing very loudly at the table," Staci said. A favorite song was "Sex on Fire" by Kings of Leon, a driving, crunchy tune about getting it on. It makes sense as a favorite, and I can picture Tyson tipping his head back and belting out the lyrics about being "the greatest." The energy fit him, especially at that time of his life when he wanted to push ahead.

"He always seemed happy, but he had a dark side to him, like 'I'm also a bad boy, but I'm not going to show you,'" Staci said. "So we really just spent a lot of time hanging out at my place or his, and we talked. We'd make fun of how we were super-blunt and nothing was

95

totally serious. I haven't met a lot of people who are witty and sassy like that. I loved it."

At first it seemed like maybe he could keep the booze in check. But toward the end of his time in Missouri it slithered back into Tyson's being. Staci said he texted her a few times to pick him up because he'd had too much to drink, and she'd oblige, but it wasn't often or severe enough to cause her alarm. She figured he was just being responsible.

But forty miles northeast of Springfield, concern was starting to sneak into father Jim's mind. After finding stability with decent work at a distance from the bottle, Tyson suddenly decided he wanted to jet off to Las Vegas to try his hand at working the poker tables. To his dad, this restlessness was not a good sign.

"He always had this idea that he would be a poker dealer—he'd played it throughout his life," Jim said. "But his downfall is that he'd get angry, and that didn't work—not if you're playing poker. He said he was going to go to Las Vegas, but it never materialized. He was going to do that when he left Missouri, but he never got there.

"He wound up going back to California instead."

So—two years after moving East in 2008 to be with his dad, that experiment at plowing a straight-and-narrow path was over. It was 2010 now, and he wound up back at his mother's place—but by then she was living with her ninety-three-year-old mother, Gladys Percy, in Pleasant Hill, another suburb, twelve miles north of Danville.

"When he came back he was doing okay on the drinking, but it wasn't really good," said Chris Van Dyne. "I remember him showing me pictures of him in Missouri, and he's floating on the river with a Bud Light. So it started before he came back."

Chris sighed. "This is where the guilt comes in. I should have been like, 'Okay, Tyson, let's go out for a hike and do sober things.' But me being in my thirties, we just fell into a groove, and I thought since he'd gotten sober at his dad's in Missouri, we could go out drinking again. But first it was the Bud Lights, then more beer, and then a lot, and then he was back where he'd been. When he was sober, he was incredibly polite, and a considerate person. When he got under my skin, it was usually after three or four beers.

"That's life. You live and learn. I think ultimately Tyson had some demons."

All this was happening while Baron was carving out the straight life he'd had in mind for himself since late high school. And it didn't involve drinking with his brother, or over the past couple of years even hanging out with him much. Baron earned a bachelor's degree in business administration at San Diego State University and started mapping out a career and a marriage and a life far from Danville.

While Tyson was once again starting from scratch in a new home in Pleasant Hill, things started to look up again. He got a job working at a cell-phone store—and he found a new passion. Acting.

TYSON JOINED THE ACTING troupe at the Pan Theater in Oakland in late summer, and over the next year or so he snagged roles in a series of short plays. This improvisation theater was based in a small performance space, and the troupe consisted of about a half dozen actors.

In group publicity photos at the time, Tyson looks healthy, happy, engaged. The theater didn't pay—the actors actually paid dues of about $70 a month—but it was a great place to learn some chops. His drinking, along with that taste for cocaine, was by now cementing its grip on him again, and pretending to be someone else was a way to escape that. When he was at the theater he was all about the craft.

Plus, he thought it could help him become a better salesman. Even while floundering, he was trying to aim a bit.

David Alger cofounded the Pan Theater and still runs it. He remembers Tyson as being "a bit reserved, probably a bit younger than anyone else in the group, but very polite and respectful—and I wouldn't be surprised if Tyson joined the troupe to get more comfortable speaking, connecting, for doing sales. He struck me as reserved, introverted. A lot of people are that way; I was. Some people play tennis, some people do softball leagues. We do acting.

"The biggest thing about being in this for a lot of people is being around people on a regular basis that are not in your normal circle. And Tyson? He had a good sense of timing. People generally enjoyed working with him."

It was a good fit for the Danville guy who liked to joke around, could be a clown, but was always looking to get somewhere. This had promise.

"Tyson had an even keel, very stoic—but at the same time there was some sensitivity," his teacher and fellow actor at the theater, Alan Coyne, told me. "He looked like he worked out, and he was into his projected image. But there was a tender side to him that once you got behind that first instant of meeting, there was something more . . . well, sensitive. A vulnerability. And you get to see that in improv. You're performing without a safety net."

A few clips remain of Tyson's acting stints there, and he is somewhat stiff but engaged in them. One in particular stands out—eerily. It's from a scripted fourteen-minute play by playwright Jami Brandli, called Looking for Bruce, and only two actors are in it. A woman is looking for her cat, Bruce, who ran away around his seventh birthday. Tyson plays the cat.

Watching the clip, my heart actually started to race a little. It's like this play was prescient.

Tyson stalks the stage in jeans and a white T-shirt, and he's grim, imposing. He's got short black hair and a beard. Stocky and muscular, his role is to be a defiant cat who doesn't want to come home, who's chosen to live outside, live the free life.

Less than a year later, that's what he'd be doing for real. In the play, the cat jokes that he gave himself a Mohawk—and that's what Tyson did after he hit the streets in San Francisco, posting the photos on his Facebook and alarming all his friends as he began to disappear from their lives.

In the play, the young woman playing his owner is taping up posters outside near a trash can and a park bench when Bruce the cat suddenly strides up. She goes to hug him and he wards her off. He's tense.

"I slept behind a tattoo parlor last week," Tyson-as-Bruce tells his owner. "That's right, a tattoo parlor. . . . Didn't think I'd travel to the rough parts of the city, did you?"

The owner says, "No. I didn't."

"You wouldn't understand. You know, I've been eating out of garbage cans for the last ten days?"

She goes to hug him again, and he wards her off. "Bruce—are you drunk, Brucie?"

"Maybe."

The crowd laughs. Watching the clip, I blanch.

"It's morning," the woman says.

"Morning, night, afternoon. Makes no difference. I'm on my own schedule now."

Again, I wince at the prescience.

As the play goes on, Tyson-Bruce lies down by the trash can on the stage, then chases after some catnip on all fours like a cat and eventually curls up on the park bench with his pretend-cat head in his owner's lap. He's convincing in the role. A bit menacing, a bit feral. I can't help thinking this play was running through his head as an almost-subconscious script for where he was headed. His cousin Stephanie guesses somewhat the same.

"I know Tyson . . . well, this is something he said when he first started going off the rails ten years or so ago," she said in 2022. "He said he didn't fit in, in society. He couldn't work a nine-to-five. He just didn't fit in."

He kept that disconnect to himself at the theater, though, Alan said. "I'll tell you, he was an interesting actor. I enjoyed performing with him, for sure. That solidity is nice to have onstage. That calmness—you knew what you were likely getting when you were in a scene with him. He didn't overact or go to places that he didn't need to go to. . . . I never felt he was overperforming, playing in some direction that was just playing to the crowd. In improv terms, yeah, I'd say he was good. I think everyone felt like that in the group about him.

"I don't know what pulled him into this [acting]. He did have an interest in film and television acting, though, and may have been interested in improv because of that. I could see him being in a lot of cop roles. He had the right physique for it. He could be quiet, in that strong way."

That's just what he wound up doing for at least one gig. Tyson pops up in a December 8, 2011, episode of Investigation Discovery channel's true-crime show I (Almost) Got Away with It. Filmed in the Bay Area, the episode is called "Got to Make a Dummy out of Sheets," and it details the exploits of Christopher Mallos, a slippery robber who knocked over stores in Florida and Georgia in the 1980s and escaped from prison over and over before finally getting locked up for good with five life sentences.

The show features interviews with the imprisoned Mallos and the cops who chased him, and actors reenact scenes to fill in the blanks. Tyson, in suit and tie, plays Sergeant Steve Hounchell of the Pinellas County Sheriff's Department, one of the detectives who finally nabs the thief. It's not a speaking part—a voice-over narrator carries the dialogue—but the bearded, short-haired Tyson is imposing and convincing as the stalwart sergeant.

In the episode he looks like he does in the play about Bruce the cat: a solid, muscular guy sure of himself.

Toward the end of that year with Pan Theater, Tyson lost his phone-store job. Theater founder David hired him at his second business, a poster-distribution outfit called Thumbtack Bugle, to walk around stapling event posters on posts, dropping them off at businesses, and the like. It's a simple job, requires a lot of shoe leather, and one type of person who tends to sign on comes "from transition homes, rehab and the like," David told me.

"They'd work really hard, be stable for a while, then something would happen and I wouldn't hear from them. Seemed to happen right when things were going well, and then they slipped off track somehow."

One guy like that punched in to work one day and said he was quitting because he'd saved "his nest egg and was all set," David said. "He could not have had more than a thousand dollars, and then I was on Haight Street a little while after that and saw him passed out, sleeping alongside one of the buildings. It was obvious that whatever had a hold of him had done it again. I was sad. There was nothing I could do for him."

David got a taste of that with Tyson. "You know, he kind of drifted out of the group. It didn't seem like he found his path. My guess is he was on one path, lost that, did improv, then never really found a path after that. I heard that he'd gone to jail at one point. It's surprising sometimes the way life turns for people.

"I think most of us have a support network that we can lean on. But I guess some people don't have that, or they turn to the drugs to get solace and it doesn't work."

Alan was sorry to see Tyson leave the stage. "Tyson wasn't in the group terribly long, but the way improv is, it felt longer," Alan said. "There's something about improv. . . . With scripted work you get to know people, sure, but improv is even more of that. You're not performing *yourself*, you're performing a character. You get a little more insight into people. Tyson? He was a good person to whom terrible things happened."

CHAPTER 10

Hot Guy on a Slide

2011

Tyson's friend Chris Van Dyne knew things had lurched off the rails when in late 2011 Tyson casually dropped something into a conversation one day while they were hanging out. Tyson had, for a nanosecond, a job at a falafel shop in Montclair, an upscale neighborhood in the Oakland hills, and felt like he had a bit of extra cash on hand for some fun.

"He just came out with how he got a hotel, had an eight ball, found some chicks on Facebook, and just partied for a couple of days," Chris said. He paused at the memory. "Man, that was just way out there. A couple of *days* with coke and a bunch of women in a hotel? That's when I got really worried for him."

An 8 ball is an eighth of an ounce of cocaine—or about 3.5 grams—usually selling for about $350 or more. Since it only takes about 50 milligrams to get high, that's enough dope to get high for, well, days.

"A couple of weeks later, he asked for some money, and I couldn't do that, so then I didn't hear from him again," Chris told me.

Amy Schroll had dated Tyson in the early 2000s when he was a salesman at a health gym in Walnut Creek—when she told me this, for the umpteenth time I thought, "Good God, how many jobs did this man blow through?"—and they stayed in touch off and on after it evolved into a mere friendship. She was working as a paralegal across the street from the gym back then, and being a couple of years younger than Tyson, she was jealous that he could go to bars. He liked to work out and so did she; she thought he was handsome and he thought she was cute.

"Tyson was one of those positive, encouraging people back when we met," said Amy, who now works as a notary. "It's not like he'd give you happy speeches, but he was confident and really impressed people. I saw him do improv, and he was great. He was relatable, very fast to respond to the audience. He always read people very well."

But by late 2011, the sheen was gone.

"The last time I saw him, he came to my house to visit me and some friends," Amy said. "I remember standing in the kitchen with him—can't remember what we talked about, but he didn't seem right at all. And when he left, we thought, 'Wow, what's up with him?' He said he'd come see us again, but we never saw him again. He just disappeared."

Despite the drinking, despite the occasional coke she saw him snort, Tyson had always managed to at least put on a show that he had his life together. This new behavior rang all the same bells for her that Chris had heard.

"I mean, Tyson always took care of [his] shit," Amy said. "He had nice clothes. He paid his bills. He did stuff in life that people are supposed to do to be successful. He seemed like one of those hot guys who would always have pretty women at his side, maybe hanging out on a nice chartered boat with wealthy people drinking martinis at sunset. But he just—disappeared."

Behind the façade of the working guy with serial jobs, the charming actor, the cool dude at the bar, things were finally unraveling in ways that Tyson couldn't stitch back together.

• • •

BARON, TYSON'S FRIENDS, AND I have spent years trying to figure out why Tyson wound up on that sidewalk in San Francisco where I first met him in 2019, and clearly the pathway could have been averted with better mindsets, better choices. But events do trigger actions, and a key one for him came on November 20, 2011.

That's when Tyson's grandmother died.

Gladys Percy was ninety-four by then. She'd broken her hip not long before, tripping on her bathrobe as she walked through her house, rapidly declined in health, and then, as often happens in these situations with seniors, that was the end. For Tyson's mother, Patricia, too, it was an end of sorts. She needed money, wanted to move out and head to Idaho to be nearer to relatives, so she told Tyson she was selling the Pleasant Hill house.

That would be the end of the free ride, which had become necessary because by 2011 whatever Tyson was earning went up his nose and into bottles.

Baron was by then living in Southern California, working his way up to a later job in Ohio as an industrial-plant manager. His life was on track, he was with Tasha Miller, the woman who would soon be his wife, and he didn't have time for the bits of family drama he heard were going on back home.

"When he was living with Grandma [and their mother], he still looked like a normal person," Baron said, showing me a picture of a smiling Tyson in a sweater standing with a cousin, looking—well, normal. The "tell" that things were not fully normal came when Baron got married in Las Vegas in March 2012.

Everything looks fine in the wedding photos, for the most part. Baron wears a striking white vest and tie with dark jacket, and Tyson is in a dark suit with blue shirt and yellow tie. All beam happily in the group photo with Tasha, resplendent in her shoulder-less wedding dress, and a batch of other relatives. But it's in a photo of Baron, Tyson, and their dad that Tyson's face reflects more of what was going on.

Jim and Baron look radiant, arms around each other. Tyson's expression is flat, arms at his side.

"Tyson pulled a Tyson and got drunk and was mostly MIA," Baron said. "Mom, Dad, Tyson, Tasha, and I were supposed to decorate the tables for the wedding dinner, and Tyson was a no-show. It was like that. Pretty shitty."

Tyson was still trying ever so slightly, though. He'd stopped posting regularly on his Facebook page, but he did put this up on March 7:

> My brother Baron Feilzer and Tasha Miller are getting married tomorrow and I'm getting ready to go meet them in Las Vegas. They're an awesome couple and I couldn't be getting a more sweet and beautiful woman for a sister. Welcome to the family Tasha.

Tasha commented under the post:

> Thank you Tyson !! That is very kind of you ☺ can't wait to see you. we are about an hour away. Text us when you get in !!!

The written words couldn't make up for the lived reality.

A few months later, in 2012, Patricia sold the house. Just before she did, she and Tyson got in a raging argument and Tyson punched a counter, inadvertently hitting her hand and scaring her. She told Baron, who promptly texted his brother.

"I said something like 'You're a piece of shit, if I ever see you, I'll knock your teeth out,'" Baron said. "There wasn't a lot of love between us by then because he was being such a dick. That was the last time we communicated."

The first inkling any of them had that Tyson had hit bottom was when Chris Van Dyne heard from a friend that he'd seen Tyson rummaging through a dumpster in San Francisco.

"That was when he hit the streets, right then in 2012," Chris said. "It was a tough thing to go through, seeing a close friend like that go in the wrong direction. It was shocking."

THAT PLUNGE TO THE streets was quick and predictable.

After his mom's departure to Idaho, the now-thirty-two-year-old Tyson was out of options. He was doing too much booze, too much coke. He crashed on a few friends' couches, but the addictive behavior wore everyone out. Borrowing cash and not paying it back. Coming home smashed. This is the inflection point a lot of homeless people I've known tumble to—you've rattled down all your ladder rungs until none is left between you and the dirt.

Tyson hadn't known the dirt yet, but he knew he was headed in that direction. And he figured if you have to be homeless, there's no better place than San Francisco. He thought: the booze and dope are plentiful, the cops are lax, and the homeless culture is so widespread you can disappear into it. He had a few hundred bucks in his pocket when he left his deceased grandmother's house, so he rented a cheap residential-hotel room for a few nights. But then it was the end of the line.

He found a sleeping bag outside—they are sprinkled throughout homeless alleys, easily abandoned—and started bedding down in doorways, in parks, on sidewalks.

You can trace his drop to the bottom through his Facebook page. The next post after his March 7 day-before-the-wedding celebratory one came in April, simply showing an open road and a field. Then came this, on September 3, 2012:

I AM AS HORNY AS A MOTHERFUCKER!!

You can feel the shock of his friends leap off the page.

After weeks of nothing but GIVING [sic] in jail, no surprise, jokes Kate Hauser.

jail is like summer camp but the counselors are fucking dicks, Tyson types back.

omg! You were in where???? Wtf???? retorts another friend.

October 9, he simply posted, Hot rails! And *that* was the tell—drug addiction now announced to the whole world, since his Facebook was unrestricted to viewing. *Hot railing* means lighting the end of a meth pipe, snorting the fumes through your nose, and blowing them out through your mouth—a technique that gives the quickest high you can get from the drug. Really? posted his friend Jeff Sutherland, incredulously.

The postings got fewer and weirder as the months rolled by, complete with the kind of bad grammar and punctuation that someone who attended college would know better than to put out there. If he was in his right mind, that is. Which Tyson was not. need to end this damn streaaaak comes on January 3, 2013, followed by valentines is not a holiday.. unless I get laid on February 14, followed on February 21 by a caption-less picture of himself with a Mohawk haircut, dark eyes staring into the camera, a blank expression on his face. By that point he was meth-addict thin, and one worried friend posted the comment Are you eating?

The Mohawk was especially eerie since in that Pan Theater play just a year or so before this, he played a cat who goes homeless and—yes—gets a Mohawk.

The Facebook posts end three months later, and as they progress, they take on the semblance of the journal of a man imploding. On May 9, Tyson posted a picture of himself, still with a Mohawk but this time wearing sunglasses, a tank top, and a metal-studded belt with a silver buckle the size of a CD. He's standing in a room flexing his biceps, and behind him is hand-scrawled graffiti on a stained wall that's only partially legible, but part of which reads, HA! The caption reads, **Douche mode enabled.**

A couple days later comes **I took a shower!**, and the last post is a quote from a song by rapper A$AP Rocky about liking to have sex and loving "**bad bitches.**"

By that point his captions read like pure street, like the language of so many people I've gotten to know in the tent camps and cardboard drug circles over the years and the hard people I knew on the road. You snort, shoot, or smoke enough for months or years on end, and your brain gets cooked. You think elemental—sex, food, drugs, pain, relief, survival.

Tyson's friends and family were freaking out.

"When I read that 'bad bitches' post, I thought, 'He's totally lost it,'" Baron told me. "I didn't have any idea where he was, but I knew he was in trouble." Baron began checking the jails for his brother, and Tyson started turning up in San Francisco's lockup in early 2013 for petty theft. He was doing what every street junkie has to do, shoplifting and smash-and-grabbing out of cars to pay for dope.

It's easy to sell that stuff—in San Francisco, it's an open secret that the UN Plaza, a block from City Hall, is the quickest place. So many people there hawk obviously stolen iPhones, clothing, DVDs, and everything you can swipe off a pharmacy shelf—deodorant, diapers, candy, you name it—that I dubbed it Thieves Market on a map that ran in my 2003 "Shame of the City" series, showing homeless territories in the city. The cops know about it, counselors know about it, housed people and workers who stroll through know about it, and it never really changes. Market Street, the main drag through the center of downtown, with extra-wide sidewalks, is also a popular place to sell stolen goods or things found on the sidewalk or in garbage cans, and so are the grittier streets in the Mission District and the Tenderloin. Tyson made enough doing that, as well as the usual junkie habit of chipping bits off his stash to resell to other junkies, to keep his habit up—and that soon became the driving force in his life.

His rap sheet grew. In 2013, he was arrested for passing a bad check and having burglary tools, and by 2016, he was getting arrested for car theft, robbery, receiving stolen property, passing bad checks, and drug violations.

"I'd never even seen heroin before I was on the streets and just smoked it for the first two years trying to tell myself I could control it," Tyson told me years later. "Then I started injecting. And then I was lost.

"I did things I never thought I'd do. It got to where I was just trying to survive every day. I didn't recognize myself."

By the end of 2013, Baron was seriously worried. His brother's phone wasn't working; the Facebook posts were scary and then they just ended. Tyson stopped communicating with anyone from his previous life.

"Back then, I thought maybe he was just couch surfing after he left our grandmother's house," Baron said. "I didn't think he was actually in the street. Doing all those things. It was very hard later to learn how far he'd gone down. But I had no idea for the longest time."

IN A BIZARRE TWIST, living on the streets as a drug addict triggered the first semblance of responsibility in Tyson in years. Educated, smart, raised in a class of society that expects to get things done, he became known as the guy who could handle things. He often joined homeless junkie camps along the waterfront, in the Tenderloin, and the mid–Market Street wastelands and acted almost like a traveling street counselor. Arguments? He mediated them. The best places to scrounge for clothes and tossed-away appliances to sell for a hit of meth or smack? He knew them. The guy you wanted sleeping next to you in the alley who always seemed to have one eye open? Tyson.

He usually wasn't a tent kind of guy. He was more old-school, the kind of homeless man you saw before the 2010s. Cardboard boxes, doorways, makeshift tarp shelters, were his bag. "Less crap to have to carry around," he told me.

Kevin "Biscuit" Bynum was one of those street addicts who looked up to Tyson.

"Tyson is the guy you want around when shit gets heavy," Biscuit told me. "He's just smart, you know? Stays calm. He's someone I can trust, and that's rare out here. I play guitar—I've got an electric Squier [made by Fender] and he's the only guy I could leave it with. I'd leave anything with him. That's how good he is."

Embarrassed by being reduced to living on the street, Tyson broke off with everyone he knew before. He stayed disconnected so long he even lost track of his own family.

"It got to where I didn't even know where to begin to connect again, so I didn't," he later told me.

But finally, after more than five years on the street, a belief sank into his bones, and he told his good friends living outside with him about it: He wanted to be rescued. He believed his family would someday come for him, and as he talked about it, he gave other people hope that maybe something good could rise from the hell they lived in.

Tyson just needs a chance to get back to a normal life, his friends told me in 2019.

That chance was coming. More than twenty-four hundred miles away in Ohio, Baron had been making those phone calls to jails, morgues, homeless shelters, and hospitals for several years. One time when he called, the cops told him Tyson had said he was Baron to try to slide out of a bad-check rap. Tyson did short stints in lockup, but never stayed long. Baron could never get a message to him before he was released; calls are notoriously hard to make *in*to jail—the prisoner has to call out. And Tyson just didn't do that.

But Baron kept it up, even if it someday meant finding out Tyson was dead. "He's my brother—I had to know what happened to him. It was so incredibly frustrating. Nothing seemed to work. Except for jail, which came and went, he just disappeared."

CHAPTER 11

Reaching into the Void

2019

I get a lot of letters in my job as a reporter. I'm known as a guy who writes about homelessness, and occasionally people write to ask if I can direct them to someone who can help them locate their father, uncle, cousin—whomever—who may be homeless or in a rehab program. I can't always spend a lot of time on the responses because the newspaper keeps me pretty busy with stories and projects, but I regard answering these questions as a public service. We who learn about arcane systems like the ones that help homeless and addicted people have a responsibility to be helpful when we can, I believe. And there's always a small part of me that remembers what it was like to be that sixteen-year-old kid, struggling to figure out the big bad world by myself. So I always try, directing people to outreach counselors or a program if I don't have time to actually look around myself.

It can feel nearly impossible, and a bit stressful, to find someone who's slipped off the grid. More than twenty thousand people are reported missing every year in California, and San Francisco in 2019 had around twenty thousand homeless people cycling through its streets and shelters throughout the year.[1] That's daunting enough. But I do also have a little extra emotional baggage about these things.

Another of my specialties over the years has been writing about missing people who've hit the news as crime victims, and a lot of them wind up being kidnapped children, most of whom end up murdered.

There was twelve-year-old Polly Klaas, snatched in 1993 by Richard Allen Davis, a petty criminal with a long rap sheet, from her Petaluma home during a sleepover party. Davis molested and killed her, and after her body was found (stashed under some scrap wood off a highway), the cops arrested him at a Native American reservation that I hiked into over a mountain while they were busting him. Polly became a national obsession while she was missing, the pressure of the story was intense, and her family's grief filled me as I wrote. Six years later came the kidnapping and beheading of seven-year-old Xiana Fairchild of Vallejo, whose killer, Curtis Dean Anderson, was one of the sleaziest scumbags I ever had to interview—he bragged to me at the jailhouse that he loved raping kids and asked if I could send a woman reporter for a follow-up interview so he could look down her shirt.

There are a lot of other cases. So, yeah, there's a bit of anxiety even on my end when approaching the search for someone. But I do believe in hope.

On April 17, 2019, at 6:15 a.m., I got an email that stood out from the others. It was the first time I heard from or of Baron. "Hi Kevin," it began. "My name is Baron Feilzer. Tyson Feilzer who is pictured in your recent article is my older brother and my family and I have been looking for him for some time. I wanted to ask if you could share any information you were able to get about him with me. I live in Ohio but am planning to come and find him in the next few days. I would greatly appreciate it if you could take some time to call me. Any information you can share would be greatly appreciated."

The tone, the directness, the plan—everything told me this query was different.

I remembered the hunts I'd been a part of that worked, but also the ones that turned up empty, that led to a find but changed nothing, or that ended tragically.

In 2000, I'd searched the city for weeks after hearing that one of Robin Williams's comedian pals, Doug "Dougzilla" Ferrari, was homeless—and I'd found him. I hooked him up with "St. Mike" Pritchard, another great comedian and friend of Robin's, who's dedicated his life to doing seminars around the country advising kids on how to be kinder to one another, and then I stuck with them as Mike helped Doug wrestle his borderline personality disorder into stability. The two men became pals of mine, and Robin would call me from time to time over the years to hear how my work on homelessness was going. The whole experience felt good. Like I'd done a mitzvah.

But there was also Bridget Pendall in the mid-2000s, a heroin addict whose sister Jackie flew out from upstate New York and looked with me and Brant all over the city for a week—finding nothing. Bridget was like a will-o'-the-wisp as we hunted all over the seediest parts of town—a sighting here, a friend who'd known her there, an arrest for drugs or prostitution that led to release to a program and then another disappearance. I still have no idea what became of her. A few years later Jackie died, never knowing what had become of her sister.

So much pain, so much death, so much sorrow swelled up and then lost to time. I wanted to help Tyson be remembered as saved. I wrote back to Baron the same day:

"Hi Baron—I would love to talk to you and help you find your brother; I have done that sort of thing before, having covered homelessness as a reporter for several decades. I will call in the next day or two to connect. You have my deep sympathy. I know how hard situations like yours can be."

I wanted Baron to know that nav center story wasn't a one-off for me on the subject of homelessness. I wanted to give him hope. But the city has a lot of camps and hideaway spots for outside folks, and I could tell that scrap of cardboard where I'd met Tyson wasn't his regular spot. It would be a hunt. So before I called Baron, I checked around to see if anyone knew where Tyson was.

Dr. Barry Zevin, head of the city health department's Street Medicine team, was one of my first calls. He's a careful man, whom I've known for many years, and his team roams the city helping homeless people with their medical needs—which to a large degree means helping the chronically homeless in camps and alleys with their addictions and neglected physical ailments, like abscesses or broken body parts. I'd just spent a lot of time with him for a story I did on his team's effort to bring buprenorphine—more commonly known by the brand name Suboxone—to street people to help them step down off opioids. I thought this was a terrific idea since Suboxone works quicker than methadone and is easier to detox with.

Barry told me, yes, he had encountered Tyson, but couldn't get into medical details because of federal HIPAA health care privacy laws. He didn't know where I could find Tyson, but did offer that he thought Tyson might have a lot of difficulty rehabbing—but again resisted going further when I pressed him. "Medi-Cal can cover some of the residential rehab if you can find him and get him into it," Barry said. "Good luck."

I called a few outreach counselors I knew, and they hadn't heard of Tyson. So I figured I'd run my string for now, and if I was going to help this Baron from Ohio, it would definitely have to be a shoe-leather search job.

I called Baron a couple days after getting the email and he picked up on the first ring. He had an even, friendly voice—like someone who's used to handling things. I liked him over the phone right away.

"We haven't seen him in more than seven years, not since my

wedding, we had no idea where he was, and when I saw that photo [in the article], it hit me hard," Baron told me. "I figured he was probably homeless but was hoping maybe he wasn't. I know I have to come get him."

Then Baron told me that in the time since reading my article he'd researched rehab facilities—"and I called a lot; I didn't know anything about all that stuff"—and picked one, a ninety-day residential program called Elevate in Placerville, a woodsy little Gold Rush–era town in the Sierras about three hours east of San Francisco. He started a GoFundMe page to help raise the $40,000 it was going to cost. "They don't take Medi-Cal there, so we'll need to pay for it," Baron said. "I've already got fifty-six hundred dollars. My brother has a lot of friends."

I asked Baron to give me a little background on how he and Tyson grew up, because I've always found it handy to be aware of what pitfalls might be lurking in someone's background—a murderous uncle somewhere, everyone on crack, the people I'm talking to maybe so traumatized or impoverished themselves that they might have extra challenges, violence in the home as a kid, and so on. Not this guy. He laid out a little of how he and Tyson grew up in Danville, a town I knew well, having grown up in the same area, and then he said he was a manager at an industrial plant in Ohio, with a college degree.

"How in the hell did a guy with Tyson's upbringing wind up smoking meth on the street in San Francisco?" I asked.

Baron thought about that for a moment. "This is the kind of story that's not supposed to happen in a place like Danville," he said slowly. "The odds should be in our favor. We were both heavy drinkers when we were young, and he went further, but not me. Before he disappeared, he was into marijuana and cocaine and alcohol, but now it's obviously gotten a lot worse."

Are you surprised? I asked.

No, he said. "Basically, the last place he lived was with our grandmother. She was the last one to support him—her and my mom. One night he was watching TV, and my grandma got up around ten p.m. to get something to eat. She tripped on her robe and broke her hip, and that was it.

"Tyson thought it was his fault—that if he hadn't been there, it wouldn't have happened. But it *wasn't* his fault. But that's how you feel when you're feeling useless.

"Feeling useless is what got him to where he is, I'm pretty sure of it."

There was clearly a lot more to this narrative, but I reckoned we'd get into that later. Okay, come on out and let's go find him, I said. I know where street people hang out, and it's not that big a city.

"I'm going to do this—I'm going to make this happen," Baron said. "We're going to find Tyson and I'm either going to get him into rehab, or I'm going to have to say goodbye forever, because I know he will die in the street. It's his choice. But I love him, so I have to try. He's my big brother."

CHAPTER 12

"He Needs You"

2019

Baron landed at San Francisco International Airport on Friday, April 26, 2019, at 10 a.m. An hour later, he and I were sitting at a café table on the Embarcadero with a couple of cups of coffee.

He'd hired an interventionist named Vicki Lucas through the Elevate rehab outfit to help—she was a professional trained in the ways of persuading addicts to agree to rehab, then helping figure out what programs to send them to and how to get them there. It's what an interventionist does, and Baron had done enough research to know he needed this kind of expertise if he was going to make this mission work. I figured I was there principally to guide Baron—and, yeah, maybe report. The *Chronicle* had hired freelance photographer Nick Otto to shoot pictures on the hunt because (Brant was retired by then), after talking to Baron, I'd told my editors this might actually turn into a story. It didn't have to—the real purpose here was to help one brother find the other. But I had a feeling this could be a useful thing to write about, that people could learn something from the experience.

We were a curious lot. Baron showed up in a gray T-shirt, jeans, and a dark ball cap and was composed and directed from the get-go. He still had the muscular build from his high school wrestling days, and his beard framed a kind face. Vicki was super-chatty, sturdy, and full of energy. Nick is an ace *shooter,* as we call photographers in my business—he's shot overseas, shot local homeless stories, and freelanced for the *Washington Post* and the *Chronicle,* and he lived in the Tenderloin, of all places. He and I hit it off immediately; I liked his grit.

I'd brought a map of the city and marked it with the territories where I thought we could scout for Tyson. We'd start at the waterfront, where I'd found him on that scrap of cardboard. Then we'd head uptown on Market Street, where the panhandlers and stolen-goods hawkers are sprinkled among the tourists. The Tenderloin, epicenter of homelessness, would come next, and if we were still out of luck, we'd go south to the Mission District. The Haight-Ashbury neighborhood, center of all things neo-hippie, was on the western edge of town and had scads of homeless people—but they were mainly old drunks and young people trying out what they thought was a bohemian life. (I always got a kick out of seeing the old drunks berate the younger ones, saying, "You think this is cool? You wanna look like me in twenty, thirty years?") Didn't seem to fit Tyson.

My bet was that he was on the waterfront or in the TL.

We started by scouring the parks, sidewalks, and benches around the stately, storied Ferry Building at the foot of Market Street. Baron had printed out a stack of reproductions of the main picture of Tyson that had run with my nav center story, and he, Vicki, and I showed them to everyone we talked to.

First we looked for Shorty and his usual crew in their palm-tree-studded park facing the Ferry Building, but they weren't there. So we hit the edges of the garden and the surrounding plaza. We approached about a dozen people before we got a real bite—a lanky guy who said he was forty-seven years old and went by "T." He said he knew Tyson.

"I seen him the other day right here," T said, scratching his neatly groomed salt-and-pepper beard. "He's a good dude. He's got some wisdom to him and a story to tell."

Baron lit up. "Where can we find him?"

"Well, he's kind of a loner, real smart, but sleeps in different spots. You'll have to look around."

We all looked at one another. Baron nodded. Nobody said anything for a few beats.

"You miss your brother?" T asked.

"Yeah."

"Keep looking. He needs you," T said. "Me? My family passed away. Nobody's looking for me. And you stay out here long enough, like me, it gets deep. You'd be surprised at the stories. When shit happens to you, it's like a tattoo. It never leaves. It'll kill you."

He patted his chest, fingers tapping his heart. "But Tyson, at least he has you. Go find him."

About a hundred feet away, we found James Herrera, who at twenty-nine seemed a bit young to be hanging out with forty-year-old Tyson, but he brightened up at the name. He was a stringy fellow, fidgeting on a concrete planter.

"Tyson—you mean James Tyson Feilzer? Yeah, I know him. He hangs out on Market Street. Sometimes sleeps on Stevenson Alley between Fifth and Sixth, or over by the Post Office on Post Street. Good dude."

This was helpful, but only a bit. All those spots were common hangouts for street campers and addicts—and I smiled when he mentioned the Stevenson Alley location, because it's a block from the *Chronicle* newsroom. Like I said, small city.

Baron gave me a wan smile as we took off south along the waterside Embarcadero toward the spot where I'd found Tyson on the cardboard.

"So far so good," Baron said. We stopped by nearly every group we hit along the way, as well as individuals if they looked like they'd be open to talking. When you're walking up cold to street people, you need to assess quickly. Are they coherent, as in not so mentally ill that they're gabbling to themselves? Are they too high to talk? Do they look withdrawn or hostile? This isn't to say most chronically homeless people are like that, or unapproachable, but you do need to be respectful and careful so you don't get into a needlessly tense encounter by invading the space of someone who doesn't want to engage. You also have to be direct and honest. Most street folks have great bullshit detectors and survival skills, so they can tell if you're just trying to wrench a quote out of them. You have to be honestly interested in them as human beings, not two-dimensional figures, and show that you're looking for a real conversation with no judgment or hesitancy. Which for me is never a problem—and fortunately it wasn't for our little group that day, either.

Baron took to it right away, even though he had never done anything like this before. He'd stroll up smiling and say, "Hi, how are you doing? Got a second?" If the person was lying down on the sidewalk or a bench or the grass, Baron would bend low and gently tap the person if he or she seemed to be lightly dozing.

Then he'd pull out the picture of Tyson and say, "Have you seen this guy? He's my brother."

Every time, you could tell his heart was skipping a few beats while he waited for an answer. My heart was skipping, too, as I watched him work and repeated the same routine alongside him with the folks I queried. I knew we'd get good leads, but along with them came flurries of fuzzy ones. One woman said he was in a fleabag hotel in the Tenderloin, another said he slept outside on Second Street, another said he was sleeping around North Beach. It was all over the map.

Stringy James called us—yes, many homeless folks have phones, provided free through nonprofits with government money so they can keep in touch with counselors, family, and the like—and gave us the name of a Tenderloin hotel he was sure Tyson was crashing in front of, so we split up and headed in that direction, about a twenty-minute walk up Market Street. I took a parallel route, threading through the Financial District of business offices, figuring I'd hit a few camps I knew of on the way, and Vicki, Nick, and Baron went straight up Market. About halfway to the TL they ran into a heroin addict leaning against a light pole. He called himself Seven. Sure, I know Tyson, he said—you can find him at the Drug Users Union, an unsanctioned safe-injection site for street addicts, up on Turk Street in the Tenderloin, in about an hour. Thanks very much, Baron said. We'll head up there—but if he's gone, there's $20 in it for you if you can connect me later with him. Seven nodded, but it seemed clear he was most interested in just doing the right thing.

I met our group at the Drug Users Union that hour later, and sure enough, no Tyson. But there was Seven, otherwise known as Shawn Swanson, relocated and sitting in the middle of about a dozen ragged junkies in front of the injection office. He didn't see us at first as we started talking to those on the edge of the group, but lurched to his feet when he heard us say Tyson's name.

"You have to find him, man, you have to find him," Seven said. "Tyson has been convinced beyond what normal people usually are that his family is looking for him. He's been saying that for a few years now. Lots of people are stuck out here.

"I lost faith in it; my family's done with me. But Tyson? He needs to be with people who love him, not brother junkies. He's smart. He just needs the chance."

Seven was different. If he hadn't told us he was homeless, and if he hadn't been sitting on the sidewalk both times we met him, we could

123

easily have mistaken him for being comfortably housed. He wore a jaunty Irish walking cap, his blue jacket and pants were clean, and he presented like someone who was just taking a break from work. Well-spoken, neat white beard. We liked him.

Baron and Vicki wrote their phone numbers on one of Tyson's photos that we were all toting and gave it to Seven.

"Call us, please, if you find him," Baron said.

"You bet, brother," Seven said.

Several others in the group nodded vigorously. "Yeah, Tyson's a good guy," one said.

"Find him," said another.

We shook hands all around and headed deeper into the Tenderloin, past the usual tableaux of degradation and people trying hard to live with dignity and grace. The TL, with its hodgepodge of immigrants, artists, working folks, and poverty, is a constant source of inspiration and anguish to San Francisco. Tent camps and addicts shooting up, smoking, or snorting dope dot the district, sometimes taking up entire alleys or block-long stretches of sidewalk. Outreach counselors regularly approach people offering shelter or housing—when they can, that is, since there is never enough—and the cops and public works cleaners regularly sweep groups and camps away, which just means they move to another spot a few blocks away.

The TL also has a rich, very cool history—music icons from Billie Holiday to the Grateful Dead sang there decades ago, and it still has vibrant music halls drawing modern bands. In the mid-1900s up through the 1970s it was the LGBTQ hub of the city, and in the early and mid-1900s its dozens of residential hotels housed working singles before they got married and moved into apartments. Those old hotels—the movie *Vertigo* features a classic example—were great back then, but today they are bottom-end housing or rehabbed complexes used for supportive housing for formerly homeless people.

If Tyson was anywhere, I reckoned, he'd be here.

We wandered for hours, finding plenty of people who knew Tyson—at least in passing, as a fellow street denizen—but no Tyson. Jessie, lying with a bulging backpack in front of the public library that looks onto City Hall, told us she'd just seen him on Willow Street, a short stretch of blocks that is probably the most consistently clogged, camped-on strip in the Tenderloin, with clusters of tents and fentanyl addicts smoking and shooting up all around them. It was also right below the window of Nick's apartment.

"Wouldn't be surprised," Nick said dryly.

While we were walking around, I decided to sling out a call to Kevin Adler, who in 2014 founded Miracle Messages, a nonprofit that connects homeless people to their families by phone or video. I've written about a couple of Kevin's endeavors—one was an expansion of Miracle Messages to connect people isolated in COVID-era housing—and he's usually got a pretty good ear on the street. Plus he has a big heart and remembers whom he runs into.

Ever heard of Tyson Feilzer? I asked.

Kevin took in a breath. "I sure have. Met him on the street a while back. He was a good guy, and I really felt bad for him. He said, 'I haven't seen my family in a long time and I'd love to reconnect.' So right there we got him on the phone with his stepmom and dad somewhere back East—but it didn't work out." The tone immediately went to the parents suspecting that Tyson was calling for money (which was not an unreasonable assumption, given his history and addictions), Kevin said, and Tyson "stormed off."

The call was made in June 2018. Tyson's dad, Jim, later told me he was "sorry it turned out the way it did. . . . We weren't ready then when we got that call."

"I think Tyson felt insecure and sheepish," Kevin said. "A lot of people out here do—they feel embarrassed, even self-loathing. It's a hard thing to connect again. That's why we do what we do."

Kevin said that when he talked to Tyson, he'd been sleeping at Second and Market Streets. "Let me know if you find him. I'd like to know he's okay."

Walking endlessly and talking to hundreds of people is exhausting. And nothing like what ordinary housed people do.

"This is surreal," Baron said at one point. We were standing at the corner of Sixth and Market Streets, a notoriously seedy corner at the end of a block of low-rent hotels, homeless supportive housing, people hawking their stolen or found stuff on the sidewalk, and drug dealers and users shambling all around. Down the block, a couple of men were screaming at each other, something about one owing the other money for a gram of something, and the only reaction around them was a few people looking on bemusedly.

"Yeah, *surreal* is probably the right term," Baron repeated, scratching his chin and gazing at the screaming men. "I don't know how there could be so many people in such pain here—in such terrible conditions. I can't imagine how people would be okay with this."

Vicki stared at the sidewalk a moment. "If we find Tyson, we're going to have to get him up to the rehab center right away," she said evenly. "When they're this far gone, when they say yes, you go. If you wait, they're gone and you've lost them."

I knew that, and I think Baron had caught on to that. But it was good to articulate it. This was a rescue mission with time pressure.

We put six miles under our feet before we finally decided to give it a rest at about 9:45 p.m.

"We'll hit it early in the morning," I told Baron. "I'll call you." He and Vicki headed to the Hilton Hotel they were staying at in the Financial District, and Nick and I headed home.

I was a little discouraged. But hopeful. There were too many traces of Tyson out there for this not to work out.

CHAPTER 13

Get in the Car

At 10:15 that same evening, Seven strolled up to one of his usual haunts in the Tenderloin, where a conglomeration of street people were shooting up, smoking up, selling stuff, and just hanging out, at the corner of Larkin and Willow Streets—that same alley the woman at the library had mentioned. Tyson had just finished dumpster diving for women's clothes to sell on the sidewalk and was chilling.

"Hey, your brother is looking for you," Seven said.

"No shit."

"Yes, shit." Seven pulled out his phone and called Baron. He handed the phone over to Tyson.

On his end at the hotel, Baron turned on a recorder—which he then left on throughout the evening. He wanted to capture everything so he could remember it best.

"Hi, it's Baron."

"This doesn't sound like Baron," Tyson said.

"This is Baron—your *brother*." A moment of silence. "Okay, ask me a question. What do you want to know?"

"What was the last time I talked to you?"

"Wow, I don't know. I sent you a Facebook message saying I didn't ever want to talk to you."

"No, it wasn't—it was at the wedding. So where was the wedding?"

"Las Vegas."

That seemed to soften Tyson up.

The conversation was quick. Baron didn't want to spook Tyson by saying anything wrong on the phone, so he told his brother he'd been looking for him all day and got to the point. "How do you feel about coming in off the street?"

"Okay."

"Okay, I'm coming to get you."

Baron called me and Nick, who was at home, right away and said, Okay, it's on.

I'd just made it back to my house twenty miles east in Walnut Creek, so I jumped back in the car and gunned it toward San Francisco. If I kept to 80 mph with a few surges above and below, I could make it in twenty minutes, I told Baron. They would get to the corner in ten minutes in a rental car they'd stashed at the hotel.

Baron rounded up Vicki at the hotel, and while they headed to the TL they went over the plan. Get Tyson into the car as quickly as possible, tell him they have a hotel bed, shower, and food waiting for him, and have "the talk" in person as quickly as possible—asking if he's up for rehab, is he fully tired of street life? Does he want a new life? And I had a role to play, too, as a journalist.

"We're just going to tell him, we're just going to say, 'Look [with] Kevin—let's finish the story,' you know?" Vicki said. "Kevin will follow up on [the article], and you know, you've got to go through treatment. It's part of it, and then you'll go home and then there'll be a story about you, about all this. I'll word it real appropriately."

"Yeah," said Baron. "Yeah."

This might not work right away, Vicki reminded him. She breathed a little prayer. "I know you don't [pray]," she said, looking over at Baron. "But I think . . . for both of us."

"Thank you. We believe in something, you know—we just don't believe in church."

"You know if Jesus existed, apparently he didn't believe in organized religion, either," Vicki said. "Yeah, he didn't. He didn't walk with the rich. He hung out with sinners and poor people, right?"

"Yeah . . . he preached outside."

I thought about that later, when Baron told me about the conversation he and Vicki had and I listened to the recorder he'd flicked on and carried. I'm not a religious guy, either, but I do believe in a spiritual responsibility to be nurturing, decent, kind. And Jesus was, as a rabbi once told me, at the very least a cool street preacher. Good philosophy. Living outside. Homeless. A good guy to be paying attention to at a time like this.

On my end, every minute dragged like an hour as I gunned my car along Highway 24 through Oakland and across the Bay Bridge before plunging into the Tenderloin. I got lucky and wasn't pulled over anywhere. I made it to the corner in twenty minutes all right, but by then Baron and Vicki had already made the ten-minute dash over to the corner—and just before them was Nick, who did indeed luckily live in an apartment just above where Tyson was hanging out. Nick dashed downstairs to shoot pictures just as Baron rolled up in the rental car.

"What kind of world do we live in where you're worried someone won't come and find you?" Baron mused as they slowed to the corner, searching the sidewalk for his brother.

"That's him," Vicki suddenly called out. "Right there."

Baron jacked open the door and stepped out. Tyson slowly rose to his feet as this clean-cut-looking man, the brother he hadn't seen for so many years, walked over. Seven stood nearby and watched.

It was 10:36 p.m.

TIME FROZE JUST LONG enough to hear the crunch of discarded needles and glass meth pipes underfoot. Long enough to hear the low murmur of a dozen or so homeless people sitting or sprawled on the sidewalk all around them in the darkness. Long enough for Baron to focus in on the face of this brother whom until this evening he hadn't been sure was still alive.

Tyson spoke first. Quietly. "Hey, Baron."

Relief and sadness swept over Baron, but he knew he had to keep his cool. Don't mess this up. Keep it simple. "How you doin', man?"

Tyson stared, miles of hard times in his face mixed with a note of disbelief. Seconds passed.

"Nice to see you," Tyson said, and stuck out his hand.

"Nice to see you—gimme a hug," Baron pulled him close.

At Tyson's feet were piles of clothes he had fished out of trash cans all day to sell later on the street. "Want me to watch that stuff for you, Tyson—take care while you take time with your family?" Seven asked.

Tyson nodded.

Vicki had parked the car and walked over. She told Seven they brought the $20 they'd promised him.

"Thanks a lot, man," Seven said. "And you know, hey, we're all glad you guys came."

"Awesome," said Vicki.

"Thank you," said Baron.

"You guys did an amazing job," said Seven.

Tyson got ready fast. All he had was a small backpack with a few things in it.

"Want to go for a ride?" Baron asked.

"Yeah." Tyson got in the car.

Vicki ducked over to Seven and handed him the $20 and a pack of cigarettes.

"You didn't have to do that," Seven said softly. "We just want him to have a chance. Let me know what happens."

"We will," Vicki said, then she got in the car with Baron, Tyson, and Nick.

It was a quiet few minutes' ride to the Hilton. Tyson asked how his mom and dad were doing. Basically fine, Baron said. How's your wife? Tyson asked. Fine was the answer. Then, just as they pulled toward the hotel driveway, Baron came out with it, the biggest thing he had to share with his big brother: "Hey, I think I told you I have a daughter now, right?"

"No, you didn't. Actually, you might've just told me that. Congratulations. What's your daughter's name?"

"Penelope."

Tyson echoed it back softly: "Penelope."

"Yeah. She's three and a half years old."

Tyson absorbed that bit of news, while in the front seat Nick told me they'd arrived at the hotel. I was now just a few minutes away, and I switched my route to the Hilton. They all got out of the car and headed upstairs to the room. They were into a few minutes of chitchat, showing Tyson the article I'd written and the photo that had tipped off Baron that I'd interviewed his brother, when I walked into the room.

CHAPTER 14

He's Cooked

've been part of interventions before, some that worked and some that didn't.

I was on the phone with a dear friend of mine, Dan Reed, a few nights before he died, and that probably set the tone for me on these things. Dan was a terrific reporter whom I'd worked with at the *Chronicle* on murder stories including the Polly Klaas case, and who then competed with me when he went to the *San Jose Mercury*. He had a crack sense of humor and was an elegant, complete writer. Dan was also a terrific drummer, and we jammed, talked about doing a band together. But he couldn't shake the bottle, and it got so bad that when we flew separately to New Orleans on a scandal story involving the Louisiana governor, he crashed in my room because he couldn't remember where he'd booked to stay. I told him to take this as a sign—that if he didn't clean up, the liquor would kill him. He said, Yeah, yeah, yeah. His marriage and job fell apart and he wound up in a cheap motel in a part of Oakland where we used to cover drive-by shootings.

He called me from that motel on New Year's Eve 2009, while I was out to dinner at a fancy restaurant with my wife. He was in hell. Sad. Separated from his wife, no job, crappy motel. "You can shake the booze, Dan, I know you can," I told him. "Come on, you're smart. You've written about people losing it. You know how to do this."

"Yeah, I know." His voice got a little of that old derring-do Dan in it. "I'll be okay. I'll do rehab. I just have to get to it."

Eight days later, he was dead. Broke my heart. I'd had people in my life drink themselves to death before, and I'd certainly covered plenty of people in the street who died of booze and drugs. But my reporting mate, a writer who had a similar sense of humor and approach to life as mine? A guy whose reporting was as good as any I've ever known or read? It made me realize that sometimes, despite everything you try or hope, addiction won't shake off. Death will win. But not always. You have to keep trying anyway. I'd already felt that way, knowing other friends of mine who did manage to get clean and stay clean. I hold that feeling close when I try to help other friends or family who struggle with the bottle or needle or pipe, and in those numberless How-about-you-getting-clean? conversations in the street.

So when I walked into Tyson's hotel room, I wasn't nervous. More like determined, with just a touch of anxiousness. After spending so much time with Baron, meeting his brother, learning about their lives, I really wanted this to work. Yes, I was a reporter in this situation, and the intervention was being done by Baron and Vicki. But I cared and wasn't going to be afraid to let Tyson know that.

The thing is to not come on strong in a situation like this; let the process work naturally. So my first aim was to not get in the way.

Vicki was sitting on a windowsill, Nick was leaning against a wall, and Baron and Tyson were sitting side by side on a bed.

"Hey, well, look at this, huh?" I said, walking to the bedside. "I just saw you a week (or so) ago!"

"Yeah," Tyson said with a chuckle.

"How are you doing, huh?"

"I'm good. Thanks a lot, I appreciate it."

I gave him a hug, patting him on the back, and we pulled apart and looked at each other a moment. His eyes were clear; he must have shot up or smoked recently enough to be steady. Some might have mistaken the look on his face for defeat. I saw it as relief. A growing feeling of rescue mixed with a bit of trepidation.

"Did these guys say they were looking for you . . . ?" I asked.

"Yeah," Tyson said quickly. "Yeah, good article, by the way."

"Good quotes!" I said, and the room broke into laughter.

That was the moment I knew this was going to work out. This was a guy who wanted what his brother had to give.

I NEEDED TO ASK a few questions, but mostly I was going to just listen. And be positive. Be supportive of the process that Baron and Vicki were here for. "What I liked when we were talking is that you were being straight and you were being smart," I told Tyson.

"Well, thank you," he said.

I told him his thoughts about putting a navigation center on a prime real estate spot were insightful. Not just on the face of it, but because he had obviously evaluated the subject and wasn't giving me a knee-jerk answer. "I could see that you were thinking about something other than the next thing," I said.

"Yeah. I mean, when there isn't a solution to a problem, a lot of the time people will try to figure out what they would do, you know, or what would be a good solution, instead of just wanting something to get fixed. And trying to think of what would getting fixed look like and just naturally trying to solve the problem—even if it's not something that will ever actually happen. Yeah, at least I know what it is that I would like to have."

He looked bone-tired and was just on the edge of rambling, with a lot of *you knows* thrown in. But he was coherent. The same smart man I'd met on the sidewalk a couple of weeks before.

Vicki ordered pizza, and I told Tyson I wanted to write a story about him working to get his life back. "You seem like a guy who got kind of tired of sleeping in the street," I said, trying to help nudge the door open to the whole rehab pitch.

He didn't need the nudge. "Oh, yeah, very much, you know, I hate being homeless, you know?"

That was Vicki's cue. "So do you want to end that now?"

"Yeah."

This was the key moment of any intervention, where some addicts say sure, but let me take care of something first—which pretty much means they'll be gone once they hit the door. Others just say no way. We knew Tyson had tried to kick dope before and failed, which is totally typical—most addicts need several tries to get clean, with the relapse rate being around 60 percent, according to the American Addiction Centers.¹ So that runaway impulse could clearly be there.

But it wasn't. All of us saw that Tyson was "cooked," as street counselors say, completely tired of the street and drugs, and ready to take a hard try at getting clean. And to hear him tell it, he'd never really given up.

"A couple of guys said that you've been saying for several years that you thought your family was going to come looking for you," I said.

"Yeah, yeah. I just felt like that was something that was going to happen. Pretty much why I stayed in the same spot, mostly. . . . I could have gone to Oakland or some other place, but I stayed here in San Francisco because I wanted you to be able to find me. I just felt like my family would come for me someday."

Baron's eyes were wet. Tyson's voice stayed flat, like he couldn't believe this hope of his had actually come true.

Vicki rolled out a little detail about driving up to the rehab facility in the Sierra foothills town of Placerville the next day, and we all chatted about how he might get some medication—Suboxone—to stave off dope sickness until he got there. No sell job was needed. He was in.

He rattled off a quick street résumé of sorts: I'm hooked on heroin and crystal methamphetamine, Tyson said. Didn't start shooting up until he'd been on the streets for two years. Became homeless not long after his grandmother broke her hip and died and mom sold the house they were living at in Pleasant Hill. Been to jail a bunch of times for short stints on car theft, drugs, and shoplifting and detoxed behind bars but went straight back to dope when he got out.

This rehab spot in the Sierras is going to be nice, Vicki told him— all about mindfulness, hiking, getting in shape, detoxing gently on Suboxone. You'll like it.

"Okay," he said. "Who . . . who's paying for it?"

Everyone sat silent for a second.

"Pretty much everybody that knows you," said Baron.

Tyson stared straight ahead. "Wow," he breathed.

"So when his [Kevin's] article came out, I started this GoFundMe." Baron showed Tyson the page on his phone, showing about $40,000 raised by that moment. "And between, you know, mostly between 'em . . . your friends . . ." Baron's voice choked up and he couldn't finish. Then he was crying. "Ninety people," Baron squeezed out.

"That's amazing," Tyson said.

"People love you," Vicki said quietly.

Tyson didn't need any more convincing, but Baron had come prepared, and there was more to show. He pulled out a packet of photos and a piece of paper. The photos were of a happier past—Tyson as a baby, the family on vacations, and the brothers looked over them together, Tyson turning them over and over in street-grubby hands.

"I have a letter here from Dad," Baron said. "Let's take a look." He began to read, voice choking up again every few sentences.

Dear Tyson,

    I'm writing this letter because I love you and because I can't be there today. I'm sorry. When you were born, that was the happiest day of my life. And that will never change. I need to reinforce my feelings about you as my son. You were my firstborn son and that can never change. I was the first to hold you and bond with you when you were born. You were loved in that first moment and you continue to be loved to this day. I regret you did not hear that enough.

    I have fond memories of the life you spent with me growing up, our fishing trips with the Feilzer clan and trips to the beach with the Cooks. I remember watching you grow up with Stephanie and Jason as your cousins. I remember when you caught your first fish and how envious I was that you could surf and I could barely stand up for a second. I loved watching you play baseball, soccer and football. Win or lose, you were the happiest kid on the team. Your life hasn't been easy and you have faced hard times.

    As a father I want only the best for you and your brother. I fought to have you in my life and to be there to witness your successes, but also to help pick you up when you stumbled. Drugs and alcohol played a major role in these hard times. Like the night I got a phone call from the Danville Police Department that you'd been picked up for drugs. At the time,

I was angry with you for that situation. But I am grateful that you chose to call me first. 11 years ago, when you wrote me that your life was out of control and you needed my help to get your life back on track, and with Becky's agreement, you moved to Lebanon. You were able to improve your life. And I was proud of your effort to do so.

When you moved to Springfield, once again, alcohol and drugs brought you down. Drugs and alcohol have not helped you, Tyson. Addiction is a disease that can be treated. Please be willing to get that treatment.

Tyson, I have been so proud of your accomplishments. You have had good jobs and many opportunities. You are so personal, intelligent and easy to love. But today you exist on the streets and my heart aches for you. Becky loves you like you were her own son, and she and I have prayed that you find a way off the streets.

A reporter chose to interview you for an article about the homeless problem in San Francisco, and a picture was taken of you. Your Uncle Fred, who still reads the Chronicle, saw the story, told his son, who told his cousin, who loving you, put a string of events together. You probably have no idea how many people love you and believe that you deserve help out of your present situation. We didn't abandon you, Tyson. We just didn't know where you were.

I don't believe in coincidences. The time has finally arrived for you to decide whether to accept this help and agree to the treatment being offered. I want you back in my life. Our family wants you back in their life. I will love you either way. But I want to be able to see you again. To be able to tell you I love you in person and not in a letter. You have a life still worth living. Please choose to live it.

Baron finished reading. The brothers sat silent. Tyson stared at the floor.

"Dad really cares," Baron said. "And he doesn't say he loves you very easily, you know? Dad wants you back."

Long pause again.

"Yeah," Tyson said slowly. "I definitely want to be back."

Next, Baron called up his phone's pictures and flicked through a few of his daughter, a lively tyke with a button nose and pleasantly impish smile.

"Have you met this little girl yet?" I asked Tyson.

"No."

"Well . . . you're going to have to get well versed in Disney movies," Baron said. "I assume you haven't seen *Frozen*?"

Tyson smiled, his first that night. "No, I haven't seen *Frozen*."

"Well, you're going to have to watch *Frozen*," Baron said. "At least a million times."

Next, Baron played a video of Penny. Her words were a bit garbled on the recording, but the takeaway quote was "My name is Penny and I miss you."

"She's adorable," Tyson said.

"Yeah, she's—she's great," Baron said. "She hasn't met Mom or Dad. You can be the first one she meets."

"Okay," Tyson said in a near whisper.

Baron breathed hard, tears running.

WE HAD A FEW more minutes before the pizza Vicki had ordered would arrive, and Baron gave me a sidelong look that seemed to indicate the ball was in my court to keep the conversation going. So

I asked Tyson what he was really thinking when Jessica and I had stopped to talk with him on that scrap of cardboard.

"I was just happy to have, you know, an ear," he said. "To be able to, you know, to speak to somebody who's interested in the same issues that I was, or am, because it doesn't happen a lot."

"When you're on the street, people just look at you like you're part of the landscape with nothing to say, right?" I said.

"More than that—you don't get treated very well. . . . I have literally been told that it doesn't matter what I think or say, you know—I'm homeless."

"People beat you up or spit on you or that kind of stuff?" I said.

"Yeah . . . you know the whole 'Get a job' thing. You get pushed around a lot. I'm not somebody who tolerates stuff like that, and that can be really difficult because the natural inclination is to not believe me, because, you know, you're homeless or, you know, a drug addict because of, you know, things people have done previously."

What came next was a reminder of how self-aware he was. "You know, it's definitely an earned reputation that homeless people have, let's face it," Tyson said matter-of-factly.

He picked at a nickel-size abscess on his right forearm, the kind I've seen over and over in street people from dirty needles—the kind Rita's boyfriend Tommy had, and that Rita herself had. They are always trouble. "This is what happens when you're on the street," Tyson said. "You get sick. You get infections."

I asked him what he thought of the difference between the high-toned Danville he'd grown up in and the gutter he'd learned to call home.

"Definitely didn't prepare me . . . for living on the streets," he cracked.

Everyone laughed.

"No shit," said Vicki.

"We'll really have to work on that," added Baron.

But seriously, Tyson said—what does it all mean? I felt my heart jump. I could hear it in his voice. An evaluative guy like this—he was already looking to a different future.

"I keep looking for a lesson—what's the lesson? What's the point? What was the reason for this? I mean, it happened to me and there often is not one reason. And that is one of the most difficult things to deal with because it's, like, why did I have to go through this?

"You know, why do I have to have suffered through days without being able to get out of the rain or without food? Being dope sick? Why did I even have to be addicted to heroin in the first place? Just to feel, you know, to feel good enough to, to think about it another day?

"And God's silent. He's not going to explain himself to me."

"Well, some people say that you hit the bottom so that you can appreciate that you actually climb back up again," I said.

"Yeah, there've been so many bottoms, it boggles the mind," Tyson said. "The bottom is a relative position."

We were back to the same thoughts we'd talked about on that cardboard scrap at the Embarcadero. The pizza was due any minute, and I wanted to leave the brothers and Vicki to themselves so they could eat, really relax—and Tyson could finally take his first shower in God knew how long.

"I'm gonna leave you guys to be brothers," I said, standing up. I hugged Tyson. "You know what? I think you've got a shot. I really think you do."

"Thank you."

"You're not just a lost guy—you can actually do something."

"I hope so."

HE'S COOKED

As I hugged Vicki and then Baron goodbye, I could see the crying lines on Baron's face being replaced by something heading toward happiness. My heart melted. I hugged him extra long, and then Nick and I left.

Vicki waited until Tyson was in the shower to finally exhale completely.

The tape recorder Baron had turned on back when he got that call from Seven and Tyson earlier in the evening was still on. I grinned when I heard the playback later.

"You did it, dude!" Vicki told Baron.

"I can't . . . I can't believe it."

"He was ready."

"Yeah, he's ready."

"I think the whole thing about 'Oh, he's going to do a story' made a big difference on him going into treatment," Vicki said. "That's going to be a good story."

"Yeah, it really is."

PART 3

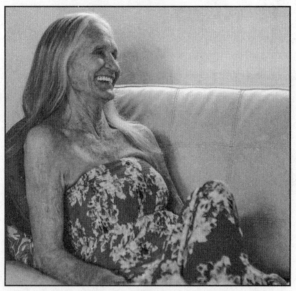

Rita, in recent years, looking restored and healthy in Florida even as she fought cancer.

(Photo courtesy of Brant Ward)

Tyson, restored and healthy in Ohio

(Photo courtesy of his brother, Baron)

CHAPTER 15

Rita—a Full Smile

2004

R ita's new life began in mid-April 2004, in the spare bedroom of Pam's country bungalow on the outskirts of DeLand, a charming town north of Orlando with about twenty-six thousand residents. Downtown has quaint stores, restaurants, and bars, where Pam's gardener-carpenter husband, Rick, was a popular musician (still is), and a lot of Rita's family lived in nearby towns (and still do). Rita already knew it well, having visited family quite a bit, sometimes staying for periods, in those early years before she left for California. It was a perfect little spot to start over—no drugs, no panhandling needed, nobody around to tempt her back to using dope, no sleeping on cardboard. No worrying about surviving moment to moment. Her government disability check and public medical assistance were plenty for what she needed for now.

The first tell that she was on the right track was when Rita painted everything in her bedroom in calming hues, with white for the rattan dresser and blue for the table next to her double bed. Pictures of her kids hung on the walls, and she put framed photographs of John Lennon and Bob Dylan on her dresser and nightstand.

NOTHING IS EVER SIMPLE read her pillowcase. The jarring contrast with the concrete hell she had just escaped from scared her, but through hours of meditating alone about her dilemma and reading

147

through the Bible, her resolve to heal solidified. She tapered off methadone, kicked crack, and become drug-free in a couple of months—pretty astounding, considering the long grip heroin and crack had had on her. She had truly been ready to quit.

For now, the recovering process was mostly down to just her and her sister, and Rita's daughters. The rest of the family, still traumatized by her long absence, would take a bit more time. It usually does when a lost soul returns.

As she settled into her new life, Rita talked by phone to Little Bit and Little Bit's tough-guy boyfriend, named Twenty, Bobby Ray, and other former Homeless Island streetmates, encouraging them to kick drugs and get off the street. She spent much of her time at a local church and frequently attended Alcoholics Anonymous and Narcotics Anonymous meetings.

She went back to her Key West–era diet of fish, vegetables, and fruit. As 2004 closed toward 2005, her T-cell counts normalized with the help of AIDS medications, and she was once again strong, bicycling everywhere and fit enough to show a glimpse of the ace gymnast she'd once been.

Tommy's death had jolted her, but most important, she woke up to what life should be and could be. Loving her family. Living healthy. Not waking up dope sick or hungry.

And that was how it all sat when I finally called Pam. It was a quick talk. Enough time had gone by that Pam was finally okay with the idea of me checking in.

"You'd be amazed how she's changed," Pam said.

"It'll be nice to see you," Rita suggested.

"I'll book the flight," I agreed.

• • •

I GOT TO PAM'S house in DeLand around noon on December 15, 2004. I knew I'd be able to tell within minutes if the rehab was really sticking.

It clearly was.

"Well, waddya think?" Rita said, her toothless smile seeming to fill her face as I got out of my rental car. The woman I saw before me bore little resemblance to the ravaged apparition I knew just a year earlier on Homeless Island. There was a calm in that wrinkled face that I'd never before seen, and I teared up seeing it.

"Rita, you look great, really," I said.

She hugged me, arms less bony now, and put her head on my shoulder.

"Doesn't she look great?" Pam said, putting an arm around Rita. "She's learning to be a friend to herself again."

Rita patted her stomach. "Look at me, I'm fat now!" She cut loose the kind of laugh she hadn't been able to sink into for years. "I've gained twelve pounds! It was amazing, feeling the toxins leave my body. I can think straighter now, too." She laughed again—I hadn't heard her do that two times in a row ever. "When I was on the Island, I couldn't even tell you who the president was, so I have some catching up to do." Now she watched the TV news and read local newspapers— a real luxury, she said.

Rita gave me a little tour of the house, tearing up when she got to her bedroom and pointed out the pictures of her five kids on the wall. She sat on her double bed and opened one of her journals at random.

"'I thank God for keeping a small flame of hope in my heart that maybe there was a better tomorrow,'" she read in a soft, unhurried voice. "'I pray for a healing miracle. I used to have a panhandling sign in California which said, "I need a miracle," and I got one. Recovery.'"

Back out in the living room over cups of herbal tea, I asked her why she finally agreed to take the help, which had been there all along—all she had to do was take it from the outreach counselors or reach out to family. Shame and pride had a bit to do with it, she said. But mostly it boiled down to surrendering. Admitting she was beat by the street.

"It was just time for me to go," she said with a shudder. "I was finally tired of the street—too much tragedy, too much loneliness, too much sorrow. But I couldn't get cleaned up by myself."

She gazed over at Pam for a long moment and smiled. Pam smiled back.

"Thank God, my family didn't give up," Rita said.

"We knew we could never force her," Pam said. "She had to be willing to take that chance at another life. I always knew she would someday, and we never stopped loving her, but I guess we had to wait until she hit bottom."

Joy told me over the phone that her mom's biggest challenge now was "finding a purpose, because like so many homeless people she got to where she didn't think she was worth anything. But we tell her that her purpose is enjoying her life.

"She always had so much love inside for us, even in her worst times, and it hurt me to know she was lonely and sad." Joy paused for a moment. I could sense her emotionally struggling on the other end of the line. She pulled in a deep breath.

"Now I don't have to hurt anymore," she said slowly. "I am so proud of her."

Later, Rita sat in a black rattan chair under a huge oak tree in the backyard, which looked out over acres of woods and meadows stretching off like a watercolor painting, and watched the sun sink. She held her bronze-furred kitten, Smeagol, in her lap and her eyes were calm, hands steady, as she stroked the cat. Her blond hair had luster again, the wrinkles had softened in her face. She was nothing like the fidgety street beggar I knew a year before.

I told Rita what Joy had said, and Rita let a long silence sit between us. "That's nice," she said quietly.

Then she looked down at the kitten and smiled. "Just think: somebody dumped this kitty on the road six months ago, and we took her in. She was skinny and wasted out, needed some real love.

"Kind of like me, huh?"

ONE THING MISSING IN that first year, though: a full smile. Her years of street life and addiction had rotted all twenty-eight of her teeth. It's a common, crippling problem for street junkies—that "meth mouth" of drug and sugar rot sets in, teeth get bashed or chipped in beatings, or the addicts fall down in drug or booze stupors. With unsightly mouths, they can't get jobs and their self-esteem is stunted, but fixing the problem is often out of reach since surgery and dentures cost thousands of dollars. Rita couldn't easily afford that.

Her work helping Pam paint furniture didn't pay a lot, and between that and her monthly federal disability check (AIDS, hepatitis C, and the ravages of street life qualified her) of $550, daily expenses got met and not much else. Federal Medicaid funding didn't cover dental work. She was poking away a few bucks to save up the $3,000 she reckoned she needed for a set of dentures, but it was slow going.

My story in the *Chronicle* about her resurrection in Florida ran in January 2005, and San Francisco dentist Dr. Tom Jacobs read it. I'd mentioned Rita's need for teeth in the story, and Tom—who'd helped disadvantaged people with dental care in the past—called me. Connect me with Rita's family and I'll see what I can do, he said.

He got on the horn with Pam, who connected him with Dr. April

Flutie, whom Pam and Rita had been talking to about getting dentures (she was Pam's family dentist), and voilà. Turns out April—whose husband was a cousin of NFL star quarterback Doug Flutie—had also done dental work for disadvantaged folks, and she wanted to help Rita, but dentures and the surgery she needed were a bit steep for pure solo charity.

The two dentists decided to pool their resources.

It was quite a job. Rita's teeth had deteriorated so badly that raw nerves were exposed, and prepping her mouth required pulling all the old stumps, fixing the gums, and chipping and filing her decayed jawbones to accommodate dentures.

April did the work, Tom kicked in cash. The tab was $7,000. Rita didn't pay a nickel. The dentures were in by springtime. April said she always wants to help in situations of need, and with a charming, grateful Rita and with Tom chipping in, "this was a perfect situation."

April said, "Against her beautiful tanned skin and blond hair, she needed a white set. She looks great."

Tom told me the whole effort had a spiritual tinge for him. His wife was fighting cancer, and he'd been talking to his priest "about what directions God leads you in" when he read my story. "I guess this was one of my directions," he said.

"Rita—she's a really nice lady. Sometimes you don't know where to offer charity and where not to, and this one seemed like an obvious case. It's so wonderful to be able to give directly to a person like Rita. We could really see how she was working hard on her life."

Rita didn't take any of this for granted. "I'm not used to seeing my mouth look so beautiful. It's been about ten years since I had a whole set of teeth." She stitched April a quilt in gratitude, profusely thanked both dentists—and particularly liked hearing that Tom had felt a bit of divine motivation, because by then she was fully reconnected with her spiritual beliefs.

"It's like God is continuing to bless me after getting my life back," she said.

From then on, every time she smiled, her entire face lit up, and her teeth were dazzling. It's amazing what a decent-looking set of choppers can do for a person's self-esteem.

ONCE SHE'D SETTLED INTO her new life in Florida after her rescue, Rita kept her distance from the San Francisco Homeless Island crowd—and, crucially, heeding her own concerns and the advice of all of us who knew her, she never went back to the city. She was rightfully afraid to reenter the toxic street environment where she'd sunk into hopelessness: "I know I can't go out there," she told me. "It's hard, but I know it's how it has to be." She was happy to talk on the phone, and until finally all of the Islanders lost touch in the late 2010s, she urged them to take whatever help the city had to offer.

Those city efforts got Little Bit into supportive housing, which led to rehab and the first healthy life of her adulthood. Michelle, too. Twenty, who in 2003 was standoffish and rough, ready to fight anyone who messed with his girlfriend, Little Bit, became an evangelical convert—inspired by Rita's dedication to Bible study in sobriety. Rita was thrilled by all of it. "Twenty, I never thought I'd see him like that," she said. "And Little Bit! Michelle? Thank God. Really."

Little Bit had the most spectacular resurrection aside from Rita's— and it was government programs that finally did it. She'd detoxed in hospital beds and done residential rehab after jail so many times she lost count, but finally around 2008 she had a new boyfriend, named Andre, who lived in the Raman Hotel, a supportive housing complex run for formerly homeless people, and for once this boyfriend wasn't a dope fiend like herself. She started crashing there with him, the on-site counselors took her under their wing, and finally—finally—the out-reach took hold. She got on methadone, started pulling a government disability check, and adopted three pet rats, which she named Baby Boy, Kasper, and Squirrel.

"She did a complete turnaround, and she could have become a drug counselor," her case manager, Kermit Burleson Sr., told me. "I wouldn't put any limits on her."

She lasted one year. I tried to see her a couple of times, but we missed each other. And then I ran out of time—in September 2011 she died of kidney failure when the damage of street life finally caught up with her. She was only forty. It's a common thing; I have seen it over and over. You come in off the street, clean up, get more relaxed, and then the survival-mode body defenses that somehow kept you alive for years outside relax, and boom. Something brewing for a long time, like kidney disease, or new such as pneumonia, swoops in and kills you.

Rita was more than lucky in that regard. She was a near miracle. When I told her about Little Bit dying, she became very quiet. Didn't cry. Too much death over the years—too much expected death—for tears to come right away. But she sighed heavily.

"I've evolved from being happy to being spiritually happy, and maybe Little Bit had that knowledge by the time she died," Rita said. "I pray she did."

The outcome for Vina, the one-legged Islander, was more typical. After Homeless Island disintegrated, she occasionally gave in to street counselors and took a "transitional"—i.e., temporary shelter—hotel room, but never stayed for long. And she resisted every offer of help from her father and her childhood best friend, Gina Lindow. Gina had reconnected with Vina in 2004 after reading my Homeless Island story—Gina called me to ask where to find her, then sent me a phone card (needed back then) for Vina to use, which Brant gave to Vina in the street. Gina then flew to San Francisco and begged Vina to come back home to Oregon, where they grew up, to give stability a chance. But even though Vina took brief stabs at shaking her heroin addiction, usually after going cold turkey in jail for low-level drug busts, they never stuck, and she was always driven by the drug demon to stay in the haunts she knew.

One thing she did do was pull it together—tidying up the tent or hotel room—when her daughter Ashley Farrell visited. Vina would sweep the dirt, pile the clothes, push the clutter into a corner. She still had pride.

"She was always honest with me, and when I'd come with my friends, she'd make us lunch, tell us to eat right, be her funny, energetic self," Ashley told me. "I know what it's like to be homeless, to feel the worst hatred you can from people, to feel there is no hope left. But there is hope."

Mostly though, there was anguish.

After Gina flew to San Francisco to reconnect, she had that hope that Ashley spoke of. "It was the same Vina," Gina told me. "We talked mom stuff, and she sat there and brushed her hair like she always did and smiled and had that same big heart. She scared the crap out of me wheeling that chair in traffic like that, and I told her, 'Vina, this is pretty hard-core.' She just said, 'Oh, Gina,' like it was no big deal. She was brave. Always still the same Vina I'd known."

I kept visiting Vina again and again, finding her on the street or in those subsidized rooms, urging her to get clean and take her friend's help. Sometimes she'd cry and say she'd give it a chance. Sometimes she'd snarl at me and tell me to "fuck off."

"I wasn't always like this," Vina told me in spring 2015, sitting in her wheelchair at the spot that used to be Homeless Island. "I was a mom with a place to live. I was an artist. I was a good student." She sat silent a moment, staring at her leg stump. "A lot has happened. I would love to get clean, I love my kids, but . . ." Her voice tapered off.

When she finally died of a heroin overdose that summer at age fifty, she lay on a slab at the medical examiner's office, unclaimed by family, until I learned of her death and called Gina.

And then there was Jill May, who mostly stayed in the nearby seedy Tenderloin neighborhood but occasionally slept at Homeless Island. She was addicted to crack and heroin and got her dope money from turning cheap tricks in alleyways and cars. She was one of the most notorious street hookers in San Francisco in the late 1990s, early 2000s, a rail-thin wraith with a deeply lined face, screeching at cars and passersby when she was dope sick, and at night crashing on the sidewalk, splayed out on blankets or in cheap sleeping bags. But in those moments at 3:00 a.m. when her head was clear and conversation got real, Jill was thoughtful, caring. Smart. I thought she was marvelous. She loved to journalize her thoughts in reporter's notebooks I'd give her, but I only got to read a few pages because she'd lose them within days. I remember she wrote something about how she missed her kids—she had three, all taken away young to be raised by other people. And how people should avoid drugs. Hopeful stuff, forgotten when the need for heroin and crack pushed her back to her seamy reality.

Jill had tumbled to the streets when she and her pimp, Ricky "Slick Rick" Smith, got buried in their addictions and he couldn't handle his stable of prostitutes anymore. The children she had were with him, and he hit the streets with her; the kids were raised by friends and family. Rick generally tried to protect her, but too often he was out making cheap drug deals so he could cut the stash with baby powder or some such and keep enough extra to sell for the next hit. Sometime in 2007 Ricky stiffed a drug dealer on $150 worth of crack, and she—yes, a woman drug dealer—dragged Jill to the city's southeastern waterfront, doused her with gas, and lit her on fire, watching Jill scream her way to death in front of her. Jill was forty-nine years old.

After her killer was convicted in October 2013, Jill's family and Mike Philpott, the San Francisco police homicide inspector who nailed the case, and I all went to the spot where Jill died and had a ceremony. Ricky had been clean for four years by then, jolted to his senses by the horror of what happened to Jill, and he came with the kids.

Parts of Jill were still stuck in the asphalt. We placed a podium over that spot. I sang a song I'd written years before called "I Will Think of You" when an old girlfriend died of cancer right around the time my father-in-law died of a cluster of health ailments; I sing it at funerals for people who are special to me. The bridge goes like this:

There's nothing left to hurt you now,
What's done is done, just let it all go by.
You can't make sense of something that makes no sense at all
And now we learn the meaning of goodbye.

It fit the moment. But learning and feeling the meaning of good-bye, something I've specialized in for far too many years, doesn't help the hurt much. It's still there.

"Our best Christmas present will be you moving inside," Brant and I used to tell Rita and the other Islanders when we were all hanging out on the cement as the traffic roared by. All these years later, it's gratifying that Rita gave us that Christmas present.

But depressing to realize how few of her friends made it.

OVER THE NEXT COUPLE of years, Rita kept making and painting furniture with her sister, earned a therapeutic-massage license, and started working at a health nutrition store in town. She pedaled eight miles a day into town for the job, and more all over town—"keeps me in shape," she said. We talked on the phone, and she sent me pictures of herself in which she soon looked so healthy there was no residual sign of the street life left in her face. Her body tightened up with the exercise, and the abscesses were a distant memory.

Pam slowly reintroduced this prodigal daughter/mother to the family as she healed, and it made for a gradual reunification. The kids and siblings all saw her long dark period as a cautionary tale about what not to do, but they didn't throw it in her face. They simply had too much grace for that. Amazing people. She was lucky to call them family.

"My mom was just so helpless and couldn't make the right choices after she'd been out there so long," Joy told me. "Tommy may not have been the greatest boyfriend, but he unfortunately was the nicest she ever had after our dad. We didn't really know where she was, and it always hurt me so much to know she was probably so lonely and sad. I'm so proud of her now."

Rita's mother took the longest to get used to the idea that this wayward child of hers might be back on the right track, but Rita's kids—now fully grown and earning livings—warmed up quickly. Like me, the whole family needed some time to go by before believing this transformation, this rehab, would last. First the months rolled through, then a year or two, and Rita didn't waver. Her mother reconnected lovingly with her, the siblings reconnected, Rita got jobs, got new and sober friends. She got the new life she should have had all along but for the twisted road she took. But then, how many people have straight lines to happiness and success? Some roads are just more twisted than others.

"You never do know what path people will take in their lives," her old high school friend Marsha said when we talked about Rita's descent and rebirth. Then Marsha stopped to ponder that thought for a long moment.

She sighed. "But I'll tell you this—Rita was always very strong. You could see that in her, pretty or popular or not."

As the years unspooled, Rita and I kept in touch with phone calls, emails, letters, pictures, Christmas cards. Every new picture looked better than the last—Rita on the beach with her kids, Rita in stylish clothes at a family gathering, Rita backlit on a waterfront looking twenty years younger.

Rita earned a massage certificate at Angley College in DeLand and started giving chair and table massages. She got a job working at the local Health Foods for Life, moved into her own apartment, and decorated the walls with inspirational sayings. She rode her bicycle everywhere, visited her kids in Miami, Key West, and Costa Rica—lived the life her soul had been waiting for.

One December card from her in 2009 said on the front, *Certain times help us see with clearer eyes the gifts we have in life . . .* , continuing on the inside with *And I find that one gift I really treasure is knowing you. Happy Holidays.*

"Kevin, the card speaks the feelings inside," she wrote. She then referred to "righteousness and holiness in truth" with "my new self walking in that direction. Home.

"May you travel along with joy in your heart. Sing praises this holiday season. Life is good!! Bless the earth, love and touch each other's hearts. Missing you at special times like these. Things are good. Love you lots, Rita Grant."

Her shifts at Health Foods for Life were flexible around her appointments for massage clients, and one of her main gigs there was painting cheery signs for the front of the store with messages like THANK YOU FOR COMING! It was taking the old panhandling cardboard-sign skills to a legitimate new high, and store owner Bob Lewandowski loved it. She also ran a massage chair at the store — and worked on Bob's back when it ached.

"When she came back here from San Francisco in '04, it was amazing," said Bob, who at eighty was still manning the store cash register in 2022. "She became super-spry and healthy, did cartwheels outside for fun. She was perfect for this place."

Rita also met Bonnie Leonard at Bob's store, and they became great friends — she's the one who told Rita there was a vacancy in her apartment complex and helped her move in. They both wound up at the same church and shared health food cooking tips.

"When Rita makes up her mind, she is very strong," said Bonnie, seventy-seven. "I could never be homeless like she was, but she is physically strong, too. Obviously had to be.

"The only thing irritating is when we'd go to a restaurant, she'd ask a million questions — 'What's in the water? Is it [whatever dish they were ordering] organic? Where did the avocados come from? Were the apples grown locally without pesticides?'" Bonnie sighed. "But that doesn't really matter. I just love her personality. Very spontaneous. Free as a bird."

One of their favorite things to do was to go dancing — especially when Rick had a gig in town. There's a video on Pam's phone shot in 2018 of one of those gigs, when Rick's band, 'Lectric Weiner, played the Abbey restaurant and packed the place with family and friends. In the video, the band hits a peak with a jazz-rock jam, and Rita grabs one of her little nieces on the dance floor and twirls her around. Rita thrusts her arms in and out, face absolutely beaming, breathing in the moment like a treasure.

"That's who she became," Pam said, tapping the video with her finger as she showed it to me. "*That's* Rita."

• • •

RITA'S DAUGHTERS ALSO DID well and visited their mom frequently, reconnecting, making up for lost years as they had their own kids and had careers.

Faith—the driving engine of the family, ever the senior sibling—had earned a BA in government and Latin American studies from Smith College, then an MA at Florida International University.

In April 2018, Faith married the love of her life, Leo Zini—a Brazilian-born graphic designer who likes to surf. Naturally, the wedding took place in Key West. It was a beautiful kick-out-the-jams affair, held in the island's classic old Fort Zachary Taylor with gourmet food, *American Idol* singer Les Greene and his band, Patrick and the Swayzees, belting out dance tunes, and everyone dressed to the nines in island shirts and dresses.

Rita felt like she was spreading healing, not the one needing to be healed. Her oldest daughter was marrying her successful marketing-company partner, and Rita was there not as *the formerly homeless mom* but as the loving mother, health nutritionist, and therapeutic masseuse. She wore a snow-white dress that shone almost as brilliantly as Faith's off-the-shoulder lacy gown—but most of all, Rita was grateful for the simple fact that she was alive and able to be present for this joyful celebration.

Years before, in those street days, she would never have been able to pull herself together enough to come, even if she had known about it. This time, she posed for all the family pictures with the bride and groom, looking radiant. In one of those shots, she's standing with Faith, one blond beach babe next to the other, both beaming, holding a gigantic bouquet of tropical flowers in brilliant reds and yellows.

They looked beautiful and they felt beautiful.

Doug Jr. was there, looking healthy and happy in the wedding party of guys decked out in short-sleeved white shirts with pink island motifs. Like his brother, he was an island guy, buff and tanned with six-pack abs and a winning grin.

The whole family was there, from the sisters, kids, and cousins to even Diver Doug—who, cleaned up off dope for years now, lived 350 miles north of Key West on the coast with an orchard of papayas, mangoes, and avocados in his yard and still dove for fish.

It was exquisite. And normal, in the conventional senses of the word.

"I was so very proud to have my mom there," Faith told me later. And she meant it.

"I'm almost a real person, not Pinocchio anymore just waiting to transform from what I used to be," Rita excitedly told me. "And I take nothing for granted. I pray every day for my friends who haven't made it off the streets like me."

Faith had been a legislative assistant for Florida Democratic congresswoman Kathy Castor and now runs a digital media and design firm with Leo. Faith gave birth to their son in 2020, and they lived in Key West until moving to a suburb of Orlando in 2023. They also have a second home in Costa Rica.

Joy stayed in Key West, became a massage therapist to celebrities, found love with a landscaper named Edward "Eduardo" Willis, and has two sons with him. She also has another home in Costa Rica—which has been pretty handy for her mom. Rita had great times visiting her daughters' getaways over the years in that Central American country covered in rainforest, mailing me pictures of her smiling self on the beach.

Penelope, a fine singer, lives on the Gulf Coast of Florida, works as a waitress, and is an avid devotee of yoga and rollerblading.

The girls still look like the beach kids they grew up as, tanned and lithe and happiest when their feet are in the sand. And Rita now doted on the grandkids—her voice raising an octave when they talked on the phone, asking what toys they're playing with, what they're eating, how Mom and Dad are. Simple grandma stuff. No birthday went gift-less.

RITA'S SONS WERE A slightly different story.

Mark "Scooter" grew up to be an electrician working in Miami, then started going to Florida International University. Rita moved down there briefly to be near him, when he was a freshman. She worked in a bakery, and in January 2008 she came off her shift to find him dead of a heroin overdose in his truck outside the bakery. The family says he had kept away from the drug for a long time, but he slipped. He was twenty-one.

Doug Jr. grew up to be a waiter, a plumber, and a bartender. He met his wife at Faith's wedding (she was Leo the groom's sister), and they were still relative newlyweds living in Key West when he did a favor in June 2019 for a friend whose father had just died—drove to the dad's house to help his pal clear it out. They found some fentanyl, and after years of being sober, Doug sat in a car with his friend and decided to give it a casual try. Both of them overdosed on the hyper-powerful drug and died on the spot. Doug was thirty-six.

Heroin was bad enough, with its various surges in just about every decade since the 1960s, coming alongside surges in meth in the 1990s and the ever-present scourge of crack, which never really went away. But the synthetic opioid fentanyl? It's the worst yet, up to fifty times more powerful than heroin and carrying a hair-trigger ability to kill with minuscule amounts. Of the one hundred thousand–plus overdose deaths every year in America, nearly 70 percent are related to fentanyl. And that drug only clawed its foothold into the American *substance use disorder* (the term preferred by health professionals) world in the 2010s.[1]

With each boy's death, Rita felt as if a part of her died, too. She'd talked with both of them in the years since she'd reconnected about getting clean, staying clean. Just look how her redemption had worked, she'd say. And yet, ultimately, though they tried hard, theirs didn't.

But after so much pain, so much horror, in the streets and in her ruined life before its resurrection, Rita absorbed the blows without letting them crush her. Having come through hell and back, even while mourning she could see a bright side in her street-worn way.

"Having both of them die absolutely broke my heart. I did what I could, and it didn't stop it," Rita said when she called to tell me about Doug's death. "We all make our choices. My son made his choice, like his brother, and I guess I have to live with that, we all do now." She sighed. "But at least I'm alive to live with it. I have to appreciate that."

There was guilt about all those wasted years, yes. And regret and embarrassment—but it was the rebirth, the forward motion, that mattered most now. She lived in the moment, and the moment was good. Since getting sober, Rita had leaned more on her religion, going to church and reading the Bible. Long talks with her daughters and her sisters also helped.

She had finally learned to take care of herself.

CHAPTER 16

Baron—Rolling to Hope

2019

"He should be fine for the night, and then we'll get him up to the rehab place in the mountains," Baron had told me when he first got to San Francisco and was outlining his plans for the intervention if we located his brother. Baron was still hopeful when the evening wound down after finding Tyson. Vicki wasn't so sure. She was right.

That night, Tyson slept in one of the double beds, Vicki in the other, and Baron took a foldout bed. The plan was to meet up with the men's cousin Stephanie first thing in the morning—she would drive in from her home in Stockton—and she would then take everyone to the Elevate rehab center in Placerville. When Tyson got up, the group grabbed a quick breakfast downstairs, Stephanie arrived, and he was ready to go. For a few moments. Then, sure enough—just as Vicki and I had feared, he started getting sweats and shakes. He was dope sick.

It was 7:30 a.m. Vicki's sources and my sources had struck out the night before when we called around to see if they could get him hooked up on methadone or Suboxone before heading up to the mountains. And now it was too early in the day to try again. So Vicki did what you do in a situation like that. She let the street addict, the guy who really knew the landscape, lead the way. "We need Suboxone, or maybe methadone," she said. "Not heroin. We're done with that. Can you do that?"

"I know where to go," Tyson said quietly.

They all got into Stephanie's car.

The problem was solved in ten minutes in front of the Hamilton shelter, the main shelter in town for homeless families. Everyone but Vicki and Tyson waited in the car, and the two of them came back with a short strip of Suboxone. Ten dollars. Yes, it's not just illegal drugs that get sold on the streets—it's pretty much everything. You can score the typical Suboxone dose of 2 mg or 4 mg just that easily if you know where to look, and one dose usually lasts for hours. This being a street sale, Tyson couldn't be sure how big the dose was, but the assumption was it was 2 mg since that's the usual $10 hit. He stuck it under his tongue, it dissolved in six minutes, and the shakes stopped.

"This is so much better," Vicki said. "It would be terrible if you OD'd on the way to rehab after your brother found you." By that, she meant getting dope sick, and Tyson somehow getting away and scoring the wrong kind of hit in a hurry—anything can happen when desperation sets in for a junkie, and they both knew it. Tyson smiled. "Yeah."

Vicki had another appointment and couldn't join the ride to the mountains, so she left while Baron, Stephanie, and Tyson headed out on the two-and-a-half-hour drive. After the initial excitement, the talk grew quiet. Then it dawned on Tyson that he now had relatives with wallets and access to a few treats he hadn't been able to put his hands on in years. They stopped at a Starbucks and got a strawberry coffee drink with whipped cream. Venti, the biggest. Then McDonald's for a vanilla milkshake. The biggest.

He downed them both in three minutes, and each time he felt a little better and a little more chatty. "Guess you didn't have too much in the way of treats when you were outside, huh?" Baron noted with a smile. Tyson grinned back.

Next, Baron dialed up Penny on a video chat and handed the phone to Tyson. It was a big moment for both of them—uncle meeting niece and vice versa. The little girl took it right in stride, as little kids do, and pretty quickly they were playing. Like uncle and niece. Like normal life.

"Peekaboo!" he boomed. She giggled and hid her face. "Peekaboo!"

Another thing he sure as hell didn't do in the street.

When they got to Placerville, they stopped at a Walmart and stocked up for the rehab stay: jeans, suitcase, alarm clock, underwear, shirts, running shoes, an MP3 music player. The basics. Then they finished the ride to Elevate.

"You know, this one is only for a while, and then we get you to a longer-term place," Vicki told Tyson by phone when they got to the door. "There's one ten minutes from my house."

"I don't work well with others, especially in the condition I'm in," Tyson said.

Okay then, Vicki and Baron both told him. We'll get you a good place somewhere with lots of space.

Intake took twenty minutes, and Tyson started to get dope sick again, so out came another dose of Suboxone—this time legit, at least. The jitters calmed down again, and with hugs all around he went inside.

Vicki called me to catch me up after the drop-off, and she was pumped, talking in an excited stream. "I believe he's done—he's hit bottom and he's stopped digging that hole for himself. He's put his shovel down. I believe in his heart of hearts he's done. I've seen more acceptance and willingness to change in him than anyone I've ever seen. Now I've got to look in Ohio to see what kind of opportunities are there. I think he could work with the homeless. He can do this!"

Baron was next with a phone call: "I think he's gonna do it. I think he's learned lessons he needed to learn."

BACK HOME IN OHIO, Baron's wife, Tasha, started girding herself emotionally. This was really happening. The brother-in-law who could be charming, a pain in the ass, and a lost tragedy all at once was coming to Ohio, and she would be part of the healing.

"I wish we had known sooner just how bad it all had gotten for him," she told me. "We all got raised to pull yourself up by your bootstraps, but what do you do when you just can't?" That's when family comes in, she said. We'll be ready here. We're fixing up a room he can stay in.

But first, there was rehab to get through. Not a slam dunk, despite all the hopeful signs.

The plan was to take seven days to detox off the worst dope hunger, still taking Suboxone, then a few weeks to acclimate, and then off to a longer-term rehab place yet to be chosen. Lindsey Conway, his counselor, couldn't put him on the phone—patients need to keep the focus inward, so we don't encourage phone calls, he said—but Lindsey sounded positively chirpy when I called four days into Tyson's stay. "Tyson's getting a lot of rest, enjoying having his own room," he said. "He's very respectful, very kind, enjoying having meals at a regular time. We're getting him back to a state where he can heal."

And, yes, that was true for several days. But when the Suboxone dose got reduced, a normal step toward weaning a patient off, Tyson freaked. Hurting for dope, his first impulse was to get a hit. Placerville's a small town in the middle of woodsy nowhere, so he strode out of Elevate, made his way to Highway 50, the main road heading in and out of town, and stuck out his thumb.

The staff got to him before any drivers did, and they cajoled him back inside and dosed him enough to calm him down.

"Okay, we have to move a little quicker to the next step," Baron told him. Vicki had already referred Baron to a rehab chain that sounded great, so he just pushed it and booked it quick: Oxford Treatment Center in Etta, Mississippi. Within two weeks Tyson was there.

This time there were no hiccups. The Oxford Treatment Center was a sort of Eden for addicts—cool rustic brick-and-wood buildings set on one hundred acres in the Holly Springs National Forest, with a kaleidoscope of amenities to make you feel engaged in interesting things while you also do the counseling sessions and Narcotics or Alcoholics Anonymous meetings. The pictures alone made it look like a resort.

There were stables for horse therapy, which essentially means hanging with the critters to focus on an interaction that's simple and calming. There was a fitness center with weight machines, a ropes course, an art-therapy studio. and tons of spots to wander around in the trees and get your head clear—including a lake lined by trees with benches set here and there. Patients lived in cabins with roommates, and the counseling ran from the usual cognitive behavioral therapy to eye-movement desensitization, which uses eye-movement techniques to help process memories and deal with trauma. Which, after years on the street with needles in his arms, Tyson had plenty of.

Within a few weeks, Tyson looked like a different man. He gained more than ten pounds from eating right, and a new serenity had set in on his face. None of us could yet call him; rehab rules blocked that. But he started posting photos online, and I thought, "Damn, this might actually work."

• • •

THE LOST AND THE FOUND

ON MAY 16, 2019, Tyson started a new Facebook page, right after arriving in Mississippi, and used it as an open-air journal, with his friends able to chime in as he went along. The first photo was pure Tyson, a goofy shot of his nostrils—quickly followed by the real shots to show how he felt, a couple of pictures of him standing in shorts next to that lake at the rehab center. It was bucolic.

On May 17, Tyson posted:

> Thanks for all of the well wishes everyone. I'm in a rehab center and having a hard time processing so please don't be offended but I definitely need all of the support I can get. I'll be sure to correspond more as time goes by. Love. Tyson Feilzer.

Eighty-three friends immediately "liked" the post, and thirty-two commented. Among them was Vicki:

> There's no rush Tyson. . . . We didn't become addicted in one day, so remember, easy does it. . . .

And his mother, signed as Patsy:

> Tyson this is wonderful. You are safe and doing well. You look terrific and sound happy. Keep it up I can't wait to talk and see you. Love without a doubt!!!

And this, from me:

> The only thanks I'll ever want is seeing you healthy, Tyson. You are smart, strong and capable, and after everything you've seen and lived, you will have a lot to offer the world.

He responded:

> Thank you any how Kevin. I'll give you a call in a few weeks to check in. You and my brother saved my life without a question. You are a tremendous man.

I posted a heart in return.

He didn't call, but I was sure we'd connect.

On May 21, he posted:

In case some of my people haven't heard this part of my story.
Baron Feilzer Tasha Feilzer Kevin Fagan Eq Lucas [Vicki's
Facebook name] Jake Petrykowski [one of Tyson's
counselors] are all part of the fantastic loving team who
helped intervene in my life and have given me an opportunity
to redeem myself from some very bad decision making and
circumstance. A group of angels who clustered long enough
to grab a poor soul from the tenderloin but not long enough
to be properly thanked save for a technologically assisted
one. Thank you again and thank you again everyone who
lent well wishes or any amount of your hard earned dollars. I
don't deserve them. I hope someday that I will be able to say
with any and all honesty that I do but I can't. I can give you
a very truthful, humbled and grateful thank you very much.
Thank you very much.

Sixty-five "liked" the post, eleven people shared it, and fifteen, including me, commented. Mine was four thumbs-up.

On May 23, he posted:

Talking about drugs . . . Trigger
Improperly medicated . . . trigger
Money . . . trigger
Free time . . . trigger
Certain music . . . Trigger
Women . . . Trigger
Sunshine . . . Trigger
Air . . . Trigger
Shoes . . . trigger
Thinking about triggers . . . Trigger

There were twenty-nine comments to that one. Jeff Sutherland's was:

> That shall pass. It's going to take time as the fog lifts.
> Proud of you.

Cousin Stephanie's was another:

> Hang in there Tyson. . . . I can't imagine how hard this is.
> You've got so many people who love you and want you back.
> You are one of the most incredible people I know, I am proud
> to call you my cousin!

It just kept getting better.

On May 26, he changed his Facebook profile photo several times, one with short hair, smiling—smiling!—at the camera with sparkly stars superimposed around his head. I'm not afraid to sparkle, he posted, a pretty cool thing to hear from a street-roughened guy. Another was a shot of him standing with a horse at the stables, hand on the animal's head. Tyson's eyes are calm, he's wearing a white T-shirt and a backpack. For the first time in many years, he looked like his old somewhat beefy self, though he still bore traces of wear in the lines around his eyes. Clearly it was going to take a lot to flush out the years of hard living, but it was happening.

Then on June 1 came a jolt:

> A friend of mine died Friday. She was only here for two
> weeks but decided on Thursday, with two other people,
> that they weren't ready to get clean and left treatment.
> She overdosed the next day. I'm sorry I didn't hug you
> sooner dude, I only got to be your friend for one day.
> That wasn't nearly long enough. I'm sorry.

Thirty-two of us "liked" the post, and eighteen of us commented. I responded:

Be the survivor. Be the one who makes it out and thrives, helps others.

Turned out Tyson didn't waver. On June 8, you could hear another breakthrough happening. He posted:

The roiling in my stomach brought
To a still
The uncoiling in my soul is what I feel
The butter spread under my eyes
These are the feelings of my demise
The harder path to the pond that Walden sought
Is what I've got a long long way and not for naught
So into the breach again myself
Friends around, the enemy rout
It could have been me of the pyrrhic fight
But I feel resolute, I have won the night.
I took my last opiate this morning. Suboxone. 2mg 6.08.19
7:30 am in anticipation of 5 days clean before the vivitrol
medication.

That fetched fifty-six "likes" and nine comments. Staci Sue said:

I hope that you are as proud of yourself as everyone else is
of you.

EVERY YEAR, AROUND 2 million people are hooked on meth and 3 million are addicted to opioids of all kinds, including fentanyl.[1] There is nowhere near enough rehab treatment available for everyone who needs it—the National Survey on Drug Use and Health estimates around 90 percent of those who should get specialty treatment don't get it—so if you can get to a place like Oxford, it's gold.[2]

Francis Gerety, at fifty-three quite a bit older than Tyson, was at

Oxford at the same time as Tyson, and they were fighting the same demons with the same trepidation. They hit it off right away. The way Francis remembers it, they both were pinching themselves a bit for their good luck.

"When I got there, I thought, 'Wow, I think they made a mistake—are you sure I'm supposed to be here?'" Francis told me. "My impression was amazement. They have a lake and a treatment center where detox and medicine takes place. And yoga. And equine therapy, horse stables—and let me tell you, the horse therapy is for real.

"The horses teach you trust. You see a twelve-hundred-pound animal and you think predator, but really, he's scared. I found myself up there every day feeding the horses apples. Tyson would go, too."

Tyson, an addict who less than a month before had been dumpster diving for food and clothes, feeding food to a horse. That was a twist.

Francis was there for meth addiction—"a horrible drug," he said with a sigh. "Tyson and I were both in the same situation, needing to kick the drugs. My family was done, tired of my shit. I'd lost everything but my insurance. I didn't even have a pair of shoes. I was living in Gulf Shores, Alabama, in my van, and I set it on fire with everything in it. I OD'd and wound up in ICU. That's how I ended up in Mississippi."

Addicts going through the jitters and stress of trying to get clean can be testy and even nasty. But now safely away from triggering situations, Tyson was pretty chill.

"Tyson was a good guy to the people around him," Francis said. "I didn't see him treat anyone unkindly. He knew where he came from and that it was a blessing to be there. Oxford is a beautiful place, nice people, and he was overjoyed to have reconnected with his brother.

"He was very, very happy to have reunited with family. He was optimistic in his recovery and reconnecting with friends. He and I were having trouble speaking after he left here, hard to get ahold of him, but, man, I was pulling for him."

It was a cautious hope. Francis did get clean and is clean today, but he knows three people from his rehab stint with Tyson—including Nolan Neal, who was a celebrity from *America's Got Talent* and the rock band Hinder—who have died. Fentanyl killed them all.

"It's like this—once you're in recovery, things become better, you get a place to live, a job, a girlfriend," Francis said. "The memory of your last use is no longer in the forefront of your mind. And you start to think you're in control again. But it's always just one day at a time. It has to be. You have to stay with it."

Tyson's pal Jeff Sutherland managed to snag a quick, private Facebook Messenger chat with Tyson on June 21:

How you doin buddy? Jeff said in the chat, which he shared with me. "I've missed you. Thought about you a lot for the past 9–10 years. Stick with what you're doing, it takes a while but the fog does lift I promise. It took a while for me as I was doing meth every day for ten years. One day you wake up and you are yourself again. It's an amazing feeling. You are an amazing person Tyson. I am so happy to see you make this journey to a better life. Keep up the good work and call me anytime. I'm here for you man. Love ya

Tyson's reply came less than two hours later, at 4:53 p.m.:

Thanks bro. Goin on vivitrol. It's been rough. Heroin and crystal

Jeff's response, twenty-five minutes later:

That's a fucked up combo man. . . . Too punk rock for me. I always knew you were punk but fuck man. . . . Anyways, life is so good away from that shit. I'm happy for you man.

• • •

VIVITROL IS ANOTHER OPIOID treatment drug. Doing this instead of Suboxone would be a challenge. But the family trusted the process.

Baron called Tyson nearly every day while he was in Oxford to buck him up, and then came to visit halfway through the nearly two-month stay, for friends-and-family weekend. He was blown away like Tyson had been.

"When I went down there to visit, everyone there was smoking cigarettes," Baron told me. "I had to drive out to the middle of nowhere. My cell service didn't work that far out. And then I get to a guard shack that was like in a huge forest, and I'm thinking, 'What is this?'"

Then he rolled into the compound itself.

"There was a lake in the middle where you could fish, there were the horses, the buildings were great—and I thought, 'Wow, this is a really nice place. One where you could go to get well. This is good.'"

And it was rooted in reality. Compassionate, but not just touchy-feely good times. You have to act like an adult if you're going to rehab, and that's not always easy—especially for addicts, who were able to do whatever the hell they wanted out in the open air for years on end.

"The one thing Tyson didn't like was the rules," Baron said. "Like, he wanted to skateboard there, and that wasn't cool. I mean, he's a man-child, really. So he's out messing around with a skateboard, and everyone's jealous. Then some counselor says, 'You can't have that here,' and took it away. Tyson went into a rage at the injustice." But to his credit, Tyson worked through it.

One moment that stuck out for Baron came when he got to sit in on a group doing a version of an AA meeting. "A guy stood up and said, 'Here's what it's like dealing with me—you can't trust me,'" Baron remembered. "And, yeah, I got it. So you have to be careful dealing even with your own brother. But you don't give up hope. You help, and hope they help themselves, too."

Not particularly startling revelations for a man who'd seen his brother burn every bridge and screw up every ladder for years. But reassuring. Which is what rehab, at its best, does for everyone involved. Again—rooted in reality.

After more than a month at the woodsy rehab getaway—preceded by those weeks in the Sierra detox center—it was time for the next step.

In late June 2019, Baron flew down to take Tyson home to Ohio, and it was looking good. They took a selfie on the plane, Baron beaming through a full beard and Tyson grinning from under close-cropped hair, looking healthy, like himself again.

On June 25, Tyson posted a picture from my original article about the proposed shelter, when I met him, and a happy photo of him and Baron on the plane, smiling at the camera. Tyson wrote:

> Two months and an angel of a hero brother. I love u baron.
> Kevin Fagan Vicki Lucas Baron Feilzer Tasha Feilzer Jake
> Petrykowski Eq Lucas

One hundred and thirty-eight of us "liked" the post and thirty-six of us commented. Mine was:

> You guys rock! Enjoy this next step!

"Tyson, you can make a nice life here," Baron told him as the plane pulled into Cleveland and his brother peered out the window at the sprawl of suburbia dotted with forestland. "It's really not a bad place."

"Sure." Tyson smiled. He was clean, he was on his way to a better life. He was game for this.

ON THE SIDEWALK BACK on Larkin Street in San Francisco, where the hunt for Tyson had ended and his rescue really began,

Seven and the half dozen pals who were there when Baron showed up took stock of what they'd seen on Facebook on their Obama phones, which is what they call the free, federally funded cell phones provided under a program President Barack Obama started for those who can't afford phones. They all told me that they wished they could do the same—and that their own desperate hopes were now centered on Tyson making it, even if they couldn't.

Two days after Tyson's rescue, Seven wrote a note to Baron, which Baron shared with me:

> We are all so proud of Tyson. Change is scary and it is something most of us avoid. He's facing this head on. And more importantly we love him unconditionally, high or sober, in stable housing or not. A lot of us deal with guilt and shame because we let a family member down or disappointed them when our addictions caused us to slide off the road. We don't want him feeling that way about us. We're blessed to know him and experience life with him. He's a great man.

Tyson smiled when he read this. "Okay, now I'm doing this not just for me and my family, but all those guys out there in San Francisco, too," he told his brother. "I can do this." Tyson told me on Facebook that he'd catch up with me after he was through rehab and stable.

I was stoked. His progression through Placerville and Mississippi, reflected by our Facebook contacts and through Baron and Vicki, was looking great.

This was going to work.

CHAPTER 17

Leaching Out the Street

2019

O hio rightfully brags about its thick forests, covered bridges, and the Rock & Roll Hall of Fame. You can buy a perfectly fine house with a big yard for the price of a small mobile home in the Bay Area, and the state is famous for down-home friendliness. Baron lives in Peninsula, a quiet town of a little more than five hundred residents a half hour south of Cleveland, right in the middle of one of those thick forests—the Cuyahoga Valley National Park. His home is a brand-new suburban showpiece that would easily run $1.5 million or more back in his hometown of Danville but cost a fraction of that in Ohio. Sure, it's not California. But life can be good in Ohio, he told his brother.

Tyson's willingness to give this a shot just a couple of months after coming in off the street was huge. Making it happen was a little tougher. The plan was to situate him in a sober house rather than to drop him straightaway into Baron's nest of a home with him, Tasha, and their wee one, but like everything with addiction, the details are the devils.

A sober living house, by definition, seemed like the right fit for a guy like Tyson, who had actually worked well in groups on the street and in Mississippi. It's a house full of fellow recovering addicts, all supporting one another's journey of sobriety, attending outpatient clinics and AA meetings or whatever support they need, and being loosely overseen by a house manager. If you backslide into dope or booze, you're out—which at most sober houses means you go back to rehab and can cycle back once you're clean again.

Tyson's residential rehab programs had to be paid for out of pocket, which is where the GoFundMe money was most needed. For penniless people like Tyson, Medicaid picked up outpatient medical treatment. The remaining few thousand dollars in GoFundMe money could go for sober house rent and expenses, though Baron would help pay for that to stretch the dollars so some could be saved for helping Tyson get fully independent once he was ready.

Plenty of nonprofits run sober houses, and it's a free-market hunt when it comes to picking one. Baron started looking while Tyson was still in Mississippi, and it was a good thing he started early.

"You try to google this stuff and it's intimidating," Baron said. "I'd learned a bit by then, but I still wasn't sure what to look for. I started out with city services, who pointed me in one direction that led me to another. It was frustrating. The challenge was that some places wouldn't talk to me because I wasn't Tyson."

He eventually settled on one about forty minutes west of Peninsula in the small town of Elyria. It sounded good, situated in an old church. But when Tyson moved in, he wound up sharing a room with several guys in the basement with no air-conditioning, and the neighborhood proved dicey with drug dealers a block or so away. Too much temptation to screw up.

"You've gotta get me out of here," Tyson said after a week.

Baron talked it over with Tasha, who said, "He's going to run if he stays there." They made a quick decision. They'd brought this guy all the way out from California, why not take another step? Didn't sound so great when they were spitballing plans a couple of months before, but now? Maybe things were better enough to give it a try.

"Okay, come stay at our house," Baron told Tyson. He moved into the guest room upstairs.

It would have been one thing if this were two bros in their twenties sprawled on the couch watching cartoons and downing pizza and beers. But Baron soon became more than just Dad to little Penny. He became sorta Dad to Tyson.

"Every day, you need to do one chore," Baron said as Tyson stashed his stuff in the extra bedroom in the house. "Maybe vacuum upstairs one day, downstairs the next?"

"Sure thing." Tyson nodded.

Baron's spacious, two-story house has plenty of room to roam in — giant living room with comfy couch and TV, kitchen big enough for kids to chase their toys in, wide-open deck outfitted with cozy hammocks and cushy chairs overlooking a sprawling backyard lawn with a playhouse and plenty of grass to play Frisbee or catch. Suburban ease straight out of a catalog.

And for placidity, you couldn't do much better than woodsy Peninsula, with its charming dot of a downtown and seemingly endless hiking trails.

Baron and Tasha bought Tyson a cell phone, a Kindle, and a bicycle. Try to get reconnected with the real world, maybe get a job, catch up on what normal life is, they said. "We showed him how to use all the stuff, the Kindle and the TV, and were so excited having him here," Baron said.

Tyson enrolled in an outpatient program within bicycle distance of the house to maintain his recovery meds, and he went to NA or AA meetings every day. The setup was solid.

But domesticity wasn't quite in Tyson's bloodstream. At least not yet. Or maybe he just felt like it was easy to be lax with family. The chores did not get done. The TV was on all the time. His butt was in a chair or the couch or his bed more than up getting things done.

"He did none of the chores, ever," Baron recalled, shaking his head with a combination of exasperation, amusement, and lingering disbelief. "So I had to sit my older brother down and say, 'Why didn't you?' So now I'm Dad. Tyson would say. 'My back hurts,' 'I didn't have the time,' stuff like that, and I'd say, 'Guess what? When you go to a sober house, it'll be worse—they'll really make you do even more chores.'

"So one time—one time—he actually vacuums. But the whole time he grimaces and said, 'My back hurts' and 'I can't do this,' so eventually I said okay. And he went back to watching TV."

Without the need to score heroin or meth or fentanyl sucking up his time, he immersed in his favorite entertainment as a young man—fantasy, mind candy. *Ad Astra*, the mystical Brad Pitt space-odyssey movie was a favorite. *Red Rising*, the dystopian science fiction series of novels set on Mars, was another. So was the *One-Punch Man* cartoon based on the manga series about superhero Saitama, who grows bored from a lack of challenge because he can knock out any bad guy with one punch.

"It was like having a lazy teenager in the house," Baron said. "This just wasn't working for us."

So after about two weeks of this, Baron got back on the hunt for a good sober living house. It quickly led to A Way Out Recovery Solutions, half an hour south in Akron, an industrial city of about two hundred thousand known as the birthplace of oatmeal and Goodyear Tire—and Alcoholics Anonymous. This time, the sober house was near a beautiful park, and the program promised encouragement for finding a job. The brothers checked out the house, a tidy two-story suburban home with a fine-trimmed lawn out front in a tranquil neighborhood.

Sold. Tyson moved in, and there were a couple of roommates but they were cool guys, around his age, unlike the older ones in the previous sober house, so no problem. But the responsibility thing still hung uncomfortably over his head—the street hadn't been leached enough out of his soul yet.

"The sober house required that you look for a job, and Tyson said, 'Baron, how am I going to apply for a job? I only have a bicycle,'" Baron recalled. "I said you've got a phone, you can go on Indeed.com, just start somewhere—and you know what? In a month he found a deli job."

The deli was in an Acme grocery in a nice residential neighborhood just a few blocks away, easily reachable by bike. The staff was congenial, the place bordered on upscale, and the pay was a decent $14 an hour—plenty to cover the $700 monthly rent at the sober house, with public welfare paying for medications until benefits kicked in at the job.

Nick Bianco, the sober-house manager, was impressed. "We only paid the closest attention to the guys who were standing out needing attention or were a problem, and Tyson was neither one of those," Nick told me. "He had a really cool idea about starting some kind of mission in the ghetto back in San Francisco—they call it the Tenderloin, I guess. He really wanted to help other people through the kind of trouble he'd had. Be a counselor.

"He had cool ideas. He was a bright guy and a gentle soul."

That gentleness came out more clearly now when he visited Baron's house. Living a distance away reduced conflict and allowed them all to be more cordial again. Tyson finally got to watch *Frozen* with Penny—yes, about a million times—and the uncle and the niece became pals.

A picture of the two of them playing says it all. It shows the pair sitting on a porch bench, wearing bicycle helmets and grinning at the camera. They're waving, and each is holding a leaf. Tyson posted this on Facebook with the simple caption **We both have leaves.**

The difference in your face is astounding, Staci Sue posted in a comment under the photo. **I'm so glad you're back. Stay safe friend.**

I posted my comment beneath hers: **Love this.**

That Fourth of July, the family and neighbors all gathered in the street to blow off fireworks. It was the kind of beer-bottle, "let's have fun" atmosphere that in times past might have been trouble for an addict like Tyson. Not this time. He left the Heinekens alone and stayed close to Penny, now the protective uncle.

"Careful, sweetheart," he told her as she plugged her tiny ears with her fingers. A cluster of firecrackers exploded on the pavement and she shrieked. Tyson laughed. Baron and Tasha glanced over—no worry in their eyes, at last. "Okay," Baron breathed.

Even the deli job seemed to be going great. Tyson showed up on time and was the cheery guy behind the counter cutting sandwiches and cleaning up.

"He was always nice to me, never caused any trouble, and was great to work with," Maggie Gemicki, his coworker, told me three years later. "I guess he was in rehab of some sort, but that's something very personal. We don't ask. I just know this was a great place for him."

I was talking to her to get a feel of where Tyson had worked, and the store was lovely. The deli part of the grocery store is set behind a long counter so shiny and clean you could use it for a plate. The people were so down-home warm it was almost corny—when I bought some snacks on the way out and the total was $2.12 but I only had nine cents in coins in my pocket, the clerk smiled and said, "Don't worry about it," and handed me $3 for my $5 bill.

"I'm not gonna lie, Akron has its troubles—you do hear about a shooting now and then," Maggie said. "But I can walk down the streets and feel safe. I was born and raised here, and most people are cheerful and friendly—a real Midwest sense of community. People aren't suspicious every time you ask them a question. It's a trusting place.

"It was a good place for Tyson, and we were glad to have him."

Everything was looking great that summer. "I've got my brother back," Baron told me.

TYSON DID LIKE THE stability, but just like that time with his dad in Missouri, he felt there wasn't much action—not that he wanted the kind of excitement a junkie gets by surviving moment to moment. But it's hard to lose the stimulation of being unfettered, being able to do anything you want with anyone you want, anywhere and anytime you want to.

"Look, Tyson, you can get a house here for eighty-five thousand dollars," Baron told him after Tyson had finally settled in at the Akron sober house. "Just find a job you like, work at it, and everything will fall into place."

Tyson would nod, but the old Tyson who didn't want to pay dues, who hungered to go from no money to big-deal guy in one step, was emerging again. He was antsy. He was still smart enough to know this was his only path to avoid ruin. He put on a brave face. And there were parts of the whole Ohio thing that he did actually like a lot.

A month into his recovery, Tyson had begun posting upbeat comments on Facebook, with photos of peaceful forests and of himself smiling. More than one hundred friends and relatives cheered him on.

Love the updates, one friend, Brendan, posted on July 2. **So proud of you buddy. Stay strong and I'm here if you need anything!**

Tyson posted on July 14, **You people are so awesome. Thanks for** being so supporting. I really do appreciate it. Every thumbs up and comment means so much to me. Thanks to Baron Feilzer and Tasha Feilzer and Penny for lunch today.

Meanwhile, there were little indicators that the sunny outlook Tyson gave off wasn't complete. On the day he left Mississippi, amid all the other hopeful stuff, he posted on his Facebook page a reference to "Near Wild Heaven," a song by R.E.M., with the caption **I love this song**. It's about achingly wanting things to be right, and they're not quite there. "I don't know how much longer I can take it," the song says.

That inside doubt continued to roil. The street was still baked into him. This came out in the memories that were always fresh in his mind.

"I didn't see Tyson the deli guy or the street guy, I would just sit and listen without judgment . . . and some of his stories were scary," Tasha said. He told her of one time he was "on meth or something," went into a T-Mobile phone store, "and started ripping phones off the wall." As he told it, he was "laughing maniacally," she said.

When he was in pharmacies with Baron, he'd talk about what he used to be able to steal to sell quickly. "We'd be in CVS and he'd say, 'See that bottle of fish oil, I could get five dollars for it on the street,'" Baron said. "He would be amazed they didn't lock it up. Or we'd walk by the library or somewhere like that and he'd see, like, a Giant bicycle and tell me how he used to twist cable locks until the lock popped and say, 'I could get two hundred dollars for that bike.' He wasn't stealing anything now, but that stuff was all still in his head."

There were two outdoor places where none of that static throbbed, though, similar to the parklands the brothers used to play in back in Danville and around Mt. Diablo, only with thicker trees. They were escapes to quietude like when they were kids. No traffic or temptations or triggers.

When they wanted total isolation, Baron and Tyson would head to Ledges Trail, a ten-minute drive from Baron's home in a densely wooded section of Cuyahoga Valley National Park. Once you walk past the trailhead marker in the wide parking lot, you might as well be a thousand miles from anywhere. First there's a grassy meadow, and then you plunge into a 1.8-mile dirt trail studded with knobby oak and hickory trees that winds through giant moss-covered sandstone formations. There are caves, fallen logs to climb over, rocks to clamber on, a set of steps carved into one huge sheet of stone. It's a magical, pristine place that you'd think some Disney set designer crafted—but it's real.

Penny would often tag along and climb the rocks. After the trail they'd head to a shorter route on the other side of the meadow leading to Ledges Overlook. That trail cuts through more oaks and hickories and suddenly spills you onto a sandstone cliff that drops down to what looks like a horizon of vivid green forestlands stretching out of sight.

I went there with Baron in 2022. We hiked the trail, stood on the ledge, watched the afternoon sunlight play on that endless forest below the cliff, and he fell silent.

"Tyson loved this," Baron said quietly. "He couldn't believe how beautiful it was. And it was easy—which was important, because he went from disturbingly skinny on the street to unfortunately heavy in rehab, from about one hundred fifty pounds to around one ninety, so biking and hiking was a little harder. But he still had some muscle in there."

We stared over the cliff for a long moment. It's hard not to linger when gifted with a calming, encompassing view like that. A bird twittered soft and low somewhere far behind us. The sandstone, the trees, the moment, were a definition of peaceful.

"Tyson thought the same things I thought about this place," Baron said. "We just didn't know there was this kind of thing in Ohio."

Another ten-minute drive led to Hudson Springs Park, a 260-acre gem of landscaped lawns between groves dotted with benches and kid play structures, all set alongside a huge lake. The best part of this place? It had a Frisbee golf course, a touchstone of the brothers' youth. Baron and I walked around there, too, and it was hard not to want to just lie in the grass for hours staring at the sky. The fresh air and trees breathed an air of calm beauty.

"We really liked playing disc golf here, but Tyson sucked, which was kind of funny because he was the one who played it first in Danville," Baron said. "He taught me how to throw a Frisbee well—we'd play after school before wrestling practice, and it was my favorite part of the day—but too many years went by without him playing." Baron patted one of the cages that pass for "golf" holes you throw your Frisbee into as you wend along the nineteen-spot course.

"Tyson did the whole course, though," Baron said. "He still liked the game."

So there was hope. There was progress. Tyson was going to Narcotics Anonymous meetings every day, regularly visiting the family in Peninsula. Showing up on time for work. Staying off dope.

So far so good.

Throughout his recovery, as I posted comments on Tyson's Facebook page and kept in touch with Baron, I planned to fly out to visit at the six-month benchmark of getting clean. By then, I reckoned, the sobriety and new direction would be solidified.

CHAPTER 18

Panic

2019

I t turned out Tyson had a secret he didn't know he had.

Vicki, the interventionist, said Tyson was doing well until early September 2019—about four months into recovery—when he stopped taking Vivitrol, the medication to prevent relapse. He told his family he was feeling depressed and thought ditching the medication would help. But that wasn't all he ditched.

Tyson's medical records showed that he had also stopped taking other prescriptions as well—including meds for a bipolar condition he'd only been diagnosed with in late summer. It turned out Tyson had been self-medicating with narcotics for the condition that nobody knew he had, even himself.

"We had no idea," said his dad, Jim.

"It was a shock, and we didn't even learn about it until he was in the rehab house," Baron said. "We had him see a psychiatrist and thought, 'Okay, he's getting meds now.' But he never told us he stopped so many of them."

Stopping meds is a common mistake of people in recovery. But combine that with something like a bipolar condition, and it's explosive.

"The disease—that need for the drugs—started talking to him

again," Vicki said. "He had been so upbeat before, wanted to work with me after getting clean. But it was the disease. It's just devastating."

The struggle to stay clean radiated in a letter Tyson wrote to himself as part of his rehab program on September 10: "Tyson: If you're using again you're lying to people you love and your life sucks. You were homeless. . . . I can't believe you would do that to yourself. Get your ass to treatment 'cause you'll likely end up dead."

ON SEPTEMBER 11, 2019, Tyson posted on Facebook. I'm on a bus on my way to S.F., and then turned off his phone for several hours.

Baron panicked.

He immediately called Stephanie, his dad, friends—What can I do? he asked. They had no clue. The man was on a bus headed on some unknown route on an unknown timetable. The only thing to do was wait for him to communicate.

It took Tyson five days to reach San Francisco, and along the way he texted back and forth with Baron, who agonized with him over why he was giving up on himself. In Denver, Tyson actually got off the bus and considered heading back, and an uncle prepared to go pick him up. But Tyson changed his mind and got back on the bus.

He wouldn't pick up the phone, so texting was the only communication.

Baron texted, What triggered you?

Tyson: Just couldn't see the light at the end of the tunnel.

Baron: Really? How could you not? You were going to get a car and that would get you a better job. You had a path forward.

Tyson: Path forward isn't happiness.

In another exchange, Baron suggested Tyson come back for Suboxone or another rehab medication and try again.

Tyson's response: **No, it's not medicine that's gonna fix me. It's me.**

Baron called me in a panic, and I went looking all over the city for anyone who had heard from Tyson, who would be expecting him. On the waterfront? Nothing. At his main old heroin-shooting hangouts in the Tenderloin? Nothing.

When he hit town on Sunday, Tyson stopped texting altogether. He went dark.

Turns out he went straight to the same Turk Street spot where the addicted street pals he'd hung out with were and copped a hit, according to Seven—who wasn't calling me back right then, honoring Tyson's request that everyone stay away for a while. The first two times he shot up one-tenth-gram hits of heroin—a fairly typical dose for a true junkie—but his body was so unused to it he overdosed, and Seven had to revive Tyson with Narcan, a medication that reverses opioid ODs and is liberally handed out to street addicts in San Francisco to save lives in emergencies just like that one.

Two nights later, just after midnight on Tuesday, September 17, all alone this time, Tyson shot up again—on the same block where Baron and I had found him less than five months before. On Larkin Street near Willow, in the Tenderloin. This time, it was too much.

The night was chilly. For once there wasn't much of anybody around. Tyson had scored a bad batch of drugs with a grain too much of fentanyl.

He died alone, on the sidewalk. Syringes and dope-cooking paraphernalia lay at his side. The medical examiner's report indicates someone found his body before anybody decent did and stole his shoes, jacket, and wallet. Someone else hanging out on the street flagged down a cop car, and an emergency crew whisked him to the city morgue.

The cause of death on the report: "Acute mixed drug (fentanyl, heroin and methamphetamine) intoxication." He was forty years old.

• • •

BARON GOT THE CALL the next morning.

Soon after, he called me.

"I thought he was smarter than that. I really thought that in a week or two he'd call and say he'd made a mistake and come back," Baron said, crying. "I can't imagine why he would walk away like that. His life was good here. He was sober. He had a future."

"I know he did, I know," I said, choking up myself. "Why the hell would he do this? Why the hell would he give up?"

"I don't know," Baron said in a near whisper. "He just—gave up."

I went through my day shell-shocked. I've had plenty of bad news on workdays—family and friends dying or falling terribly ill, death threats from psychotic readers—but I just work through them. That's how I am. Your duty is to do the job, then grieve after your shift when you're on your own time. So I started typing up and researching a new story about Tyson, about the ending I so had not wanted to have to write. Called the medical examiner, called experts for perspective. Did the work you do as a reporter.

I rolled all over the Tenderloin again, looking for the street people who would know more. One of Tyson's sidewalk buddies, James, left me a voicemail saying he'd talked to us when we were looking for Tyson all those months before. "If you could, let Baron know Tyson overdosed on heroin," he said. I called him back and told him we already knew.

"Tyson told me he worked in the meat department of some store in Ohio," James said, voice hushed. "He had a good life. It sucks—it's all bad."

Late that night, around 11:00, I went to the corner of Larkin and Willow to see if I could find anyone who had more information. I knew that's when his crowd would be hanging out, setting out sleeping bags, taking those last hits of smack or fentanyl before sleep. About twenty of them were sitting on bits of cardboard, warding off the foggy cold with ragged coats and Royal Gate vodka. Most weren't part of the usual crew, so they didn't know Tyson. But a few regulars were there. And it was clear Tyson hadn't been hitting his usual spots.

"I didn't even know he was back," said Roscha Grady, whose lined face made him look a decade older than his forty-seven years. "Everyone said he went home. What the hell?" Roscha stared at the ground. "Tyson is a lovable person. A good guy. Why would he come back here? Why? Who would do that when you've been given a second chance?"

Latisha Meadows was sitting next to Roscha. She waited for him to stop, then stood up. She was forty, like Tyson.

"I was there," she said quietly. "I felt sorry about him. He was just laying there dead. The cops came about one a.m. and got him. I don't know who called. I just saw him there. Dead." She sucked in a long breath. "I had respect for him. Nobody should die like that, in the street."

Roscha nodded. "How many people do I know died out here?" he said. "I don't know—ten, probably more. Too many. We were doing memorials out here for them, but it doesn't really help anything. You're just dead."

A day later I got a call from thirty-year-old Nick Atamaniuk, who had looked up to Tyson.

"It was fentanyl, I'm sure of it," he said. "Dealers are spiking everything from black tar [heroin] to meth, crack, everything we do out here. It's killing us."

Nick said he was on methadone, had moved inside. "When Tyson went home, I thought, 'Hey, I can get inside, too.' I thought he was clean, connected. I was happy for him.

"You know, I needed Narcan thirty times in the past four years, and I honestly felt like I'd been waiting for death. But now I feel like I was waiting for life. I don't want to die like Tyson. He's one who should've made it."

TYSON'S DEATH IS ECHOED across the nation, with more than one hundred thousand drug addicts dying every year from overdoses. In 2018 in San Francisco, the year before Tyson died, 177 people accidentally overdosed and died from opioids—a 31 percent increase over the year before. And that was before fentanyl really took off. It's a super-cheap synthetic that pushers add to everything now, like Nick said—fifty times more powerful than heroin, it gives you more bang for the buck.[1]

The trouble is that even tiny grains can be too much. Over the next few years, the epidemic of fentanyl exploded across the nation. In San Francisco, that 2018 overdose figure now looks like the good old days—in 2023, it was 811. In the 1980s, crack was the new nightmare drug sucking down lives. In the nineties, it was crank, or methamphetamine. Now it's fentanyl. And so far there's no stopping the waves.[2]

Add to the lethality that nasty figure from the American Addiction Centers showing how addicts in recovery relapse at a rate around 60 percent. The organization says opioid addicts who relapse "often overdose because they don't realize their tolerance is lower than before."[3]

So Tyson fit.

Seven finally answered his phone a day after I learned of Tyson's death. He was living in a shelter now, he said. Heard about Tyson from a friend, who'd heard from a friend. Street telephone.

"He seemed a little depressed when he came back here," Seven said. "He said he just wanted to get high. You know how it's hard to fight opiates off—God knows I know for myself. And his tolerance was down. I had to do Narcan for him on Sunday when he got here, and then on Monday—but he kept using. That overdose—I don't think it was intentional. He didn't want to die. He just wanted to get high."

Seven said he was the first one Tyson contacted when he hit town Sunday. He went to the Drug Users Union on Turk Street to find Seven, and sure enough, he was there.

"I said, 'Look, we're happy to see you even though we're not happy to see you,'" Seven said. "'We'd really hoped you'd get clean, but at least you came back to people who loved you, to a place you also consider home.'

"I don't know what was in that last hit, maybe it was fentanyl—that's killed so many of us out here. Whether it was just heroin or not, it was too much. It's hard on your soul—you feel so joyful when it works, when someone can get away like that and start over. It's such a shame. Everyone out here is so broken up."

But right up to the end, Seven still believed his friend could fire up another second chance. "He was talking to himself about how it was so stupid what he'd done, leaving Ohio like that. He was mad at himself. When he sat down next to us, he felt bad. You could see it in his eyes. He wasn't proud. If he'd been able to last a couple of months, I think he would've gone back to his brother. Right from the start, he felt horrible for what he did to his brother."

We chatted about that. About how much Baron did. About how unusual it was.

"Look," Seven said, "Baron did everything a brother could have done. He loved him, and Tyson loved him back."

EVER THE RESPONSIBLE MANAGER, Baron didn't wait for Tyson to reach San Francisco before posting on the GoFundMe page to the

192 donors who'd helped fund Tyson's rehab with what turned out to be $43,720 in donations (which covered a lot, but couldn't pay for everything). Baron felt a duty to keep them in the loop.

I'm telling this to you all not so you lose faith in helping people like Tyson, Baron wrote on September 13, two days after his brother had left Ohio. I'm telling this to you all so you know that we did what we set out to do. We pulled Tyson out of the street, got him free from drugs and gave him a new lease on life. Tyson chose to give it away. . . .

I love my brother and hope that he finds his way back to society again. You are all amazing people and I hope this doesn't discourage you from helping others again.

Then came Tyson's arrival to San Francisco, the radio silence, and a call from the cops to say Baron's brother was dead.

"I would definitely do it again—go find him, bring him here to Ohio, help him get clean," Baron told me a few days after the end, when he'd had a chance to process it just a tad more. "There are different ways of looking at it, but here's how I see it: I got to show Tyson what life could be like. We got to have some good times, and he got to meet his niece. That was good.

"There's also a part of me that says if I hadn't gotten him clean, he might not have OD'd," he added quietly. "I'm going to have to think about that."

I went back and looked at the notes from Tyson's intervention on the night we found him, and one passage stood out for me. *Irony* may be the word for this. Or maybe it's just goddam sad:

"Naloxone [also known as Narcan] is the 'save your life' drug," Tyson says, sitting on the hotel room bed next to Baron as we all talk about how addiction ensnared Tyson on the street.

Vicki: "Right."

Tyson: "So if somebody overdoses, then you . . ."

Vicki: "Right. I have it in my backpack upstairs."

Tyson: "Yeah, I had somebody need it the other day, so I had to give one away to save somebody's life. Yeah, I saved several people's lives with Narcan."

TYSON'S COUSIN STEPHANIE HAD seen this coming from a long way off.

"Baron told me on one of the updates he gave us that Tyson was bipolar, and he had been getting treatment for it," Stephanie told me. "Things seemed okay, but, yeah, I would imagine he was not taking his medication. And that probably is what precipitated the spinout."

But the thing is, like so many in this kind of "dual diagnosis" drug-abuse, mental-illness condition, the toxic combination had roots. The trick is seeing it soon enough, and clearly enough, to flag so you can get the person to a psychologist, a doctor, a hospital—anywhere. But that's tough to pull off. Tyson's careless behavior through childhood into adulthood could have been a clue, but unless you know what to look for, it's a bit of a mystery.

The Feilzer family was like so many—you think someone is just going through a phase. Being rebellious. Finding his way. Why would anyone suspect there would be serious trouble in the future? Tyson was functional enough to be a credible actor, hold a job, be charming—not off-the-charts out of control much of the time.

But there was serious trouble. And seeing its tendrils early didn't help.

"It was the worst thing we could have expected [Tyson dying], but given everything, all the things involved with him, was it really that surprising?" Stephanie said. "We just didn't think it would actually end that terribly, the way it did. I always thought he'd have another chance."

It took her two years to be able to face it, but after spending that warm summer day in 2022 with me, Stephanie went to a desk drawer she hadn't excavated since Tyson died. She shuffled through a batch of papers and found the letter she'd written on October 25, 2019, more than a month after Tyson died.

She didn't know whom to send it to back then. It was too raw, too soon, to share with anyone. So it went into a drawer. And stayed there, pretty much forgotten. She mentioned it to me when we talked, and I said, hey, I'd like to see that.

I still get choked up reading it.

Dear Tyson,

I wanted to be able to say good-bye to you at Pinecrest a couple of weeks ago, but the first of many massive power shutoffs cancelled that. So, I am trying to say good-bye in the last place I saw you, my car. I have to get a new car, it is time, so I have to let go of part of my last memory of you.

If I had known I'd never see you again that day in Placerville, I might have come inside. I wanted to give you and Baron privacy, and I was certain at that point there would be another time. At the very least, I would have given you one more hug.

My son cried for you the other night. He never met you, and knew you were gone, but you were too abstract in his life to make much of an impact when I told him.

And then we lost ourselves to our memories. The whole family was at my mom and dad's house and the stories started coming out. Of camping mostly, but others as well. Like you vaulting over the bushes near the basketball hoop because you didn't want to walk to the other side. The hedge is much bigger now, it would be a challenge. William listened intently. He loves old stories about mom and uncle Jason growing up. You became less abstract, real even, and he mourned for a life he never knew. I was at a loss to explain to him how someone so young and so once full of life was gone. I told him you loved his pictures I posted to Facebook, and that the two of you would have gotten along well if you had met. He's smart, imaginative and quick-witted himself, just like you were.

It's a surreal nightmare. I shake with anger at you for making my son cry. I shake with anger about how you hurt your brother and your niece—she doesn't even know yet. Tasha and Baron haven't had it in them to tell her. There are days that I wonder if this was all some sort of plan—I know how brilliant you really are—maybe you knew you were done all along, and considering your interest in the articles about you, maybe you had a need to make your name known before the heroin took you. I hope to all hope that is just a stupid thought, a product of my chronic overthinking. Because if it isn't, you really are an asshole. I really don't think you are an asshole, though I've screamed at the top of my lungs so many times at you. Hate is too strong of a word, though I have been tempted.

And I know—and everyone else knows—that I would never hate you. I want some of this sadness to go away, and sometimes the anger and near hate is what gets me through my day. I can't spend all my time crying and dry heaving in the bathroom, which is what I did the morning I found out.

I lost my Uncle Dom the same day. I had told Jason just two days before that if Uncle Dom died the same week you overdosed, I was going to lose my mind. Not only was it the same week, it was the same damn day. Sometimes I hate being right.

In the span of two days, I had to tell my brother that his cousin was dead, and later his uncle, tell my parents their nephew was dead, and write my uncle's obituary. I've been lost in my head ever since.

I still miss you. I always will. We had been holding vigil for you for years. Friends of yours would contact me through Facebook wondering if I had any word of your whereabouts. Other family members and I would check county jail inmate listings periodically just for confirmation you were alive. The arrests were never good news, but at least you were still out there.

Now that you are gone, I feel like there is a huge hole in my childhood. I am not sure I will ever shake it. Wherever you are now, I really hope you are finally rid of your demons.

Good-bye my dear, lost cousin.

AFTER THE DEATH AND the flurry of grieving from coast to coast, Baron went to the sober house in Akron to clear out his brother's things. He found a journal. In it was this entry, dated the day Tyson and Baron left Mississippi to fly to Ohio:

6-25-19
Oxford Treatment
Etta, Mississippi

Tyson—

I am writing this in the hopes that you (I) have remained sober. If you have and you are receiving this approximately six months from when you wrote it, then your life should be incredibly better than it was in the six months preceding it.

You have just begun an incredibly long process of rehabilitating yourself which was initiated by the grace of god which manifested itself in the form of your brother Baron reading a newspaper article written by a good man named Kevin Fagan.

You will be well into your step work with N.A. and A.A. and you will have a sponsor. You will have a job and hopefully you will have kept in touch with Vicki Lucas and Kevin Fagan like you said you want to.

You have thought about being an interventionist and starting a small business. Running a pedi-cab and working at a bike shop were things that were an interest to you right now.

Most of all Tyson I hope you are still 100% sober because that is the key to your happiness. Stay away from San Francisco for awhile and toxic relationships and don't fall for the old tricks and make the same old mistakes. The Devil loves idle hands and details but he also has a lot of the same friends you do.

Don't forget about all the people that loved you when you did not and how they believed you were worth healing. They spent a lot of money on you, earn it.

J. Tyson Feilzer

As the words unfolded in front of me, tears spilled down my face. Six months: That's when I was going to do a big check-in on him and the family. Hoping he will have "kept in touch" with me: he did, but only through those Facebook back-and-forths and the passed-on messages through Baron, with the promise of a real conversation later. Which never came.

And now death had closed that door forever.

CHAPTER 19

To the Stars

2019

There was no talk of graveyards for Tyson. A free-spirited soul like his needed a free-spirited place to be remembered at, and Baron knew exactly where that should be.

He got permission to put up a mini-complex of memorials for his brother in one of the joyful places where everything came together for them as boys grown to men, playing just like they did in the years before life slid into hell—the Frisbee golf course at Hudson Springs Park. Baron chose the symbols carefully, and $3,000 he'd held over from the GoFundMe donations to help Tyson buy a car—which Tyson never got around to—covered them.

A birdhouse rises high on a pole, a peaceful place for free creatures to rest on their way to wherever their wings take them. A plastic-wood bench with ironwork arms and legs and a plaque carrying Tyson's name and BELOVED SON, BROTHER, UNCLE on it stands nearby, giving the same rest to those who can't fly. In between them is a tree with a red brick at its base.

Carved into the brick is:

> James Tyson Feilzer
> Per Aspera Ad Astra
> 02.27.79–09.16.19

The Latin translates to "through hardships to the stars." It's an ancient phrase, quoted in Tyson's favorite dystopian science fiction novel series, *Red Rising*.

Baron and I visited in 2022 so he could show me the memorials. After strolling the Frisbee course, we stopped in front of the birdhouse, which sits on top of a fifteen-foot pole. Five purple martins hopped in and out the holes. "That's the kind of bird this house is meant for," Baron said. "When we talked to the park people about doing the bench, birdhouse, and tree, they said this would be a great place for it." He closed his eyes and listened to the martins chirp. "It *is* a great place for this," he said softly.

He walked over to the broad-leafed deciduous tree, which was eight feet high when he planted it and now shot twenty feet into the air. The soil around the brick at the base was worn out and dry, so he replenished it with new dirt from a bucket he'd brought. Then he carefully arranged purple, pink, and white crystals around the brick, along with a small rock Penny had painted in blue and black to look like a ladybug. Baron treated the offerings like holy objects, patting them tenderly as he put them in place.

Baron remembered how when he and his brother walked the lake and soaked in the quiet, things got just a little clearer—both here and at the Ledges park.

"He could see the potential here," Baron said. "He really could."

He stared hard at the ground. "He pissed it all away. He had a better chance than most. Maybe he was on the street too long, maybe he didn't have the right personality. I don't know."

Silently, Baron walked over to the bench and sat down.

"At first, I'd be upset when I came here, you know, sit here and wish it had all gone differently," he said after a few moments. "But now I'm happy that we did what we did. If he were here, I'd tell him

I miss him. Tell him that sometimes he was a fucking asshole. But I'd tell him that I forgive him. And that I love him."

THE OUTPOURING OF GRIEF on Facebook and in calls and letters to Baron after the death was overwhelming.

Brendan posted on Tyson's page:

> I'm sorry I couldn't do more
> I'm sorry I wasn't there for you when you needed someone, anyone.
> I'm sorry you battled so hard.
> I love you and I'll see you on the other side Tyson.

Staci Sue posted to Baron:

> Thank you. For this. For trying so hard. For loving him so much. For everything you did for him. His disease got ahold of him and refused to let go. I have no doubt that if love could have kept him here, he would have outlived everyone. I'm sure he knows just how much you care and were willing to do whatever needed to be done. Again, thank you.

And then there was Baron, who didn't post a lot on social media during the whole journey, but put this up on his page on September 18 with a link to "Bro Hymn," a 1991 song by California punk rock band Pennywise, written by band member Jason Thirsk in memory of friends who died:

> When I didn't know where Tyson Feilzer was, I would listen to this song and think about him. It's one of my favorite songs. Now that I've lost him I've decided this is my song for him. If you don't know it, I suggest listening to it very loud to get the most effect. Tyson, my brother, this one's for you!

The lyrics could have been written for Tyson himself, talking about having friends with you to the end, and life being precious.

"When I was flying with Tyson, he said being cold was one thing, being hungry was another, but going months and months and months without anyone making eye contact was the worst," Jake Petrykowski told me in 2022. He was the rehab counselor working with Vicki who got assigned to accompany Tyson from Placerville to the Mississippi treatment center of horses, yoga, and a lake. "I'd heard that before, but from him—it was just so very sad. He was a very kind guy, very kind eyes, and he very much sounded like he wanted to recover. And along the way, we started singing 'Amarillo by Morning' at some point as we were heading to that Mississippi treatment center and had a great time. It was all so hopeful.

"When I heard he'd died, I was crushed. Now every time 'Amarillo by Morning' comes up, I think of him."

The pain had still not ebbed for Tyson's cousin Jason in 2022.

"I was so happy for him. He was doing so well. He was happy. Everything seemed to be going fine," Jason told me. "I know he got clean, but it's that draw, that addiction. He'd been out of society so long he wanted to use and go back to what he was comfortable with. That sucks. Everybody afforded him a really good opportunity. Ninety-nine percent of the people in the streets won't be afforded that same opportunity."

Jason wrestled with one main regret. When Tyson got on that bus back to San Francisco, "We were all imploring him not to do it. Everybody was calling and texting. But he didn't return my calls. The last thing I sent him was a text—and it was cold. I said, 'Hey, man, you go back to SF you're going to die.' And I never heard anything back until my sister called me to say he had died."

I could tell what was coming next, because I've heard dozens of people in death situations tell me they feel guilty over the last words they said to a loved one. So I asked Jason how he copes with his feelings over that last text.

"I don't," he said, voice catching. "I'm going to feel bad about it until the day I die. That was the last thing I said to my cousin, the guy I looked up to for so long. I told him he was going to die, and he did. I'll go to my grave regretting that one. Still hurts. I should've told him I love him and he should come stay with me. But I didn't."

The catch in the voice gave way to tears. "I still miss him," Jason managed between sobs.

BARON'S WIFE, TASHA, HAD been wary of rescuing her brother-in-law, but she'd begun to hope against hope that maybe this time— finally, this time—this new picture of Tyson that emerged in Ohio would last. Maybe, she thought, just maybe she could trust his recovery as he started to become his old self again. She'd cried, she'd argued with Baron about the chances of this working, and then she finally surrendered to the hope. It was a gradual process—and when it all crashed, she was not just sorrowful. Yes, she cried. But she was angry.

"At first Tyson didn't know how to act with Penny, but then he started playing with her and cracking jokes," she told me after his death. "At the end, he got along really well with her. I texted Tyson when he left, 'Please don't do this to her.' He didn't answer back."

Tasha paused for a long moment. "There's just nothing you can say," she said. "There are no words."

Baron and Tasha sent me a Christmas card in 2019, which came a few months after Tyson died, featuring happy pictures of themselves with Penny—and one shot of Tyson after he went through rehab, sitting and smiling with his father. The card had quotations from their favorite books of the year, plus one from Penny, by now four years old: "I made a wish to the moon that it would give me a star that I could hold in my hand and it would always shine bright in the dark."

Two weeks after Tyson died, the longtime family cat, Aslan, also died. Baron and Tasha couldn't bring themselves to tell Penny her beloved pet was gone, so they told her Aslan went up to the stars. The grief for the parents of losing both Tyson and the cat, and showing a brave face to their little girl, was agonizing. But she was too young for the bald reality. They had to be the parents. She believed the fairy tale. Penny took those stars seriously. As only a child can.

Then Penny started asking more about Uncle Tyson. "I want to send him some pictures," she told Baron one day. A few days later: "When can I send Uncle Tyson a letter?" It didn't stop.

"At first we told her Tyson went back to California, but she just kept wanting to send him photos," Baron told me. "So finally we told her Uncle Tyson also went up to the stars. Now she goes out every now and then and yells up to him—'Hi, Uncle Tyson! I hope you're happy up there! I love you!'"

Baron stopped and let that sink in not just for me, but for himself. "There's something about hearing her yell into the cool, dark night like that," Baron said, voice even and low. "It's so pure."

I burst into tears. So much promise, so much waste, so much sadness. So much innocence. I cried for a long time. I still cry when I think about it.

CHAPTER 20

Rita—"I've Beaten Worse"

2022

The same year that Tyson died, 2019, Rita reconnected with an old friend from decades before, Gregg Blanchard, and they fell in love.

She'd had boyfriends since coming back to Florida, but this one struck deep. She moved into his five-bedroom house in Gainesville, a sizable college town about an hour and a half north of DeLand. Gregg, a seventy-three-year-old retired building contractor, grew his own food, ate organically, and had an unreconstructed hippie view of spiritualism—which fit the free-spirited beach girl, who was now approaching seventy.

"Rita came along at the right time for me," Gregg said when I called after they moved in together. The pictures they shared showed a towering man with a long, flowing white beard. "He treats me right," Rita said simply.

A little more than a year later, in 2021, Rita was feeling a bit weak and went in for a checkup. And there it was: glioblastoma, an aggressive cancer that sprouted a painful brain tumor. Around the same time, she had a seizure. Her doctor gave her one year to live.

Pam called to tell me, and I called Rita. "After all the crap you survived on the street, through drugs and disease, conquering every challenge and thriving the way you have for the past couple of decades, *this* crops up?" I said. "What the hell."

"Hey, it's what it is," Rita cracked. "I've beaten worse."

"Well, let's see. I think you're right. You beat AIDS, heroin, crack, hepatitis C, and being homeless. You can lick this."

She laughed. Really laughed. "It's been a good roller coaster. If I die, I'll be dying with a happy heart."

That was a bit tough to hear. I let a moment hang there.

"Come on out for a visit," she said. "They tell me I have a year to live, so you'd better move fast."

Turned out she had much more time than that, thanks to the support system she'd assembled as a stable, nonaddicted person. At seventy, she had a fighting chance to beat this cancer, and she took it full on.

Led by Pam, the sisters kept on Rita about making it to doctors' appointments. Faith and the other daughters applied the same pressure. Rita had surgery to remove the tumor from her brain, and when she decided chemotherapy made her feel too sick, Gregg—being more of a Mr. Natural than a fan of conventional medicine—steered her toward getting onto RSO, or Rick Simpson Oil, a highly concentrated mix of medicinal marijuana cannabinoids. That it was made of pot derivatives didn't bother her; medical marijuana was legal in Florida. And this sure as hell wasn't crack or heroin, she told me with a laugh—"I get no temptation to do the bad stuff, so it's good." After surgery and the RSO treatments, the cancer backed down. Gregg took on the role of caregiver at their home, with family regularly visiting and pitching in.

None of it meant she was done with cancer. But it became clear she had more time on the clock. So the family planned to make a big deal of the next Mother's Day, in DeLand, counting on her staying strong until then. I booked a flight for May 2022 to be there. Rita and I had kept our close contact all these years, but I hadn't seen her since those rescue stories I wrote in 2005. Exchanging scads of pictures, talking on the phone, and writing is one thing, but being there in person is something different. We needed that.

My first stop was DeLand, to catch up with Pam before she and I drove to Gainesville, to Rita and Gregg's house.

As I pulled into the dirt driveway to Pam and husband Rick's home, I felt like I was driving onto a tropical paradise vacation rental. They lived in a long white storage barn that the two of them had, with their own hands, converted into a charming cottage over the past three years—just like they'd hand-built their vacation house in a jungle in Costa Rica years before that.

The living room was a tidy array of comfy chairs, a white leather couch, and beach-themed art on the walls. One corner was Rick's music nook, with a computer and keyboard, and a stairway led to a huge loft where their daughter, Amanda Grace Johnson, was staying in between residential-chef jobs. Outside, two horses grazed alongside a pond. Gigantic trees and ferns and other bushes surrounded the property, making it a private getaway.

This all made perfect sense when you know Pam and Rick. They are a definition of bohemian self-doers, and their handcrafting showed everywhere in the house—huge double-paned windows, dark-stained wood flooring with wide grains, wooden countertops, white cabinets with glass doors. It was a showpiece. Before she retired—Pam was now sixty-five and Rick was sixty-seven—Pam had kept up her work as a photographer and restorer of hand-painted furniture, and her artistry showed everywhere in the house in details of fine woodwork and tropical scenes on the walls. Rick grew bananas, grapefruit, avocados, pomegranates, and tree spinach around the house—this bunch, like Rita, always ate healthy.

Pam somehow looked like she hadn't aged a day, and she had that same steady no-nonsense gaze she had in 2004 when I first met her.

"Rita's managed to hang in there really well, but get ready," Pam said. "She was doing real well, still doing handsprings, before the cancer, but now it's made her pretty weak."

We sat in the living room having coffee with Rick and Amanda, who after ending her international modeling career had become a chef in Los Angeles, where she also did charity work with the sprawling homeless population, partially in honor of her aunt but also because she inherited the family's good heart. Now thirty-eight, she did chef work for private clients—and was part of the family-wide network of relatives cheering on Rita to stay healthy and fight this latest health challenge.

Amanda also inherited that no-nonsense directness of her mother. I asked her what she, a generation removed from Rita, thought derailed her aunt way back when.

"My aunt Rita had a hole in her that she couldn't fill," Amanda said immediately. "She started out with everything—well, not really, but she had it good. She was beautiful, talented, athletic, and smart, but if there were two choices, she'd make the wrong one. She was attracted to the bad boys because she had a hole in her that she couldn't fill."

As the days unfolded in my visit to Florida with Rita's sisters, daughters, and friends, I heard that same refrain over and over. There was no illusion about what had led Rita to ruin all those years ago—or about what had led to her salvation.

Fully abandoning the street, taking the help of her family, having the strength to stick with it all these years, and finally making the right choices were the only reasons she was still alive, they said.

Best of all, it's what Rita said, too.

• • •

AS WE DROVE UP to Gregg and Rita's house in Gainesville, the first thing that struck me was the veritable forest surrounding this rambling five-bedroom house with such thick underbrush that you could barely see the outside walls from the street. A gigantic live oak towered over palms and avocado and peach trees, and two station wagons and a van sat in the sprawling front yard. It was about as far from the harshness of Homeless Island as you could possibly get.

Rita met me at the door in a red sundress decorated with blue flowers. She walked slowly, clearly weakened. But she was radiant, and her face ignited into a huge grin when she saw me. A wave of emotion came over me as I gave her a hug, and she kissed me on the cheek.

"Ah, Rita," I managed.

"So great to see you again," she said into my ear, holding the hug for a long time.

Inside, the home was a throwback to the 1970s. India-print blanket on the couch, a giant stained-glass circle looking something like a dream catcher on the all-windows main living room wall, a purple semicircle entrance to the kitchen, lots of wooden furnishings, and artwork everywhere. It was full, but organized and clean.

Rita sat on the well-worn, comfy couch and I took a long look at her. Her hair was now mostly white, a recent thing, and lines were more pronounced on her face, but she was still thin and fit. When she smiled, which she did often, the lines softened and her brown eyes shone.

"I'm trying to get stronger, but I've fallen a few times, and the other night I hurt my arm." She pointed to a cane at the edge of the couch. "I have to use that thing sometimes. I'm just glad to have Gregg here to take care of me."

Gregg brought in cups of herbal tea. "Everybody remarks on how strong she really is." He handed us the tea. "I've tried to keep a clean and healthy environment here. I want her to stay strong." He sat down and put an arm around her.

"Just think—this woman went from being a beggar on the street to someone wearing beautiful clothes and having a career helping heal people through massage," he said. "I've had a great time getting to know that."

Rita leaned her head on his shoulder. "I'm not done yet."

Brant flew in a couple days after me, after Pam and I brought Rita back to stay at Pam's house for the Mother's Day brunch. She met him on the porch in that same red-and-blue sundress, and as I watched them hug, the transformation in both hit me hard. We were all nearly twenty years older, with variously graying and white hair and a few more pounds, and what felt like a couple of lifetimes of lived experience—her rejuvenating and maintaining, Brant and me covering more endless tragedies and dramas through our work.

"Where are the alligators?" Brant cracked, pointing at the pond alongside the house. "This is Florida, right?"

"They're right out back," Rita said, kissing him on the cheek.

That evening, Pam left Brant, Rita, and me alone on her back porch. It was the first time the three of us had talked since 2003 when we sat amid the pigeon shit alongside the roaring traffic at Homeless Island. The sun set vibrantly pink over the pond and the fruit trees and palms, while Brant and I drank beers and Rita had a bottle of Perrier. It was idyllic.

"We were a pain in the ass, weren't we?" Brant said. "And when those stories came out in the paper, it was hard to see it, wasn't it?"

Rita sighed. "I didn't really read those stories until I got back to Florida. I think you guys did good. Look, it helped me."

"I have to ask—what was the big attraction of the drugs for all those years?" Brant asked. "I've always wondered. I always thought a lot of people just partied too much, then just didn't know when to stop partying."

"Yeah, that's part of it. My trouble was hanging out with the wrong guys all the time. And the drugs? It's just something you do. You think it's fun. But I had low self-esteem. Bad choices."

They thought about that for a long minute. We all stared at the sunset, the beautiful light with no sound around but a couple of horses whinnying in the distance.

"I'm just glad I made it and now I have something to live for," Rita said.

WE SPENT THE NEXT couple of days going to family gatherings swirling around the Mother's Day brunch, which drew Rita's daughters Faith and Penelope and several sisters and turned out to be the biggest get-together they'd had in a while. They ate at one of the finest joints in town, called The Table, and Rita the health nut had avocado toast, eggs, and—gasp—prime rib. Rita's sister Lynda cracked everyone up talking about how much she loves K-pop and the music group BTS, sister Debbie pulled up a video of "Gangnam Style," and the group danced in their seats and laughed.

The brunch bunch did no talking about homelessness or drugs. It was all tasty food, summery dresses, and cheerful conversation. Faith had flown up from her home in Key West and rented an Airbnb, so after brunch everyone went there to hang.

I had never before seen the whole family together, and in between the typical catching up we had a chance to ask a few questions. That once again underscored the family dynamic of being totally frank. And thoughtful.

"We've always been about family, no matter how much things

blew up, and my mom did make some terrible choices," Faith said as we sat on the couch at the rental house. "But now look at us all these years later. We are still a family."

Faith, the leader of the kids all their lives, was now looking after the biggest kid of all—her mom. At forty-six, she looked ten years younger than her age, like all of Rita's children—but she carried herself with the command of a kindly CEO. She continually had Rita's arm, making sure she didn't fall, patting her back, reassuring her when she looked tired. "Faith is the glue for so much of how we all stay together," Rita said, squeezing her hand.

A lot of families might just say screw it when someone falls so low for so long, over and over, like your mom did, I said to the daughters. And it did take a long time for some of the family to come around— but they did. Why?

"It's called family," chimed in Rita's sister Lynda. "That's the word and that's what it means."

All these many years after stepping into the breach, helping to raise Faith by taking her on in high school when Rita lost the kids, Lynda was thoughtful. Not resentful, or mad. We stood in the kitchen while Rita sat on the couch with Faith and chatted with everyone else.

"It made me angry that her children had to suffer," Lynda said. "But it just came to the point where I accepted her for who she is. With family, you never say. 'I'll never see you again.'" Rita looked over and waved, and Lynda waved and smiled back.

"I'll tell you, Rita's been four different Ritas, and I've seen them all. She's the fun-loving person that she puts out there. She's the person who used drugs. I used to think she was an airhead, but she actually is a deep person—and that leads to the put-together person she is today.

"Just think of all the crap Rita's been through in her life. She's like a cat, somehow coming through it all." Lynda shook her head in bemusement. "She's the luckiest unlucky person around."

Rita knew that more than anyone else.

As I tooled around DeLand with the family, getting to know the town, I noticed that time and again if we walked past a stranger looking bedraggled on a bench, Rita would stop and chat the person up. Once when we drove by a corner on the highway and saw a couple of abandoned shopping carts with soggy clothes and food boxes in them—one of the only times I saw anything resembling a homeless camp in that area—she pointed and said, "I took some food once when people were staying there. It reminded me of Homeless Island. Very sad, they really needed help."

Pam told me that was typical. "She's always getting people sandwiches if they look like they need them, talking to people. Rita never forgot where she'd come from. My sister has a big heart."

THE DAY AFTER THAT gathering at Faith's Airbnb, I sat with Debbie, Pam, and Rita at the Dick and Jane's Café in DeLand while they looked over pictures of the old days showing the three of them clowning around, all looking willowy, sun-kissed, and carefree, the paragon of Florida beach gals of the sixties and seventies. Back on the street in 2003 when Rita and I talked about her past, these images would have seemed like they were from another universe. Now, all of their eyes lit up when they saw them—three sisters who had come a million miles and lifetimes down a rocky road, able to appreciate their shared youth again. To see it not as something lost, but restored and complete in a good light.

"I was disgusted with Rita and Steve when they left for San Francisco," Debbie said.

"How could you not be?" Rita said.

Debbie stared straight at me. The good memories may have been restored, but the pain of the bad days wasn't entirely buried. "I couldn't understand how she could live like that and leave her young children. It was a nice little family, despite the drugs," she said.

Rita's eyes blazed. "You mean she [Rita] made her bed and just gotta sleep in it no matter what?" she snapped.

Debbie kept her gaze on me. She clearly wanted to get this point out, and it was leading to something other than the resentment. "No, I was just disgusted back then. But underneath it all you still love your sister. And then when Pam and Joy brought her back and Rita went to that massage school . . ." Debbie paused to hone her thoughts. "I started seeing what she was doing. I was proud of her. It was amazing to see someone who had gone through all of that and come back from it."

Rita exhaled slowly. "It wasn't anybody's fault that I fell all the way down there. It was on me."

Debbie, still looking at me: "Yes, it took a lot of time and work, but she did it. She was fearless."

Pam, looking at the two of them, and then at me: "Rita did the work. I was no hero—it was all her. Like I always say. *All* her."

Finally, the two sisters looked at Rita and smiled. They'd made their point. Rita smiled back quickly, then stared off in the distance. Sometimes contemplating the miles and years and heartaches stings. Then she shook it off. It only took a handful of seconds.

Brant flew back to California the next day, and Faith, Pam, Rita, and I all started driving to Key West. It was time for me to see where the growing up and the dissolving had happened.

• • •

SINCE KEY WEST SITS at the end of the 125-mile-long chain of the Florida Keys islands, getting there is a marathon drive across forty-two bridges past some of the prettiest turquoise water you'll ever see. The first stop was Duck Key, to pick up Joy from the spacious ranch home she shares with Eduardo and their two small sons. They all wore year-round tans, fit from hours in the water, and were itching to take a boat ride to lunch the minute we got there.

Faith and I helped Rita into Eduardo and Joy's powerboat; the cancer fight had left Rita a bit unsteady. There were plenty of seats for everyone, and as she settled in, it was like Rita's whole body took on an electric charge. She sat up straight, eyes eagerly on the water ahead, shaking with anticipation. Here was the eternal beach-and-boat girl, always ready for the ocean—and in her weakened condition, it was like medicine. Eduardo fired up his Mercury Racing four-stroke engine and the craft leaped ahead. Rita held her hair back with her right hand and let out a little yelp of delight. Joy put her arm around her mom to steady her while the boat surged to 40 mph, but Rita didn't need the help. Being on the water made her feel strong.

She cranked her head around to look at me, sitting behind her. "Love this," she mouthed.

Eduardo, who's spent his whole life on the water, grinned as Rita turned back to look ahead. "She needs the salt air," he said. "It's in her blood."

From then on, it was as if Rita were attached to a generator. After lunch on the water at a tiki-bar-turned-restaurant, we piled into the car and made the final run to Key West. On the way we passed a park where the family scattered some of Doug Jr.'s and Scooter's ashes, a restaurant where Joy had worked, spots where car accidents in the family had happened. This was family history land. Rita beamed with every memory.

Rolling past the million-dollar bungalows that used to be fairly cheap, the tourist-friendly streets of island bars and shops selling art and clothing and everything else you might buy to take home after a vacation, Rita and her kids radiated a sense that they were *really* home. Which for Faith was true, since she still had her spacious house in town. But there was an awareness of layers of years, emotions, happiness, sorrow—everything that real *home* brings. This was their common crucible.

"My mom came down here with my dad to live the free hippie lifestyle, and for years they actually had that," Faith said. Everywhere we went there were those family landmarks. We ate organic-veggie sandwiches and smoothies at their favorite health food store, strolled the plaza where they busked as youngsters, drove by the spots where they'd stayed with Jeff and Diver Doug and hung out with Popeye, talked about how back then Key West was an island of misfits and castaways.

There it was again, I thought—the two islands in Rita's life. This one and Homeless Island. Misfits and castaways. The difference between twenty, thirty years earlier was that Rita had finally learned that the misfits and castaways don't have to involve needles, bags of heroin, and nights on a sidewalk. There are healthier ways to be alternative. There can be salvation.

Inevitably, we ended up on Simonton Street Beach, gazing at Christmas Tree Island, shimmering six hundred yards away among the anchor-out spots where they'd spent years on those liveaboard boats. It was a typically balmy and tranquil day; sailboats bobbed on the water and seabirds cried overhead.

Joy and Faith stood on a tiny concrete boat dock on either side of their mom, with Pam and me behind, and looked out silently for a few long moments. Now, all these decades after the pain that ended their little paradise here, they could appreciate how good things were—when they were good. How much they had loved one another. How much they loved one another now.

A knowing smile crept to Rita's lips.

"That was it," she said quietly. "That's where life was what it was supposed to be. We lived on boats just like that. When we wanted dinner, Diver Doug would jump in the water and bring up lobsters or crab, the kids swam like fish all the time. Nobody told us what to do and we lived like we wanted." Faith put a hand on Rita's shoulder. This was the place where Rita used to bring the kids ashore in their skiff to go to school or just visit town. Back in those earliest times when life was seemingly oh so simple.

"Yes, Mom, there were some good times," Faith said. "You were a good mom."

"Are you afraid of dying?" I asked Rita, looking straight into her eyes. She looked straight back—and then, as so often, she chuckled.

"Nah. It'll be nice if I make it to the next Mother's Day, but I've had a great life now. I've reconnected with my kids, my sisters, my mom before she passed. And seriously, I wouldn't mind seeing my friends in heaven."

She put a hand on my shoulder and squeezed. "I'm leaving it up to God."

CHAPTER 21

What Matters

2023

In early January of 2023, Rita suddenly lost almost all her energy. Her brain got foggy, she struggled with her words, and she couldn't walk. She now needed more intensive care than Gregg could give her by himself in Gainesville, so Faith drove up and brought her mom to her home near Orlando in the small city of Winter Park.

Faith set up a hospice bed in a spare bedroom. The sisters and other daughters assembled, and for days they sat with Rita, lay on the bed with her, prayed with her. Gregg came and recited the Twenty-Third Psalm. Pam played recordings of some of Rita's favorite songs—Bob Dylan's "Lay Lady Lay," Billie Holiday singing "I'll Be Seeing You."

"She's mad at God," Pam told me. "This just kills me—she was so alive and so full of life and did so well for so long. She's my best friend. . . ." Her voice trailed. "Ah," Pam said slowly. "It's just heart-breaking."

I called the house and Faith put me on speaker, where Rita's voice was disturbingly faint. I told her to stay strong, and I read her passages from this book.

"That's nice," she whispered after hearing a part about our visit to Key West the previous spring, seeing Christmas Tree Island and remembering the liveaboard-boat life.

Then: "I'm a little tired now, think I'll sleep."

It was the last thing I ever heard her say. She died on January 24, 2023, a Tuesday, around 9:45 p.m., with family surrounding her. She was seventy-two. I got on the phone with Faith, and we both cried for fifteen minutes.

"I wish I had more time with her, more time for her to be with my son growing up," Faith said between sobs.

IN 2005, WHEN RITA'S story ran, then–San Francisco mayor Gavin Newsom—today, governor of California—told me my *Chronicle* stories helped inspire him to create Homeward Bound, a program that reconnects homeless people to friends or family if both sides are committed to making a fresh start work and pays their way home. By 2022, Homeward Bound had sent 10,800 people home from San Francisco—and the program had been replicated all over the United States, from Portland to New York, reuniting thousands of people with their loved ones. Studies showed that just over half stayed with the people they were bused home to, with the rest either not arriving, abandoning their destinations, or not responding to queries about how it had gone on the other end. But half of 10,800 having a legitimate shot at stability with something resembling home? A hell of a lot better than staying in the street indefinitely—and cheaper, at an average $180 per person per trip, compared to the $100 a night a nav center shelter bed costs.[1]

It has helped people.

"Never knew it," Rita said in 2022 when I told her about Homeward Bound. I'm sure I let her know about it back when it was founded, but that was a long time ago. She was more focused on getting well and healthy than on whatever the bigwigs were doing back in San Francisco at the time—and besides, she didn't have a raging ego. That kind of news just didn't rise to the top for her. But she did allow herself some happiness in knowing she inspired something good.

"Everyone needs a second chance," she said. "I'm glad that maybe what happened with me helped."

Also back then, Newsom stepped up massive efforts to pull homeless people like Rita off the street with a range of programs including a ten-year plan to end chronic homelessness, begun in 2004 soon after my "Shame of the City" series with the Homeless Island story ran. The idea was to bring the chronics street numbers down to zero, and he beefed up street counselors, community-aid gatherings, and funding for supportive housing. His lead street counselors—tough-as-nails reformed drug addicts like Rann Parker—dug in hard trying to rescue Rita's Homeless Island friends.

The ten-year plan didn't come close to hitting that zero target, but it made a lot of headway, even though some of the push—particularly a program enacted in 2004 called Care Not Cash, which stripped most of a homeless person's welfare check away and used it to help house that person instead—stirred controversy, with activists calling it heavy-handed.

To a large extent—again, with the federal, state, and local funding mix never rising to the levels they were before being slashed forty-odd years ago—all the efforts over the past couple of decades have felt like shoveling sand into the tide. Yes, progress gets made. And, yes, there are sincere intentions and efforts by the trainload. But in San Francisco, the official biennial count of around six thousand to eight thousand people being homeless on any given night has been stuck at that mark for decades, with only occasionally significant dips.[2] Too many of those thousands of homeless people who land supportive housing units don't get enough case management to help them fully rise above whatever problems put them out on the street to begin with, so they hang out in the street, panhandle, sometimes even pop up tents on the sidewalks—and they look homeless, even though they aren't anymore.

In 2021, Newsom asked me to go with him to a couple of encampments that were being cleared out by the city's special team of counselors and street cleaners based in what is optimistically called the Healthy Streets Operations Center. He was governor now and was ramping up efforts on homelessness by billions of dollars, so he'd been joining clearance efforts around the state to highlight his dedication to the issue. He and I had gone to homeless camps together, without press and staff gaggles, back in 2004 when he was formulating his mayoral street plans, and this felt a bit like that.

We talked policy, plans, funding, and more while he swung a broom and chatted up the crews and campers at a couple of tent clusters that had held maybe twenty people, but had emptied to a few after warnings the day before that the sweep was coming. Then I brought up Rita and the Homeless Islanders.

"Really? She's doing well?" the governor said, face brightening when I told him Rita was alive and had blossomed for years in Florida. "That is so good to hear. That's what this is all about—getting people off the streets and into healthy lives." He watched the public works crew tossing trash into their truck while one guy pulled down his tent.

"People want to see progress, and these camps are unacceptable—not healthy for the people in them," Newsom said. "There is no compassion in leaving the status quo."

When I later informed Governor Newsom of Rita's death, he recalled with admiration the woman who'd helped inspire him to create Homeward Bound and said that, even in death, she continues to inspire. He said he was "touched by Rita's courage and strength."

"Faced with unspeakable obstacles, Rita remarkably turned her life around and inspired the City of San Francisco to enact policies to better serve individuals experiencing homelessness," he said in an email to me. "Rita reminds us that every person struggling on our streets and alleyways has a story, and that no matter how difficult the road ahead may be, there's still hope for a better future."

Well put. Hope—despite the horror of the journey, the setbacks, the loss of faith, the distance of years. It's always there.

THE DIGNITY OF EVERY human being—it's also still there, even when it's buried beneath grime, dysfunction, and hard times. In 2019, I got a call out of the blue from a writer in New Mexico named Craig Barth, saying he had given a ride up California's central coast to Monterey to a hitchhiking homeless woman back in 2004, and that she had affected him so deeply with her road-worn elegance that he had just written an essay about her all these years later. "About a year after I gave her that ride, I ran into your articles about Rita and realized, 'Wow, that's the same woman,'" Craig told me. "I just thought you'd like to see what I wrote."

Craig's heartfelt essay recounted how when he first encountered Rita at a roadside stop north of San Simeon, he thought she looked like a weathered wooden statue with a "heavily lined, weary, expressionless face." When she asked him for a ride, she said she'd been in San Diego and was headed back to San Francisco. As they rode up Highway 1 together, they opened up to each other—Craig about a crippling hypersensitivity he had to chemicals, and Rita about her despair of living on the street and believing she could find her way back to stability someday.

"I've lost my way and fallen from grace, but I'll never give up," she told Craig. "I'll find a way of getting back home."

By the time Craig dropped Rita off in Monterey, he wasn't seeing a weathered, lost soul sitting next to him anymore.

"I could feel the dignity within her and sense the strength of her spirit," Craig wrote. "For me she became an object of reverence and respect."

I sent that essay to Rita, but she didn't read it until a few months before she died. She had done some hitchhiking back then, sure, but she didn't remember meeting Craig. "But then I don't remember a lot of things from back then," she told me. "It's nice that he says those things about me, though."

I thought it would be good if the two talked, but they weren't able to connect before Rita died. Then, seven months after she died, Craig himself succumbed to Lou Gehrig's disease. He was seventy-two, like Rita.

Craig and I talked several times after he sent me his essay; he struck me as a deeply kind soul. And he never stopped expressing wonder and happiness that this woman he was convinced he'd met so many years ago in such a bedraggled state had blossomed back into the self she was meant to be.

"It just shows that we should never give up on people," Craig told me several times. Amen. Like Rita said, "Everyone needs a second chance."

TYSON FELT THAT EVERY bit as much as Rita did, and he had that second chance in front of him right until the final second that he didn't. I had hoped that Tyson and Rita could meet each other someday. Now that will never happen. They will never read this book, either. It hurts to know that, but in the full picture of their lives, it doesn't really matter.

WHAT MATTERS

Tyson got nearly six good months of his life back after leaving the streets, reconnecting with family, feeling healthy, seeing his own potential again. Rita got nearly twenty years of the same, chasing her rebirth for all it was worth and loving it.

That's what matters.

CONCLUSION

Death never gets any easier to stomach. I've seen too much of it. At least that's what therapists and a few pros who study PTSD in journalists have told me. I can't change the past, but I have tried to learn from it.

At this point in my career, several decades in, I've been around death in many ways—witnessing seven executions, watching people be consumed by flames in the 1989 Loma Prieta Earthquake, seeing bodies of people shot and beaten to death, torn apart by animals, crushed in car wrecks. But most of all, as I have specialized for many years now in homelessness, I've seen the poorest of the poor die. Penniless. Lost. Mostly forgotten. Like Jill, Vina, Tommy.

The ones who live, like Rita—and Tyson, for those few months— fill you with hope, and even joy. You see that redemption is possible in everyone. Even the serial killers and mass murderers I've reported on, the monsters I watched being gassed or lethally injected in San Quentin prison's execution chamber—all of them had a soul deep inside that could be reached with the right kind of efforts. I have to believe that to keep faith in humanity.

The ones like Tyson, who don't make it, tear your heart out. And I've written so many obituaries of street people I came to call friends that I can't count them all. Why did Rita live, and Tyson die? Why do *any* of the desperate people I've come to know through my work live or die? Are their fates predetermined through nurture versus nature, brain chemistry, bad luck, good fate? I don't know, and I don't think anybody does. I believe anyone can achieve grace and rebirth, that there is always a goodness deep inside that can be lit and fanned. Experts and shrinks I've talked to through the years aren't entirely sure about that.

A comfortable upbringing of basic education, financial stability, and lack of abuse, which Tyson arguably had, presumably increases the odds that you will be set on a path toward a successful adulthood. Rita, barring some not insurmountable hurdles, had the same kind of launch in life. But it's never that simple. The seductiveness of drugs is only part of what threw these two people and so many others into the ditch. The question is why would they trudge ahead on the wrong path when they could have just stopped or crimped back before the iron grip of heavy-drug addiction locked in?

According to many studies, including a 2022 examination by Rutgers University researchers, genetic predisposition to addiction is a factor for so many who get lost—but there's also your sense of ambition, your interest in how you want to spend your leisure and work time, your personal relationships, and how you let your peers steer you. There's racial discrimination, family and individual income, the demographics of where you are raised, and where you wind up living. There is mental illness. It is rarely, if ever, just one thing. It's usually a combination.[1]

Psychologists tell me failure or success often depends on what tools you have to cope with pressure. Do you meditate? Do you get therapy to focus on the positive aspects and directions in your life, to look at deep-seated pain or conflicts to better understand what might hold you back? Take medication for attention deficit disorder, depression, or whatever else you might be struggling with? Read instructive books or articles? Develop close, supportive, and healthy friendships and romantic relationships? All of these things make a difference, but at the core it's up to you to make use of them.

There were many times I could have gone sour myself. When I left home at sixteen, why didn't I deal dope, fall into addiction, or become a thief and instead propelled myself through college the hard way, working crap-pay jobs while taking full-time classes? A lot of that had to do with my parents raising me and my brother and sister to believe education is a must-have in your life, that books are sacred necessities, that learning throughout your life is as important as breathing. And despite the difficulties we had, I was loved by my parents and I loved them, something we ironed out well when I was an adult. In that regard, I was lucky. Whatever disadvantages I had were outweighed by a set of values steering me into the career that I have. Granted, I might have been just as happy doing something that didn't require a college degree. But writing is my life's passion, so that's where I wound up. I am housed and I have a decent life.

One of the people I've come to depend on for wisdom on the treatment and housing of homeless people is Josh Bamberger, the longtime addiction and homelessness specialist in San Francisco. He helped President Obama's administration create the program that reduced veterans' homelessness nationwide between 2010 and 2022 by expanding the housing and supportive services of several federal government departments. Once, when we were talking about the conditions that make the most acutely troubled street people hardest to help—mental illness, drug or alcohol addiction, and more—he admitted that he thinks some folks are so lost that even the greatest efforts can't steer them voluntarily to independence.

"There are always going to be a few people who are outside the system," Josh said. "And it's usually around their personality disorders. No medicine, no drug treatments, no charm, no love, will let them be housed. So the only alternative is jail or a locked institution."

He's talking about a very small slice of the street population. But it's real, and though he is one of the most compassionate people I know, he is also exceedingly clear-eyed.

Rita did not need that kind of extreme intervention. I don't know if Tyson would have eventually needed it. Vicki, the interventionist Baron hired, thinks Tyson may well have required something different from the tsunami of help he got.

"Maybe Tyson was just a failure-to-launch guy," she told me. "He crosses my mind every time I go to the city. That gets me choked up—he was such a nice guy. I can't help but think, 'Where did I fail?' I can't help it, it still hurts. Even Baron asked me after he died, 'Is this my fault? If I'd left him there, he wouldn't have OD'd?'

"But you can't think that way. I told Baron you guys gave him some of the best six (or so) months of his life—you guys gave him his family back, even if just for that little while."

SOME PEOPLE—NOT MANY, FORTUNATELY—HAVE told me writing about people living in gutters and fields and streets is not worth it. That they are only problems to be shunted aside, hidden, or perhaps gotten housed and saved—but by someone else, out of view.

This couldn't be further from the truth. The old maxim of measuring a society by how it treats its most vulnerable people is as true today as ever; by that measure, we fail. And whether or not you are sympathetic to the millions of people experiencing homelessness every year, you need to know who they are.

CONCLUSION

We are in a new age of robber barons, and the problem didn't merely explode over the past few years.[2] It's anything but just a local thing—for any city, San Francisco or otherwise. It's largely the result of that long, slow burn of governmental abandonment and mismanagement of support for poor people, affordable housing, and mental health programs that ignited in the 1980s. That, plus an economic system and society that abide by inadequate low-income wages, lack of national health care, oppressive housing and rent practices, and more.[3] There is, of course, debate over exactly what went so wrong. Many nonprofit and academic studies blame it on the slashing of crucial federal social-aid and housing programs under Reagan's watch, others say the bigger problem is that government money meant for the poor gets sucked up in bureaucracy or badly diverted.[4] We also live in a country where greed has too free a hand. But the fact is the societal landscape for those on the bottom decayed, and the subsequent cascade of programmatic failures and conservative attacks on support for the lower and middle classes are a lot of what led us to where we are today.

The Western Regional Advocacy Project, an antipoverty nonprofit led by longtime activist Paul Boden, reported in 2006 that between 1978 and 1983, HUD's annual national budget was slashed from $83 billion to $18 billion, calculated in 2004 constant dollars. This shortfall was never made up in HUD's budget—which in 2022 was $54 billion—or in the Band-Aid programs that grew up around it.[5]

"If you look at the last forty years of addressing homelessness, there have been two constants: using police and private security and public works for addressing it with sweeps—and then blaming people for being homeless—and putting out plans," said Paul, who was homeless as a very young man just before I got to know him as the scrappy Bay Area protester and homeless-rights advocate he became in the 1980s. "Ten-year plans, supportive housing plans, welfare plans—everybody loves a fucking plan. But none of it addresses how we as a country are going to get affordable housing back to where it was before the massive federal cuts of the 1980s and the growth of homelessness that we know today. Housing will fix homelessness, not more plans."

And racial inequality? It's reflected in all its ugly tragedy in the street, the product of generations of Black and brown people being redlined, denied opportunity, and marginalized in ways that should have been stamped out decades ago. In San Francisco, 35 percent of the unhoused population tallied in 2022's one-night count was Black—while just 6 percent of the general population was Black. Latinos constituted 30 percent of the homeless count versus 16 percent of the general population. And white people? Their homeless count was 42 percent, versus 51 percent of the general population. (The totals add up to more than 100 percent in such tallies because some people identify with more than one category, particularly people of all races who identify as Hispanic or Latino.)[6]

The imbalance held nationally, where 37 percent of the homeless population was Black, 24 percent Latino, and 50 percent white.[7]

Same thing with gender identification. A full 28 percent of San Francisco's unhoused population identified as LGBTQ, compared to 12 percent of the general population. Nationally, it's even more distressing, with 40 percent of the homeless youth population—anyone younger than twenty-four—identifying as LGBTQ.[8]

"The fact is more people are becoming homeless than the system can handle," Ann Oliva, CEO of the influential Washington, DC–based National Alliance to End Homelessness, told me. "People are losing their housing—it's just too expensive—and existing systems like behavioral health, child welfare systems, and the homelessness system overall have trouble exiting people from whatever they might have that's temporary shelter into permanent housing."

When she was a deputy assistant secretary at HUD, Ann worked with Josh Bamberger on that effort that cut U.S. veterans' homelessness. Then Donald Trump came in as president, the focus faded, and veterans' homelessness plateaued. It stayed flat until 2020, when Joe Biden got elected and enough efforts slipped past the Republicans in the form of new affordable housing and medical VA funding that the number of unhoused veterans dipped to thirty-three thousand—bringing the reduction since 2010 to a total of 55 percent.[9]

But maintaining that kind of momentum is the hardest part. The big mid-2010s success with veterans only came with the extra health, housing, and counseling resources the VA can bring to the table. For nonveterans—even though California in particular has in recent years been easing developer restrictions and pointing new money at the home-shortage problem—it always boils back to the lack of affordable housing, which can keep people living inside.

So the poor stay poor, and the poorest fall to the streets.

These broken people live in America. The richest country on earth.

An estimated forty thousand homeless people live in the Bay Area's nine counties, and in 2021 the Bay Area Council business association estimated it would cost more than $9 billion to create enough shelter and housing to put roofs over them all—and then more than $2.5 billion a year to maintain those roofs with services and staffing.[10]

As a journalist who's worked in Britain and Australia, I'll tell you that they and other developed countries like them think we're insane. They have national health systems, we don't. They have guaranteed housing for the poor, we don't. They have mostly free college education and living-wage rules, we don't. There are nuances, and plenty of people here say what those other countries do is socialistic coddling, but these are the kinds of things that help keep the poorest of the poor off the streets in developed and humane societies. America operates under a different mindset. A more callous one.

Australia, a nation of around 27 million, has for several years now been alarmed about its growing crisis of homelessness—and what is that crisis?[11] They had seventy-six hundred people sleeping outside on any given night, which they call "sleeping rough," instead of in a shelter of some kind, according to the most recent statistics available in mid-2024.[12] Similar distress rippled through England, a country of 56 million, when statistics showed nearly four thousand people sleeping rough every night.[13]

In San Francisco, a city of around eight hundred thousand people, more than four thousand people—about half of the total homeless count—sleep rough outside, what we call unsheltered, every night.[14] And that's an undercount.

What we have to remember is that every one of those people sleeping rough is worth saving. Like Rita and Tyson were.

PEOPLE FREQUENTLY ASK ME what I've learned from all the awful and the wonderful things I've written about for more than four decades—the people, the places, the transformations. Or "How do you cope?" Well, at this point in my life, there's not a hell of a lot that I haven't already wrestled with as a writer, and there are not a lot of epiphanies coming my way. My answers have been the same for a long time now. I try to see the good in people and possible solutions in agonizing situations, and I tell myself that as a reporter I am actually fulfilling a public service.

At one point when I was back in Florida, Rita's sister Pam asked me, "This book won't just be about all the bad stuff, will it?" No, I said. You need the bad stuff for the contrast, to illustrate the journey, I told her, but Rita's narrative is at its core about rescue, rebirth, redemption.

"Okay," Pam said.

I was struck then, as I've been so many times through getting to know Rita's and Tyson's loved ones, by what a weighty thing it is for a family to let reporters like me into their lives to tell a narrative like this. Nobody enjoys things such as homelessness, drug addiction, and personal crises being aired out for everyone to see. But the point of sharing those things authentically is to help others see what can go right, and wrong, and how to deal with them. As a writer, I understand that. But what is remarkable to me is how Pam, Baron, and so many relatives and friends involved in the twisting journeys of Rita and Tyson came to understand that, too. They lived it, but that didn't mean they had to understand it. Or share it. But they did.

It would be nice to have figured out conclusive fixes to homelessness, to societal abuse, and the abandonment of the poor and the lost, but that hasn't happened. Brant and I set out to dig hard for solutions to the homelessness disaster when we took on that "Shame of the City" series in 2003, and we concluded that supportive housing, rehab, and street outreach are crucial tools in the fight. But after all Brant's photographic efforts and my writing ever since, and the millions of dollars spent and the numberless programs launched, there's no end to the crisis. I still have hope, but as I think I've made clear in this book, the atrociously unforgivable poverty our nation creates and allows to continue will hobble our efforts. Stop betraying our citizens with national and local policies and practices that crush them and perpetuate an underclass, and the problem can be solved. Until then, it's good intentions and partial successes.

But there is this: No matter how far people sink into indigence, the demons of addiction and abandonment or mental illness, there is always that grain of hope. There is always that younger self deep inside them who once had a future and could again. Looking for that hope, talking to street folks about that hope they so often lose touch with, helping my readers understand how awful it can be to be trapped in a life gone wrong and how damnably unjust that is in a society as rich as ours—that has real worth, real emotional reward. It's a relief working with that. And it helps me process what I see and feel.

WHICH, IN ONE WAY, is what writing this book has been about.

Rita and Tyson crawled into my heart like few other people I ever wrote about did. Their triumphs and disasters, joys and sorrows—not only for them, but their families and friends—were so acute, real, and moving to me that I lost sleep, exulted and grieved for them. Though our paths were certainly different, I could relate in important ways to their struggles. They stumbled through periods of self-destruction and deprivation, fought to rise from where they'd fallen, scraped their souls to find meaning and a future that made sense, kept living. Which, really, I think most people can relate to in ways small or large. Life is a mix of good and bad, and it is often hard. The best we can hope for is that the good outweighs the bad, and the easier times outweigh the hard ones. Circumstance and luck have a lot to do with that, but mostly it's up to you—how you handle the punches, how gracefully you develop the advantages. It's pretty simple.

Rita found her peace, and I love that. I believe Tyson could have found his if he had given the salvation he was always offered more of a chance after that final depression overwhelmed him.

When I try to make sense of what their two lives mean, with their similarities and contrasting endings, I have to shake my head at the bewildering mystery of where life leads us. Rita and Tyson were lost. And then their families found them, and they found themselves. The love that surrounded them, that never gave up? That's the wonder.

I VISITED THE HOMELESS Island site again in 2020, after developers had torn the whole thing out and replaced it with a high-rise building. The big trees everyone slept around had been cut down, and the city had replaced the concrete with tightly clustered bushes to prevent people from spreading out sleeping bags. The colony was long gone, but with the continuous cars on Mission and Van Ness the corner was still a good spot for panhandlers.

"How's the signing today?" I asked one ragged man in shoes with no laces as he held out his cardboard panhandling sign reading HEY YOU WOKE UP TODAY, CAN YOU SPARE A BUCK? He looked like he was in his hard-worn late thirties.

"Not so hot," he said.

"Did you know this used to be called Homeless Island?"

He nodded. "Hey, that's right, I've heard that. Aren't those guys all dead now?"

I stared at the bushes where I once slept alongside battered shopping carts, and I listened to the traffic river streaming by this island of what used to be a messed-up but close little community.

"Yeah, a lot of them are. But not all."

I turned to leave, then looked back and said, "Try not to be one of the guys out here who doesn't make it, okay?"

NOTE ON METHODOLOGY

I feel two things when I'm squatting down on a sidewalk to talk with someone who's living hard time outside, often drug addicted, sometimes only barely coherent, always in some form of distress.

First, I may be a newspaper reporter, but in that moment I am also a counselor of sorts, acutely aware that what I say, write, and do will possibly have a huge effect on people who unveil a piece of their soul to me and maybe help them understand themselves better. I have a responsibility to be kind. Helpful, empathetic, accurate. I have to listen fully, feel fully—absorb the reality of what I'm seeing and hearing. I have to get the story right, so there's a point to it beyond just painting another sad picture in news pages.

The other thing I feel is misery. And a form of simpatico. After decades of writing about street life and death along with the other hard subjects of a news reporter, I have scars cut deep from immersing in this ocean I've chosen of sorrow, violence, pain, dashed hopes, and occasional shafts of emotional sunlight. It's worn on me. I cry more easily. I am at times more afraid of life than I should be. It hurts.

But I don't have a choice in the matter. I have to do this work. Doing this reporting and writing is the most meaningful thing I've done in my life, and there *is* a point to it.

NOTE ON METHODOLOGY

This is what I brought to my reporting on Rita and Tyson and the winding paths that led them into the street and out again. And for Tyson back again.

I never pretended I was homeless with either of them. That would not only have been dishonest—it wouldn't have worked. I'm an old-school reporter. I do my interviews with a pen and notepad, and even though I had a recorder rolling during a lot of my talks, I always also took notes. Makes the fact that I'm an ink-stained guy impossible to hide. Brant and I never paid cash for interviews, either—which is always a tough subject when writing about unhoused people. I get panhandled at least a half dozen times whenever I spend more than a couple of hours trolling the streets, and, yes, I do give out a dollar now and then. But when it comes to the journalism, the ethics against cash for quotes—for anyone, housed or not—have been clear since I started out. What I've always done instead was buy meals once in a while, or doughnuts, or other snacks. And I always carry a pack of cigarettes. Yes, it's a nasty habit, but Brant and I never met a chronically homeless person who didn't smoke. So to this day, when someone I'm talking to asks for a buck, I say sorry, but it's all okay when I hand over a cigarette. It beats the hell out of fentanyl or meth, I say, and that usually fetches a smile.

Rita dug the doughnuts. I didn't spend enough street hang time with Tyson to find out if he did. But I'll bet he would have been a cinnamon-roll guy. Just a hunch based on experience.

My approach to both of these folks and their families was the same one I always use. I'm here to tell the truest story I can, to help people understand how life can go off the rails—and how it can be put right again. That means showing both the misery and the joy. I want to be a mirror, not just for my readers but for the very people I am writing about. A compassionate mirror, yes, but a true one as much as anything else.

NOTE ON METHODOLOGY

I always also had the wider context in mind. Writers like me put a spotlight on the miserable, the needy, and the broken, with the aim of helping readers, politicians, and other decision-makers better understand those who are mired at the bottom of society, and how they can be helped, rescued, restored, empowered, given dignity. If we do it right, maybe we inspire someone to push for transformative policies, funding, or programming. Maybe readers can have a bit more understanding and care for the next panhandler they meet.

My fondest hope is that this book has left you feeling that way.

ACKNOWLEDGMENTS

M y profound thanks go to Rita Grant, Tyson Feilzer, and their families, who so kindly allowed me to immerse into their lives, asking pesky questions and lacing together histories, joys, and sorrows that are intrusive by definition. It's hard letting someone in like they did, but I truly believe that by sharing their stories, they help others understand the pain, pathways, and hopes that go into the tragedy of homelessness and the ways to rise from it. They were brave and incredibly openhearted to have taken this journey with me.

I have special places in my heart for Baron for calling and asking me to help find his brother and for Pam for letting me know she was coming out to rescue Rita. Those two lit the match for everything that followed and became this book. They are heroes. They have inspired me by the goodness in their souls and the tenacity of their devotion to Tyson and Rita, and I am still amazed at how loving and resilient they and their families are.

For sharing their anguish and caring with me, I thank Tasha; and Baron's father, Jim; his mother, Patsy; his cousins Stephanie and Jason; and Tyson's galaxy of friends. They never gave up on Tyson, and for that they deserve special places in whatever they think of as heaven.

ACKNOWLEDGMENTS

I give the same thanks and wish to Pam's husband, Rick; their daughter, Amanda; Rita's daughters, Faith, Joy, and Penelope; and Rita's other sisters, Debbie, Lynda, and Valerie. They nurtured Rita's restoration, and their love made Rita's second chance in life a beauty for me to behold. I'm also grateful for Rita's friends; ex-husband, Diver Doug; and Rita's boyfriend Gregg for sharing so much of their stories and caring for Rita with me.

Everybody needs an editor, and I am lucky enough to have wonderful writer/editor friends who read through this manuscript to fix and steer the writing in much-needed ways—and to cheer me on throughout the process. Thank you, Carolyn Newbergh, Katrina Rill, Mike Taylor, Bob Loomis, Lori and Sam Hawk, Steve Rubenstein, Ed Shaffer, and Cynthia Gorney for your wisdom in this. More thanks go to my former *Chronicle* colleague Jason Fagone for not just backreading this book, but being an invaluable mentor into the world of book publishing, and a calm voice in my ear when the inevitable stress swelled.

My Simon & Schuster One Signal editors then brought this book home, first with Julia Cheiffetz helping flesh it out and then with Alessandra Bastagli getting in there with literary shovel and scalpel to shape it into what it most needed to be. Thank you, thank you, thank you.

The family I grew up with knows I so very much appreciated their support in this project, but I'll say thank you again here. My brother, Chris, and sister, Lee Ann, were time-machine memories and editors for personal-history bits, which didn't come easily for me to put down in words. And my father, Larry, and mother, Dorris, laid down a foundation that, even with—and probably partly because of—its tough parts, made me who I am today. They loved and lived writing and exulted in their son being a journalist right up to the days they died. They are in every line I write.

One of the luckiest days in my life was the day I got teamed up with Brant Ward, who is not just one of the finest photographers in existence, but a sharp-as-hell reporter, too, with a heart as big as the sun. Working with him has been one of the great joys in my life; he is my journalistic brother. And I might never have forged that brotherhood if not for being teamed up with Brant by our former managing editor Robert "Rosey" Rosenthal, one of the great visionaries in journalism and a steady fire of inspiration.

Dale Maharidge and Matthew Desmond, whom I consider comrades in confronting poverty with prose, blessed me with their relentlessly optimistic encouragement and advice. Former *Chronicle* colleague Joel Selvin was right there with me from the start, spurring me on to keep going in the early days when this book was barely a concept, and as I developed the themes, his partner, Pamela Turley, jumped in with him to give terrific counsel.

My agents, Larry Weissman and his wife, Sascha Alper, have been nothing short of delightful, and I am eternally grateful for how they believed in this book from the start. They were always upbeat, encouraging me to aim higher, smart as hell, patient with my naivete about the business. And bighearted. Thank you, my former *Chronicle* colleagues Lizzie Johnson and Jason, for steering them my way.

I do have a day job, and it's a busy one, which is why the support of my *San Francisco Chronicle* colleagues has been crucial for getting this book done. My deep thanks go to Publisher Bill Nagel, Executive Editor Emilio Garcia-Ruiz, Director of News Demian Bulwa, Metro Editor Greg Griffin, and my day-do-day assistant metro editor, Dominic Fracassa, for unflinchingly freeing me up to write and research this book at the times I needed. I also thank fellow Chronster and author John King for commiserating with and advising me on the travails of punching out dailies while simultaneously grinding out a manuscript.

There are many invaluable sources whose work to help homeless people has helped me understand the crisis as a reporter, and these have shone particularly brightly for me: Steve Adami, Sherilyn Adams, Art Agnos, Jason Albertson, Angela Alioto, Josh Bamberger, Michael Blecker, Paul Boden, Emily Cohen, Dennis Culhane, Sam Dodge, Bevan Dufty, Kristie Fairchild, Jennifer Friedenbach, Gail Gilman, Roberta Goodman, Laura Guzman, Sally Hindman, Dariush Kayhan, Jeff Kositsky, Margot Kushel, Jennifer Loving, Philip Mangano, Gary McCoy, Tomiquia Moss, David Nakanishi, Gavin Newsom, Rann Parker, Michael Pritchard, Sam Quinones, Trent Rhorer, Nan Roman, Del Seymour, Randy Shaw, Darrell Steinberg, Alex Tourk, Joe Wilson, and Barry Zevin.

And finally but not lastly, there are my wife, Carolyn, and our daughter, Molly, the joy of our lives. Both have been infinitely patient and understanding about the long hours, the frustrations, the many times away from home. But more than that, they have brought expertise to this project: Carolyn, a crack editor and reporter, with her sharp eyes on the manuscript, and therapist Molly as a steady, reassuring voice when things got shaky. My everlasting love and gratitude to you both.

F inding a homeless person who has disappeared into the street world is usually agonizingly difficult. A lot of the time, people don't want to be found. Or maybe they're hoping to reconnect with loved ones and friends from their housed and more stable days, but are too enmeshed in their street lives to reach out. Or they gave up. People sink to the bottom for numberless reasons, and the ways to look for them take a lot of effort and learning for most people.

One way to start is on social media. Scour Facebook, the former Twitter platform known as X, Instagram, and the like—and post on those sites a picture and description of whom you're looking for, with your contact information. But be careful. Sometimes scam artists see these things and contact people, demanding money for information when they actually know nothing. If you have suspicions, call the police for advice.

There are a lot of homeless-specific websites out there that try to help, and most are homegrown and regional, so hunt on the Web for ones you think might be pertinent and local. These two have been dependable nationally for years and are a good place to start:

Miracle Messages: helps unhoused people who want to reconnect with family and friends. https://www.miraclemessages.org/

National Center for Missing and Exploited Children: a resource for people whose children, homeless or not, are missing. https://www.missingkids.org/home

Next, you often have a general geographic idea of where the person you want to find is, so call the official places they might wind up dealing with. This means homeless shelters, hospitals, homeless-aid organizations, police and sheriff's departments, and jails. Call the city or county homeless department in that area.

If you've narrowed down the search geography to a specific town or area, go there personally and post flyers in the street, on light poles, at homeless-aid organizations, grocery stores, parks, wherever seems logical. Again, though—watch out for scam artists calling and demanding money for information. While you're doing that, talk to homeless people, outreach workers, shopkeepers—anyone you think might help. Don't be afraid to approach people and ask questions (unless they look truly dangerous or are having an episode of some kind that makes them incoherent).

If you can afford it, a good choice is to hire a private investigator. These investigators have access to databases that most people don't, and they're great at sifting through financial, criminal, and other records that can track people's movements.

Also, think of contacting broadcast, Web, and newspaper organizations in the areas you think your missing person might have wound up in. We don't get a ton of calls like that, but if they do come, plenty of us will try to help if we have the time. There's no guarantee. But it's always worth asking.

Lastly, don't automatically expect open arms and quick healing if you do find your homeless loved one or friend. When people wind up living outside, especially if they are chronically homeless, I liken their journey to rattling down a ladder, shattering each rung on the way.

They burn through—or are rejected by—family, friends, government aid, and everything else that can keep them from hitting bottom. So there is often a difficult history of conflict or other efforts to help that preceded the street time, and there will probably be trauma, distrust, and a range of other difficulties to negotiate. You may need to arrange drug rehab or mental health services if that's among the difficulties.

And remember that not everyone is ready to come off the street when asked, whether it's by a street counselor, relative, or friend. Helping people is rarely straightforward or painless. But neither is life.

NOTES

CHAPTER 1: HOMELESS CENTRAL

1. Nami Sumida, "San Francisco May Be Small, but It's among America's Most Densely Populated Cities," *San Francisco Chronicle*, November 29, 2021, https://www.sfchronicle.com/sf/article/San-Francisco-may-be-small-but-it-s-among-16650575.php.

2. Kevin Fagan, "San Francisco and the U.S. Were Solving Veteran Homelessness until Trump. Can the Promise Be Restored?," *San Francisco Chronicle*, November 12, 2022, https://www.sfchronicle.com/sf/article/homeless-veterans-apartments-17575222.php.

3. Sam Fulwood, "Census Workers Count 228,621 Homeless across U.S.: Population Advocates Quickly Denounce the Figure as a Gross Undercount. California's Total of 49,081 Is the Largest in the Nation," *Los Angeles Times*, April 13, 1991, https://www.latimes.com/archives/la-xpm-1991-04-13-mn-192-story.html; and Office of Community Planning and Development, Tanya de Sousa, Alyssa Andrichik, Ed Prestera, Katherine Rush, Colette Tano, Micaiah Wheeler, and Abt Associates, *The 2023 Annual Homelessness Assessment Report (AHAR) to Congress*.

4. "How Many People Live on Our Streets?," *San Francisco Chronicle*, June 28, 2016, https://projects.sfchronicle.com/sf-homeless/numbers/; "About," National Homelessness Law Center, April 5, 2021, https://homelesslaw.org/about/; and Cynthia Griffith, "Millions of People Endure Homelessness Every Year," Invisible People, October 13, 2023, https://invisiblepeople.tv/millions-of-people-endure-homelessness-every-year/.

5. Kevin Fagan, "Homelessness Looks the Same as It Did 20 Years Ago," *San Francisco Chronicle*, June 26, 2016, https://projects.sfchronicle.com/sf-homeless/overview/.

6. Kevin Fagan and Mallory Moench, "New Data Shows 20,000 People Will Be Homeless in San Francisco This Year," *San Francisco Chronicle*, August 19, 2022, https://www.sfchronicle.com/sf/article/san-francisco -homeless-population-17380942.php.

7. Trisha Thadani, "S.F. Estimate to End Street Homelessness Drops to $1 Billion as Officials Clash over Best Way Forward," *San Francisco Chronicle*, March 23, 2023, https://www.sfchronicle.com/sf/article/sf -homeless-crisis-shelter-housing-report-17850629.php.

8. Fagan, "San Francisco and the U.S."

9. Fagan and Moench. "New Data Shows 20,000."

10. "Overview of Previous HSH Budgets," San Francisco Department of Homelessness and Supportive Housing, June 30, 2023, https://hsh .sfgov.org/about/budget/overview-previous-budgets/.

11. Fagan, "San Francisco and the U.S."

12. Adriana Rezal and Erin Caughey, "Key Facts about Homelessness in San Francisco," *San Francisco Chronicle*, June 29, 2022, https://www .sfchronicle.com/projects/2022/fixing-san-francisco-problems/sf-home lessness-data/.

13. Robert Polner, "The 12 Biggest Myths about Homelessness in America." NYU, September 24, 2019, https://www.nyu.edu/about/news-publi cations/news/2019/september/HomelessQandA.html; and Shawna Chen, "Facing Domestic Violence Increases Risk of Homelessness, Study Finds," *Axios*, January 22, 2024, https://www.axios.com/local/san -francisco/2024/01/22/california-homelessness-domestic-violence.

14. Matthew Adkins, "Homelessness in America: Statistics, Analysis, & Trends," Security.org, January 25, 2024, https://www.security.org /resources/homeless-statistics/#:~:text=In%202023%2C%20nearly%20 one%2Dthird,nearly%20doubling%20during%20that%20span.

15. Jialu L. Streeter, "Homelessness in California: Causes and Policy Con- siderations," Stanford Institute for Economic Policy Research (SIEPR), May 1, 2022, https://siepr.stanford.edu/publications/policy-brief/home lessness-california-causes-and-policy-considerations#:~:text=The%20 prevalence%20is%20particularly%20high,Culhane%201998%3B%20 Poulin%20et%20al.

CHAPTER 2: RITA–SUBTERRANEAN WORLD IN PLAIN SIGHT

1. Kevin Fagan, "U.S. Supreme Court Ruling Protects Right of Home- less to Sleep Outside," *San Francisco Chronicle*, December 16, 2019, https://www.sfchronicle.com/bayarea/article/U-S-Supreme-Court -ruling-protects-right-of-14910795.php.

2. Kevin Fagan and Alexandria Bordas, "Is the Tenderloin 'Healing'? This Is What It's Like to Live and Work under an Emergency Declaration," *San Francisco Chronicle*, April 1, 2022, https://www.sfchronicle.com/sf /article/Is-the-Tenderloin-healing-This-is-what-16811218.php.

CHAPTER 4: BEACHES, BOATS, AND FREEDOM

1. "Key West History and Culture: Getting to Know the Local Ways," Vacation Homes of Key West, 2024, https://vacationhomesofkeywest.com /key-west-history-and-culture-getting-to-know-the-local-ways.html.
2. Bureau of the Census and Bruce Chapman, "1980 Census of Population—General Population Characteristics Florida," 1982.

CHAPTER 5: HOMELESS ISLAND

1. Kevin Fagan, "Homelessness," USC Annenberg Center for Health Journalism, December 12, 2008, https://centerforhealthjournalism.org /our-work/insights/homelessness.

CHAPTER 6: "SHE HAD TO HIT BOTTOM"

1. Kevin Fagan, "Bush's Homeless Czar Is a Man on a Mission / He's Helping S.F. Craft 10-Year Plan," *SFGate*, January 14, 2004, https: //www.sfgate.com/news/article/Bush-s-homeless-czar-is-a-man-on-a -mission-He-s-2812491.php.

CHAPTER 7: TYSON—CARDBOARD DESPAIR

1. Kevin Fagan, "Homeless People Excited but Skeptical about Idea for Waterfront Navigation Center," *San Francisco Chronicle*, April 14, 2019, https://www.sfchronicle.com/bayarea/article/Homeless-people-excited -but-skeptical-about-idea-13764693.php.
2. Kevin Fagan, "SF's First Navigation Center, Which Spawned Numerous Duplicates, Closes," *SFGate*, November 2, 2018, https://www .sfgate.com/news/article/SF-s-first-Navigation-Center-which-spawned -13359221.php.
3. Ibid.

CHAPTER 8: ALL THE CHANCES IN THE WORLD

1. "How Does Monte Vista High School Rank among America's Best High Schools?," *U.S. News & World Report*, September 11, 2023, https:

//www.usnews.com/education/best-high-schools/california/districts
/san-ramon-valley-unified-school-district/monte-vista-high-school-3355.

2. Kate Wolf, *"The Redtail Hawk,"* from *Back Roads*, CD (Sonoma County, CA: Kate Wolf and Dan Dugan, 1976).

CHAPTER 11: REACHING INTO THE VOID

1. "California Missing Persons," State of California, Department of Justice, Office of the Attorney General, April 9, 2024, https://oag.ca.gov /missing.

CHAPTER 14: HE'S COOKED

1. Editorial staff, "What Is Relapse: Abstinence Violation Effect & Relapse Rates by Drug," Laguna Treatment Hospital, February 27, 2024, https: //lagunatreatment.com/relapse/.

CHAPTER 15: RITA—A FULL SMILE

1. Sam Quinones, *The Least of Us: True Tales of America and Hope in the Time of Fentanyl and Meth* (New York: Bloomsbury, 2021).

CHAPTER 16: BARON—ROLLING TO HOPE

1. "What Is the Scope of Methamphetamine Use in the United States?," National Institute on Drug Abuse, October 2019, https://nida.nih.gov /publications/research-reports/methamphetamine/what-scope-meth amphetamine-misuse-in-united-states; and Mohammadreza Azadfard et al., "Opioid Addiction." StatPearls, July 21, 2023.

2. R. N. Lipari, E. Park-Lee, and S. Van Horn, *America's Need for and Receipt of Substance Use Treatment in 2015* (Rockville, MD: Center for Behavioral Health Statistics and Quality, Substance Abuse and Mental Health Services Administration, September 29, 2016).

CHAPTER 18: PANIC

1. Yoohyun Jung, "Drug Overdose Death Rates for Every US County," *San Francisco Chronicle*, August 21, 2023, https://www.sfchronicle .com/projects/us-drug-overdose-deaths.

2. Ibid.

3. Editorial staff, "What Does It Mean to Relapse?," Laguna Treatment Hospital, February 27, 2024, https://lagunatreatment.com/relapse/.

CHAPTER 21: WHAT MATTERS

1. Trisha Thadani, "Hundreds of Homeless People Board a Bus out of SF Every Year. What Happens to Them Next?," *San Francisco Chronicle*, July 29, 2019, https://www.sfchronicle.com/bayarea/article/Hundreds -of-homeless-people-board-a-bus-out-of-SF-14188436.php.
2. Kevin Fagan, "Hundreds Fan Out across SF to Do Biennial Homeless Count," *San Francisco Chronicle*, January 25, 2019, https://www .sfchronicle.com/bayarea/article/Hundreds-fan-out-across-San -Francisco-to-do-13560716.php; and Kevin Fagan, "Homelessness Jumped 6% in California Last Year. Here's Why Some Experts Are Encouraged," *San Francisco Chronicle*, December 16, 2023, http://www.sfchronicle .com/california/article/california-homelessness-rising-18557152.php.

CONCLUSION

1. Andrew Smith, "Rutgers Researchers Delve Deep into the Genetics of Addiction," Rutgers University, November 2, 2022, https://www.rutgers .edu/news/rutgers-researchers-delve-deep-genetics-addiction.
2. Irina Ivanova, "The 3 Million Richest Americans Have Greater Combined Wealth than 291 Million," CBS News, September 29, 2022, https://www.cbsnews.com/news/the-bottom-half-of-america-has-half -the-wealth-it-did-30-years-ago/.
3. Matthew Desmond, *Poverty, By America* (New York: Crown, 2023).
4. Peter Dreier, "Reagan's Legacy: Homelessness in America," Shelterforce, May 1, 2004, https://shelterforce.org/2004/05/01/reagans-legacy homelessness-in-america/.
5. *Without Housing: Decades of Federal Housing Cutbacks, Massive Homelessness, and Policy Failures* (San Francisco: Western Regional Advocacy Project, 2009).
6. *San Francisco Homeless Count and Survey—2022 Comprehensive Report* (San Francisco: San Francisco Department of Homelessness and Supportive Housing, 2022).
7. Office of Community Planning and Development, Tanya de Sousa, Alyssa Andrichik, Marissa Cuellar, Jhenelle Marson, Ed Prestera, Katherine Rush, and Abt Associates, *The Annual Homeless Assessment Report to Congress*, 2022.
8. "The Cost of Coming Out: LGBT Youth Homelessness," Lesley University, 2018, https://lesley.edu/article/the-cost-of-coming-out-lgbt-youth -homelessness.
9. Kevin Fagan, "San Francisco and the U.S. Were Solving Veteran Homelessness until Trump. Can the Promise Be Restored?," *San Francisco*

Chronicle, November 12, 2022, https://www.sfchronicle.com/sf/article/homeless-veterans-apartments-17575222.php.

10. Jeff Bellisario, "Bay Area Homelessness: New Urgency, New Solutions," June 2021, http://www.bayareaeconomy.org/report/bay-area-homelessness-2/.

11. "Population," Australian Bureau of Statistics, March 21, 2024, https://www.abs.gov.au/statistics/people/population.

12. *Homelessness and Homelessness Services*, Australian Institute of Health and Welfare, 2024, https://www.aihw.gov.au/reports/australias-welfare/homelessness-and-homelessness-services.

13. P. Kellner and William Harford Thomas, "England," *Encyclopaedia Britannica*, May 9, 2024, https://www.britannica.com/place/England; and Patrick Butler, "Rise in Rough Sleeping in England 'Source of National Shame,' Charity Says," *Guardian*, February 29, 2024, https://www.theguardian.com/society/2024/feb/29/number-of-people-sleeping-rough-in-england-rises-for-second-year-running.

14. *San Francisco Homeless Count and Survey.*

RECOMMENDED READING

ere are some books I found particularly illuminating over the years for understanding homelessness:

Journey to Nowhere: The Saga of the New Underclass—Dale Maharidge and Michael Williamson, 1985

Someplace Like America—Dale Maharidge and Michael Williamson, 2013

Sleepwalking through History—Haynes Johnson, 1991

Poverty, by America—Matthew Desmond, 2023

Evicted—Matthew Desmond, 2016

The Soloist—Steve Lopez, 2008

The Grapes of Wrath—John Steinbeck, 1939

Rough Sleepers—Tracy Kidder, 2023

Righteous Dopefiend—Philippe Bourgois and Jeff Schonberg, 2009

RECOMMENDED READING

Invisible Child: Poverty, Survival & Hope in an American City—Andrea Elliott, 2021

The Least of Us: True Tales of America and Hope in the Time of Fentanyl and Meth—Sam Quinones, 2021

And here are some of the stories I wrote about Tyson and Rita:

TYSON

https://www.sfchronicle.com/bayarea/article/Once-home less-now-found-Danville-native-13817848.php

https://www.sfchronicle.com/bayarea/article/A-brother-s -heartbreak-Finding-and-losing-14458341.php

RITA

https://www.sfchronicle.com/news/article/SHAME-OF -THE-CITY-Reclaiming-her-life-2706491.php

https://www.sfchronicle.com/news/article/reason-to-smile -rita-grant-s-teeth-were-a-raw-2633690.php

INDEX

INDEX

INDEX

ABOUT THE AUTHOR

K evin Fagan is a longtime, award-winning reporter at the *San
Francisco Chronicle*, specializing in homelessness, enterprise
news-feature writing, breaking news, and crime. He has rid-
den the rails with modern-day hoboes, slept in the streets on assignment, witnessed seven prison executions, written extensively about
serial killers including the Unabomber, Doodler, and Zodiac, and
covered disasters ranging from the September 11 terror attacks at
Ground Zero to California's devastating wildfires. Homelessness re-
mains a core focus of his, close to his heart as a journalist who cares
passionately about the human condition.